Social Media, Social Genres

T0187434

Internet-based applications such as blogs, social network sites, online chat forums, text messages, microblogs, and location-based communication services used from computers and smartphones represent central resources for organizing daily life and making sense of ourselves and the social worlds we inhabit. This interdisciplinary book explores the meanings of social media as a communicative condition for users in their daily lives; first, through a theoretical framework approaching social media as communicative genres; second, through empirical case studies of personal blogs, Twitter, and Facebook as key instances of the category of "social media," which is still taking shape. Lomborg combines micro-analyses of the communicative functionalities of social media and their place in ordinary people's wider patterns of media usage and everyday practices.

Stine Lomborg is Associate Professor in the Department of Media, Cognition and Communication at the University of Copenhagen, Denmark.

Routledge Studies in New Media and Cyberculture

Social Media, Social Genres

Making Sense of the Ordinary

Stine Lomborg

LONDON AND NEW YORK

First published 2014 by Routledge

2 Park Square, Milton Park, Abingdon, Oxfordshire OX14 4RN
52 Vanderbilt Avenue, New York, NY 10017

Routledge is an imprint of the Taylor & Francis Group, an informa business

First issued in paperback 2019

Library of Congress Cataloging in Publication Data

Lomborg, Stine, 1982–
    Social media, social genres : making sense of the ordinary / Stine Lomborg.
        pages cm — (Routledge studies in new media and cyberculture ; 16)
    Includes bibliographical references and index.
    1. Social media.   2. Digital communications—Social aspects.
3. Online social networks.   4. Internet—Social aspects.   I. Title.
    HM742.L66 2013
    302.23′1—dc23
    2013021328

ISBN: 978-0-415-82848-2 (hbk)
ISBN: 978-0-367-86723-2 (pbk)

Typeset in Sabon
by Apex CoVantage, LLC

For Christian and Vera

Contents

Figures and Tables

Figures

Tables

Acknowledgments

There are many people to whom I owe thanks for the inspiring conversations and general encouragement that have fueled the development and writing of this book.

First of all, many thanks go to the fifteen Danish social media users who agreed to share their social media experiences, and their data, with me. By peeking into their daily practices of checking, connecting, and communicating on social media I learned so much about the multifarious ways in which social media are part of the ordinary activities that make up everyday life.

Thanks to Kris Lund from the ICAR lab at Université Lyon 2 and ENS-LSH, who hosted my research stay there in 2008, and to Gregory Dyke for helping me create the social media data archives that play a key part in the empirical analyses in the book.

I want to thank my former colleagues at the Department of Communication and Aesthetics at University of Aarhus, and my colleagues at the Center for Communication and Computing at University of Copenhagen with whom I have had many discussions of social media as communicative phenomena. Special thanks to Kirsten Frandsen, Niels Ole Finnemann, Anja Bechmann, Maria Bakardjieva, Charles Ess, Klaus Bruhn Jensen, and Rasmus Helles who have all provided insightful comments on earlier drafts of several of the chapters, helped me push my argument, and given good advice at various points during the project.

Finally, thanks to the anonymous reviewers for providing critical and useful feedback, and to Felisa Salvago-Keyes and the people at Routledge for their support.

1 Social Media in Everyday Life

I begin my day in front of my laptop, with a cup of coffee. When the browser opens, it displays my personalized newsreader, on which are aggregated my most important online activities: my email, my Twitter and Facebook feeds, and my favorite blogs, along with my preferred news sites and the weather forecast. I check my personal and professional email, and my Facebook and Twitter accounts regularly throughout the day. When I am out, my iPhone enables me to check these on the fly, along with handling calls and text messages. There is nothing extraordinary in my use of the internet—in fact, I am like most people I know. For many of us, internet-based communication has become ordinary, pervasive, and inextricably embedded in work tasks, coordination of activities, entertainment, and the maintenance of relationships in everyday life. Hence, the internet, in conjunction with other media and the mosaic of social practices in which we engage, may be considered a resource for organizing and making sense of ourselves and the social worlds we inhabit.

A few years ago, these developments were not self-evident. 'Social media'—internet-based applications such as social network sites, blogs, microblogs, and location-based services, to mention just a few—were on the verge of becoming mainstream, led by sites such as Facebook and YouTube, and to some extent, by blog portals such as Blogspot. Since then, new services have blossomed, peaked, and faded, and social media have diffused more profoundly into the everyday, often as venues of interaction around the ordinary, as platforms of interpersonal communication and sociality in everyday life.

This book explores the meanings of social media as a communicative condition for users in their daily lives. It is the outcome of 6 years of research on social media, driven by a practical interest in how social media become parts of the social fabric of meaning in everyday life, and how they are negotiated and appropriated to suit individual users' needs.

THEORIZING SOCIAL MEDIA AS COMMUNICATIVE PHENOMENA

To begin understanding and theorizing social media as a communicative phenomenon, this book takes as its point of departure the historically very well-developed theoretical and empirical discipline of audience studies. In common with audience studies, the book shares an interest in understanding media use among ordinary people in everyday life—a topic that is examined from various ontological, epistemological, and methodological standpoints in the audience studies literature. In its qualitatively oriented forms, audience studies focus on the relationship between media texts and media users in specific contexts, in terms of *media reception,* that is, media usage patterns, and how individuals and social groups make sense of and through media texts. In qualitative reception studies, the interplay between user and media text is understood as a process of sensemaking, where the content and textual traits of the media text activate the receiver's cognitive, affective, bodily, and social capacities, including the activation of relevant genre knowledge. In other words, the text forms a potential space for interpretation, in which the recipient's subjective and socially informed interpretations are actualized. The tradition of reception studies is useful in beginning to understand the meanings of internet-based communication for users in everyday life, because it emphasizes the *relationship* between the media user and the media text as the analytical focal point.

At the same time, social media present a theoretical challenge to the classic producer-text-audience-models that still guide audience studies of television and print media. These studies assume a text or media product sent from a producer to one or more recipients, who have limited feedback options (Livingstone, 2004). First, social media as an area of study challenge the notion of text. On social network sites, blogs, and so on, there is no 'pre-produced text,' just a technological framework or communicative template facilitated by a service provider (i.e., a company such as Facebook, Foursquare, or Twitter), which must be 'filled' through active user engagement. In social media, the text rests on user contributions; it is emergent, editable, and undergoing a continuous process of development, revision, and change. Second, although audience studies have long operated with a notion of the media recipient as an active, meaning-making agent, the idea of 'the active user' assumes a radical form when the media user becomes the media producer. Users of social media may be productive and creative, not only through conversations between users, including interactive and ongoing communicative exchanges of content bits and relations (Livingstone, 2004), but also through ongoing elaborations of the interface, its aesthetic, its functional capabilities, and its connectivity to other software and platforms (Bechmann & Lomborg, 2013; also Finnemann, 2005). This implies that the concept of a text must be expanded to encompass not only the communicative contributions of users, but also the software dimension of social media.

To address these fundamental challenges, this book develops a framework for conceptualizing and studying social media, by *rethinking key analytic concepts from the discipline of audience studies* for the study of internet-based communications among ordinary users. Specifically, the book proposes a conceptual framework for defining and analyzing social media in terms of 'genres' (e.g., Andersen, 1994; Berkenkotter & Huckin, 1993). This perspective implies viewing the communicative practices unfolding on *social media as enactments of genre* that contribute to an ongoing negotiation among users about the meanings, purposes, and conventions of their social media use. Moreover, these genre enactments are seen as inextricably interwoven in *the fabric of meaning of everyday life* and society at large.

The concept of genre is particularly useful for studying social media, because it encompasses and bridges the gaps between the three traditionally separate components in the communication process: producer, text, and recipient. 'Genre' is a crucial concept for understanding the relationship between an individual user's cognitive activity and capacity, and the properties of media and texts in given social situations. 'Genre' denotes a certain 'horizon of expectations' that manifests itself as a set of textual conventions, guiding media producers and recipients toward alignment and mutual understanding in the communicative process. Media producers draw upon genre knowledge to produce texts that adhere to—or transgress—certain conventions, and thus are likely to fulfill or challenge the expectations of the audience, and the recipients use genre knowledge to select and make sense of relevant media content. Skilled participants often deploy genre knowledge in a commonsense and tacit way, and experience a communicative situation as unproblematic and inherently meaningful. For example, we recognize a blog as a blog, an entertainment show on television as entertainment, and know what to expect from each of these genres. Thus, in everyday life, we typically enact and experience genres competently, according to our existing stock of knowledge. However, when encountering a new genre, we must acquire relevant genre knowledge by adjusting our existing socio-cognitive understandings, or inventing new ones, to master and make sense of the communicative situation (Bakardjieva, 2011). I use the concept of 'genre' to characterize social media as involving an ongoing negotiation of expectations and conventions among participants, in a collaborative effort to make sense of given forms of online communication.

The theoretical foundation for the conceptual framework of genre is a cognitive approach to media reception, which highlights genre as a cognitive category, or device for sensemaking. The cognitive perspective has been mainly developed and applied in empirical reception analysis by Scandinavian scholars, under the heading of 'socio-cognitive reception theory' (e.g., Bruun, 2004; Höijer, 1998), which inquires into 'sensemaking,' a core concept of user agency, here primarily associated with users' cognitive efforts to comprehend and ascribe meaning to texts and media. Socio-cognitive reception theory combines a cognitive-psychological understanding of the active media user with a classic, humanities-based interest in textual meanings and interpretations. I develop this socio-cognitive framework in a more sociological direction, by introducing a pragmatic understanding of 'sensemaking' as embedded in, and enacted through communicative practices, rather than as an individual's mental process (Cicourel, 1973; Garfinkel, 1967; Moscovici, 1994, 2001). I offer a theoretical qualification of the possibility for cross-fertilization of reception analysis and pragmatic, social-psychological, and sociological theories of knowledge and expectations as inscribed in communicative practice, by emphasizing interaction and negotiation as key dimensions in situated instances of making sense of social media. Together with the concept of genre, this perspective on sensemaking forms the theoretical basis for understanding and studying ordinary social media users as producers.

Against this theoretical background, I pursue three overarching research questions in this book:

- How may social media be conceptualized from a genre perspective and what are their specific characteristics?
- How do participants negotiate social media as genres through communicative practice?
- What meanings do participants, understood as socio-cognitive agents, ascribe to their use of these genres in everyday life?

It is important to note that the intention here is not ontological, that is, to say that social media *are* genres. Instead, the goal is conceptual and analytical: it is to explore what may be gained from studying social media through the lens of genre. I explore the genre perspective through both theoretical and empirical inquiry. The theoretical framework is applied and discussed in three in-depth empirical case studies of blogs, Twitter and Facebook as key instances of social media in everyday life. Specifically, these empirical case studies involve analysis of how users 'do' and ascribe meaning to social media in and through communicative practice (as manifested in textual interactions) by invoking, negotiating, and adjusting relevant genre knowledge over time.

The theoretical framework and empirical analyses have been developed and refined in tandem. To understand social media as mediated everyday phenomena, and the genre knowledge deployed and negotiated to navigate them, a fundamental premise of the genre-based approach to social media is the importance of looking at the 'human interpretive practices' that play out in actual, situated instances of genre enactment (blogging, tweeting, etc.) (Livingstone, 2004). Therefore, the research questions are driven by empirical case studies of genre in action.

Through the application of the genre framework to personal blogs, Twitter, and Facebook, I explore how users jointly organize interaction, negotiate appropriate behavior and topics, and orient to one another in and through their communicative exchanges, to make sense of the three genres. I also examine how genre enactments and expectations link social media use to broader everyday life patterns, concerns, and interests. The empirical contributions of the book are secondary to the aim of conceptual and analytical development—the case studies mainly serve to illustrate, clarify, elaborate, challenge, adjust, and evaluate the framework of genre in the study of social media.

Nevertheless, the empirical analyses that make up a large proportion of the book are illustrative and valuable in their own right, as qualitative studies of how ordinary users engage with social media for personal purposes. I do not provide an authoritative description of the blog, Twitter or Facebook as communicative genres. Instead, from the standpoint of audience studies, I use genre to examine how Twitter, Facebook, and blogging function and become meaningful to users in their daily lives. That is, I probe the experiential and social qualities of the three genres in action—and in context. For this purpose, the genre perspective offers a rich analysis of sensemaking and negotiation between media users and given social media texts.

RESEARCH DESIGN AND CASES

The empirical basis of the book consists of three iterations of qualitative, empirical case studies of social media use in Denmark: a case study of personal blogs, conducted in 2008; a complementary study of Twitter, in 2010; and a third study of Facebook in 2012. Considering the facts that Denmark and the other Scandinavian countries have some of the highest internet and smartphone penetration rates, are among the most digitally literate, and have consistently been among the first to mass-adopt new media and genres (cf. Castells, Fernández-Ardèvol, Qiu, & Sey, 2007), this geographical area is of special interest for studies of social media, even while recognizing the cultural specificity of Scandinavia.

The empirical case studies build on two main types of data: web archives of communicative practices on social media, and qualitative interviews with the involved bloggers, Twitter users, and Facebook users to contextualize their online practices and relationships, and determine what functions and meanings these are assigned in everyday life. In keeping with the focus on 'the internet in everyday life,' including social media as venues for everyday communication, I have restricted the empirical focus to 'ordinary users,' that is, I exclude individuals who blog or tweet professionally in their capacity as employee or expert, and focus solely on those who, as private individuals, communicate about their interests, experiences, whereabouts, and so on.

By drawing on case studies, the analysis was designed with a comparative strategy in mind. Comparative analyses of multiple cases are a pivotal means of developing a nuanced theoretical argument and analytical framework that are applicable across contexts (Stake, 2003; Yin, 1994). Personal blogs, Twitter, and Facebook were chosen as complementary cases of everyday communication on social media, to ensure richness and breadth in the data, and thus a solid foundation for developing and refining the framework of genre. When I initiated the first case study in 2008, blogging was already a well-established, mature, and somewhat studied phenomenon. In contrast, in 2009, when I was preparing the study of Twitter, the service was still only slowly beginning to gain a foothold, that is, it appeared to be an emerging and relatively unstable genre—certainly a 'risky' object of study, because it might not have become popular at all at an international scale. In 2010, when studying Twitter, and even more so in 2011, when preparing the Facebook study, social media were becoming increasingly portable, owing to a skyrocketing smartphone and tablet diffusion. Portability potentially has consequences for the way in which social media communication is embedded in everyday life. Hence, Facebook was chosen as a case in part to explore the interplay between media platforms and communicative practices in the ongoing negotiations of genre.

Contrasting cases is not only an important means for theoretical development; it is also analytically useful. Comparing and contrasting cases is particularly useful in this book, to make visible the way in which the capabilities and constraints at the software and interface levels of the three case genres influence usage patterns and genre expectations. Moreover, comparison helps highlight limitations of the usage variations and social purposes served by a given genre. In contrast to most of the existing comparative literature, which compares the internet and social media to print and electronic mass media (e.g., Bruns, 2008; Finnemann, 2005; Lüders, 2008) or interpersonal, face-to-face communication (e.g., Baron, 2008; Herring, 1999a), I examine variations within the spectrum of social media. When other media and genres are not used as benchmarks for the analysis, it allows the characteristics of social media to shine in their own right.

COMMUNICATING THE ORDINARY: MEDIATED EVERYDAY COMMUNICATION

The discourses surrounding the internet are often flavored with notions of the new and the extraordinary. Bruns (2008), for instance, claims 'Web 2.0' is the driver of a societal and cultural transformation, in which users become empowered 'producers,' collaboratively engaged in knowledge production and innovations on the internet. Jenkins (2006) similarly speaks of the internet in terms of participatory culture and democratization, in which ordinary users acquire power and a creative voice, vis-à-vis media institutions, politicians, and so forth. Much of the hype is rooted in the internet's inviting ordinary users to generate and distribute content on a public platform without a professional gatekeeper, thereby enhancing the capacity of ordinary people to have a voice as citizens in public debates, for instance. Currently, 'social media' are at the center of such hype.

Regardless of its potential, the celebration of the internet as new and revolutionary marks a stark contrast to the habitual, mundane communications that dominate the internet habits and practices of many ordinary users. The proliferation of 'social media' in an already media-saturated everyday life highlights the role of mediated everyday communication among private individuals as a core attraction of these communication services: we share experiences and knowledge of topics of common interest, catch up, coordinate, and hang out online for the mere sake of one another's company. Hence, the internet also represents a 'mediatization' of the mundane communications about the everyday (Finnemann, 2011).

I understand everyday life in terms of social practice—it is socially organized, negotiated, and imbued with often tacit meaning, as vividly described and studied in phenomenological and microsociological theory (Cicourel, 1973; Goffman, 1959; Schutz, 1971; Schutz & Luckmann, 1973). Everyday life denotes the realm of the ordinary, that is, the daily rhythm of familiar, habitual, and unproblematic human activities and experiences. Everyday life involves a 'taken for grantedness' (Ling, 2012) as it proceeds along its course: we draw on a given stock of knowledge, including working typifications and recipes for action—*genres,* accumulated through socialization and experience, to move naturally and unproblematically through situations. Occasionally, we encounter problematic situations that disrupt the habitual routine, and prompt us to generate new typifications and paths of action in response to the change in conditions. Hence, through our actions and engagement with the world, we actively mold, reify, and ascribe meaning to everyday life (Schutz & Luckmann, 1973). Communication plays a substantial and crucial role in the ongoing constitution, negotiation, and sensemaking of the social reality of everyday life.

What characterizes everyday communication? I consider everyday communication to refer to personal, deinstitutionalized communication (Cicourel, 1973: 70; Lüders, 2008; Meltzer & Musolf, 2000), in the sense that it is symmetrical and bidirectional, often spontaneous, and void of formally instituted obligations and prescriptions. According to Lüders, personal communication presents a contrast to mass communication, which operates under professional conventions, is typically produced within the institutional and commercial logic of mass media outlets, and implies a clear separation between senders and a mass of faceless recipients. To describe everyday communication as deinstitutionalized does not mean that it is not scripted. However, the scripts of everyday communication are informally negotiated by interlocutors in communicative practice. The works of Garfinkel (1967) and Goffman (1959), and those of their successors in conversation and discourse analysis, provide detailed descriptions of the highly typified social organization and unfolding of mundane, everyday communication, and the establishment and management of the interaction order in various encounters and social situations.

Everyday communication may evolve around personal interests, daily routines, experiences, and 'small talk' (Meltzer & Musolf, 2000). Furthermore, the function and objectives of everyday communication are often highly social. Much of it is centered on establishing and maintaining a sense of mutuality and togetherness, and a common 'definition of the situation' (Goffman, 1959), rather than on the content of communication in itself. Simmel's works on association and sociability offer vivid accounts of the norms and forms of social communication, and its accomplishment of togetherness that is freed from friction and conflict, and serves the fundamental purpose of social affiliation (Simmel, 1971[1910]). Jakobson (1960) dubs the relational functions of communication 'phatic,' using Malinowski's concept (1923) to describe how social communication serves to establish a common frame of reference, and mark the quality of the relationships among interlocutors, as opposed to a 'referential' function that serves to center communication on a given topic. Jakobson elaborates on how different factors and functions may dominate different types of communicative situations, with the social function being dominant in everyday, mundane communication. As this book will demonstrate, Jakobson's concept of phatic communication and Simmel's concept of sociability are essential to unpacking the ordinary uses of social media (cf. Chapter 7).

THE INTERNET AS A MEDIUM FOR EVERYDAY COMMUNICATION

In her review of the internet in everyday life, Bakardjieva writes, '. . . the everyday life worlds into which new technologies are drawn do not remain unchanged. New elements and dimensions are added to the spatial, temporal, practical, and social arrangements of these worlds' (Bakardjieva, 2011: 70). Certainly, venues for everyday interpersonal communication among private individuals exist outside the internet: Face-to-face encounters are the basic and most prolific form, but it also occurs through mediated forms, via telephone and letter, to facilitate interpersonal relationships across space and time. What *is* new is that, with the proliferation of the internet and other digital media, these forms of communication of the ordinary are mediated through a much larger repertoire of communication channels, and different forms of everyday communication are often seamlessly interwoven into the flow of the everyday, to create a sense of 'connected presence' (Licoppe, 2004). Moreover, the internet is the first medium for *public,* mediated everyday communication. In contrast to spoken communication, which is ephemeral (and thus limited in access), the internet puts everyday communication on public display, because the archive feature of the internet makes messages persistent and accessible, despite the spatio-temporal dispersion of interlocutors.

Digital media, most emblematically the networked personal computer and the internet, combine the storage capacity of print media with the transmission speed of electronic broadcast media (Finnemann, 2011). Furthermore, they allow for the reproduction and recombining of '. . . all previous media and genres of representation and interaction on a single platform

of hardware and software' (Jensen, 2010: 69–70). Owing to these fundamental capacities, the internet as a communication medium involves almost
endless possibilities and variations.

Communication on the internet flows in a node-link network structure
that connects content and users in a globally distributed, integrated infra-
structure. In this networked structure, users can interact in one-on-one,
one-to-many, and many-to-many bases, in various constellations using various forms of software. Users can interact in real-time, near-synchronous,
or asynchronous fashions. Users may use multiple modalities (text, audio,
video, etc.), and communicate privately in more or less closed forums, or
make their communication publicly available to anyone. The different forms
of internet communication combine different characteristics. Together with
communicative genres such as online chat, social network sites, debate
forums, listservs, photo- and video-sharing sites, location-based services,
and so forth, blogs and Twitter contribute to the construction of the internet
as a mosaic of communicative forms that may be used for a variety of purposes. Everyday, interpersonal communication may assume all these forms.

Whereas the characterization of the internet as a communication medium
is by no means exhaustive, it serves the present purpose of showing how
the internet may present new communicative trajectories by fundamentally
altering the temporal, spatial, and social structures of everyday communication. For example, being publicly available, and thus possibly expanded
in reach and scope, everyday communication on the internet may blur the
boundary between mass and interpersonal communication, because messages typically associated with private, one-on-one communication (e.g.,
coordinating a get-together or sending birthday greetings) may be communicated to a much larger, and often unknown audience of family, close friends,
acquaintances, and strangers.

The specific characteristics of internet-mediated, everyday communication raise questions about the experience and meaning of such communications for users. What expectations and norms guide their online
interactions, and what is the role of digital technology in shaping them?
How does everyday life shape and take shape from the specific circumstances, expressions, and functions of such mediated interpersonal communications? Such questions are at the basis of an inquiry into social media
as communicative genres.

STRUCTURE OF THE BOOK

The book comprises two main sections: a theoretical part that conceptu-
alizes social media in terms of genre and sensemaking, and sketches the
methodological and analytical framework for empirical studies of social
media as communicative genres (Chapters 2 and 3), and a set of case analyses based on the collected empirical material (Chapters 4 through 7). In

Chapter 2, I establish the theoretical framework of genre. I open the chapter with a brief overview of the evolution of social media genres to provide a historical context for current developments and situate blogging, Twitter and Facebook in the broader internet landscape. I then embark on the conceptual development of the genre perspective, defining social media as communicative genres constituted at the junction of their concrete enactments in communicative practice, and the communicative characteristics inscribed in the software used. As genres, social media are highly dynamic, owing to the direct negotiation among participants in situated encounters, and the specific social dynamics of the networked structure of social media. In Chapter 3, I relate the genre perspective to foundational discussions in audiences and reception studies, concerning the social and psychological processes of sensemaking in the meeting between text and user in the context of everyday life. Chapters 4, 5, and 6 are dedicated to empirical analyses of the everyday uses of personal blogs, Twitter, and Facebook, respectively, as communicative genres. In these chapters, I apply the components of the genre framework, to examine the genres' compositional, thematic, stylistic, and pragmatic focuses, and push the theoretical development further by exploring possible connections between software functionalities and social uses of the genres. In Chapter 7, I synthesize the main findings from the three case analyses of genre negotiation in personal blogs, Twitter and Facebook, indicating how social media evolve at the intersection of personal experience and the publicly-displayed nature of communication. I suggest that a key driving force in managing possible tensions between privacy and self-disclosure is phatic communication and the constitution of social media as, first and foremost, spaces for sociable encounters. Chapter 8 concludes the book by revisiting the theoretical concepts of the 'active media user' and the 'text' with the benefit of a pragmatic, genre-based framework for social media analysis.[1]

NOTE

1. An earlier version of Chapter 2 has been published in *MedieKultur, vol. 27*(51). Parts of Chapter 4 have been published in my article 'Negotiating privacy through phatic communication' in the Springer journal *Philosophy and Technology*, 25(3), pp. 415–434, and are reprinted with kind permission from Springer Science + Business Media B.V. Parts of Chapter 5 have been published in my article 'Becoming a 'tweep'' in *Observatorio OBS**, 6(1).

2 Social Media as Communicative Genres

The use of the internet for personal communication and maintenance of interpersonal relationships has a history as long as the internet itself. Email technology certainly predates the internet, but the early internet made it possible to send messages between networked computers. The technology of what has become the internet was originally developed by the United States Department of Defense in the 1960s to safeguard military intelligence, beginning with the so-called ARPANET (for a detailed history of the technological development of the internet, see Abbate, 1999). In the 1970s, when the ARPANET was primarily used and developed by American universities and military, email evolved and quickly took hold as a key functionality of the ARPANET, making up 75 percent of its traffic (Rasmussen, 2007: 44). Whereas email was, in principle, meant for one-to-one communication across time and space, it made possible new software developments enabling group communication. Alongside these developments, the internet was made available to the larger public in the 1980s, with the opening of the internet to commercial and privately run internet service providers and companies (Briggs & Burke, 2002: 309, Rasmussen, 2007: 66, 198 [note 31]). The early adopters and developers of the internet for private purposes were primarily computer enthusiasts. All this sparked the emergence of a wealth of online communication genres, including mailing lists, bulletin board systems (e.g., the virtual community, the WELL, described by Rheingold [1993]) and online discussion groups such as Usenet, which facilitated asynchronous communication among like-minded strangers who wished to connect with others on topics of professional or personal interest. Early forms of many-to-many, synchronous online communication, such as groupware and Internet Relay Chat (IRC), were invented in the late 1980s as extensions of bulletin board systems, and were precursors of the 1990s development of instant messaging. All these early forms of online interpersonal and group communication were written text-only.

Multimedia communication was first enabled by Tim Berners-Lee's invention of the www protocol at CERN, in Switzerland, in the early 1990s. Based on hypertext, the www protocol aimed to integrate the internet as a network, through linking (http) and a common code (html) (Rettberg,

2008: 23). Along with the introduction of the first graphic web browser, Mosaic, in 1993, and a growing diffusion and commercialization of the internet in the 1990s, the World Wide Web (WWW) became the dominant internet protocol, to the extent that the WWW is often taken to be synonymous with the internet, even though a great deal of internet traffic (e.g., much email traffic and mobile applications) runs outside WWW.

The WWW led to new software formats and communicative genres, often grounded in the early internet genres, to be invented, extended, and refined. For instance, online chat forums, community sites, and debate forums may be regarded as evolutions of core features of both Usenet news groups and bulletin board systems (Baym, 2010: 16), whereas wiki software, which enables groups of users to collaboratively create and edit a number of interlinked web pages through a browser, became possible only with the advent of the WWW. The personal homepage, a web page created by a private individual, which typically displays content of a personal nature (interests, biographical information, etc.), is another early child of the WWW. The homepage has inspired various later developments in software and communicative genres on the internet, including the personal profiles that comprised the backbone of dedicated dating sites in the mid-1990s (e.g., match .com) and later, social network sites, beginning with Six Degrees in 1997 (for a comprehensive history of the emergence and evolution of social network sites, see boyd and Ellison [2007]). The emergence of the weblog in the late 1990s is another example of genre evolution on the internet, beginning as frequently updated homepages, which compiled links to interesting content elsewhere online ('filter blogs') or provided more essay- and diary-like entries about the homepage's owner. Whereas the earliest blogs relied on the author's ability to hand-code the site, and thus required a certain technical knowledge, from 1998 on, various easy-to-use and typically free blogging software was launched (e.g., OpenDiary, Pitas, and Blogger) (Rettberg, 2008: 24–27). This software significantly lowered the barrier to entry because it offered preformatted templates, enabling users who wished to keep a blog to simply add content (text, images, video, links, etc.) and press a button, to publish new posts on their blogs registered with this software. Whereas the personal homepage constitutes one important foundation for the emergence of blogs, the blog has other antecedents in online communication. The threaded organization of blog conversation, for instance, was previously used in Usenet newsgroups and debate forum software.

With the advent of what has been popularly termed 'Web 2.0' and 'social software' in the first decade of the twenty-first century, yet more new software developments have emerged, as have additional online genres for interpersonal communication, collaboration, and user-generated content. Software developments have sparked another generation of services commonly associated with the term 'social media.' These developments include Wikipedia; image- and video-sharing services such as Flickr, Instagram, and YouTube; social network sites such as LinkedIn, Google+, and Facebook;

microblogging services such as Twitter; and mobile, location-based services such as Yelp and Foursquare. Whereas 'Web 2.0' suggests a paradigmatic shift toward greater user participation, personalization, and collaboration, these characteristics were also present on the internet before the first decade of the twenty-first century, and new services and software, including those labeled social media, must be regarded as extensions of ongoing genre developments that may be traced back to the origins of the internet (e.g., Baym, 2010: 13–17).

Despite the increasing commercialization of the internet throughout the 1990s and the first decade of the twenty-first century, many of the developments in software and communicative forms have been 'user-driven' from the outset (Finnemann, 2005: 138–139). Many of the services that have become vastly popular over the years started as noncommercial projects, initially developed by technologically knowledgeable and visionary individuals who happened to have good ideas. Facebook, for instance, was originally programmed and unveiled by four Harvard students as a Harvard-only network, and gradually evolved into a global business and key player in the evolving social media landscape. Furthermore, new elements are continuously embedded in Facebook, including applications (games, quizzes, awareness campaigns, and so forth) developed by ordinary users and companies to pursue specific communicative purposes, and thereby augment the Facebook experience.

Services and genres are profoundly shaped not only by the software that makes up their architecture and interfaces, but by the users who adopt them, and the existing media environments in which they are put to use. Different services become popular and widespread in different cultural contexts (national, demographic, etc.; boyd & Ellison, 2007: 217–218). Although not developed with these specific target groups in mind, teens and bands were among the earliest adopters of the MySpace social network site, and these groups have consistently dominated the site since, shaping MySpace into a particularly useful site for musicians to promote their work and connect with fans, thereby reinforcing the demographic structure. In 2010, the site was relaunched, to focus more exclusively on music and entertainment, allegedly to retain the user base by establishing a sharper edge to Facebook. In a similar vein, different social network sites are popular in different national contexts and language areas: for instance, VKontakte is extremely popular in Russia and other central and eastern European countries, but is largely unknown in other parts of the world. Facebook, and to some extent Twitter, appears to be the only services to have gained solid hold across cultural contexts.

Against the background of the historical evolution of social media, the aim of this chapter is to equip the study of social media with a theoretical and analytical grounding in genre analysis, to explore the strengths and limitations of the concept of genre, and to adjust it to this particular communicative environment. First, I consider existing definitions of social media and discuss the relationship between medium, genre, and text, to clarify the relative merits of conceptualizing social media as genres. After this initial conceptual clarification, I turn to genre theory and genre studies. As a first step in discussing the concept of genre in relation to social media, I briefly review the concept of genre as it has been used in research on computer-mediated communication (CMC), and trace the theoretical underpinnings to a functional approach to genre, as developed in sociolinguistics, rhetoric, and media studies. My second step is to relate the functional concept of genre to social media as particularly dynamic genres, arguing for a greater emphasis in genre theory and analysis on interactional and negotiated aspects, that is, how genres are constituted in their *practical enactment*.

CONCEPTUALIZING SOCIAL MEDIA AS COMMUNICATIVE GENRES

The term 'social media' is often used in public discourse, by the media industry and in academic research without any—or merely an implicit—defining qualification. As we have already seen, 'social media' is associated with the terms 'social software' and 'Web 2.0,' to denote a new era of networked, interactive forms of communication, such as blogs, wikis, social bookmarking, social network sites, photo- and video-sharing, and other, primarily internet-based phenomena that have emerged in recent years. Sometimes, older communication forms, such as email, text-messaging, and mobile telephony, and online chat and games are also included in the definition (e.g., boyd, 2008: 92; Bruns, 2008; Lüders, 2008). For example, a technology-based understanding of 'social media' is advanced by boyd, who considers 'social media' to be an umbrella term for a range of digital media that may be used to interact with others through network technologies, such as personal computers or smartphones (boyd, 2008: 92). Others describe 'social media' with a view to the purpose of communication, contrasting it to mass media, in that they are distinctly intended for the interpersonal communication and personalized expression of ordinary users (e.g., Lüders, 2008: 685). This is often framed in terms of user-generated content, and users as producers. Coined with the term 'produsage,' Bruns even suggests collapsing the processes of production and usage on social media to define them by 'the collaborative and continuous building and extending of existing content in pursuit of further improvement' (Bruns, 2008: 21). Related to this, 'social media' facilitate not only classic broadcasting through one-to-many communication, but also one-on-one and many-to-many forms of communication, thus implying a more distributed—and networked—agency. Although these descriptions are useful and hint to key characteristics of social media, they do not constitute a coherent definition of 'social media' that encompasses the complex interactional and network dynamics that characterize them, and their delimitation with respect to other digital media, in terms of their communicative attributes. In the following sections, I intend to provide a coherent, conceptual grounding for social media, by defining a framework for social media as communicative genres.

Strictly speaking, the term 'social media' is nonsense, because it presumes that other communication media are not social. This is a fallacy: All media are social, in the sense that they may serve social functions. We discuss the news with our friends, families, and coworkers, we gather around the television set in the evening, we go to the movies as part of a date, and so on. Using media is intertwined with, sometimes a core part of, our social activities. Thus, 'social media' needs a qualifier describing what is special about being social in and through these internet- and mobile-phone-based services, when compared to other media.

Arguably, social media facilitate a particular way of being social, namely, a sort of everyday togetherness and relationship-maintenance among participants. This is not to say that social media solely serve such interpersonal and sociable purposes, but simply to qualify the 'social' in the label. Certainly, social media may also be used for professional purposes, such as news dissemination, celebrity branding, and so on. However, these uses capitalize on the interpersonal nature of connectivity that is defining for social media. Social media are thus distinctly social, because they are based on interpersonal communication and interactive content creation with a personal purpose, and the connection, mutual orientation, and conversation among users (e.g., peer-to-peer, or a celebrity to a fan audience) are central aspects of the social media use (Helles, 2009: 7–10; Lüders, 2008). Moreover, in contrast to media such as television or newspapers, but similarly to the letter and telephone, 'social media' are the direct facilitators of, or venues for, this togetherness—due to their interactive potential and invitation to active content contribution by the users.

As will be further elaborated in this chapter, social media are not really media. It is misleading to think of the abovementioned communicative forms as media, because such an understanding implies that various social media are based on different technologies. Social media form a subgroup of digital media, grouped together because they share digital technology, and the specific social purposes outlined previously. They may be based on different software, and have different communicative features that enable them to accomplish interpersonal orientation and interactive content creation, but digital media technology underpins them all. Therefore, I propose to conceptualize social media as communicative genres, constituted at the junction between interactive functionalities configured in software, and the distinctly social purposes toward which they are oriented, in the actual communicative practices of users. However, while suggesting it may be more appropriate to talk about 'social genres,' I continue to use the label 'social media,' because the label is already well established. I use it in the specific sense defined here.

'Genre' denotes a commonality or 'family resemblance' among texts, both within and across media, grouped, for example, according to compositional, stylistic, or thematic criteria, at various levels of similarity. The idea of 'family resemblance' posits that no one essential common feature needs to be present in all texts for them to belong to a genre. In his original introduction to the concept, Wittgenstein (1967: 31–32e) used the analogy of the family to describe cognitive, typological systems. A type may be described as a pattern of overlapping similarities: every family member shares traits with other family members (e.g., nose, eyes, height, temper), but no single trait is common for all members of the family. Transferred to genre theory, 'genre' denotes a group of texts that are connected by a network of overlapping similarities (compositional, stylistic, thematic etc.) that crisscross in different constellations and constitute the genre as a whole. Accordingly, 'genre' is a flexible and elastic concept. For instance, news journalism in different media is recognizable as a genre characterized by factual content, use of sources, and adherence to criteria of newsworthiness (Berkenkotter & Huckin, 1993). News journalism is also a subgenre within the broader genre of journalism, alongside sports journalism, and investigative journalism, among others. Similarly, the letter and the email share compositional features (both are typically initiated by a greeting, followed by a main text, and ended with a goodbye), but at the same time involve a diverse array of contents (e.g., advertisement and spam, business proposals, love notes, etc.), linking a specific email or letter to thematic genres in other media. Accordingly, a text may be inscribed in different genre systems at different levels of analysis. To describe two texts as related by genre implies that they share communicative logic and functionalities at some level of analysis.

'Genre' is not only a textual construct. Chapter 3 will demonstrate how the notion of genre is linked to a fundamental cognitive need to categorize and sort experiences and impressions as a means of navigating the social world. Thus, along with other typifications, genres may be viewed as cognitive tools for organizing experience in everyday life. Genre knowledge is crucial for taking meaningful part of communicative encounters. Genres evolve around ongoing negotiations of expectations and conventions regarding media texts and media use. Genre knowledge guides communicative processes of production and reception, and establishes a common ground in interaction. Any textual instance expresses, transgresses, and mixes different aspects of genre, prompting the media user to actualize and adjust pre-established genre knowledge to make sense of the text.

Conceptualizing social media in terms of genre is useful for at least two reasons. First, because it provides 'social media' with a much-needed defining and conceptual framework that captures how different texts within the social media environment resemble one another, and are differentiated from other texts by their communicative characteristics and social functions. The concept of 'genre' has a comparative advantage over 'media' in this respect. It is a much more dynamic and flexible concept, well-suited to describing the shifting environment, and the emergence and decline of forms of online communication, as shaped by the communicative practices and social needs of the users.

Second, the genre perspective shifts the conceptual focus from media technology to the actual communicative process through which different social media accomplish different things for the users, and, in this process, become imbued with meaning, and inscribed in the social fabric of everyday life. The recurrent communicative practices, including the expectations and conventions they embed, are emphasized as playing a central role in constituting the various social media, in an interplay with the communicative characteristics inscribed in the software. Thus, genre involves analytic tools at the level of communicative practice. By stressing genres as orienting devices that help communicating parties to reach an intersubjective understanding of the situation, the framework of genre offers an explanation of how users manage to successfully navigate dynamic and networked social media environments.

NOTES ON CLARIFICATION: MEDIUM, GENRE, TEXT

As a point of departure for distinguishing media and genres, 'media' are tied to inherent material properties (e.g., the physical architecture and expressive means of a device), whereas 'genres' are closely tied to discursive functionalities (e.g., content, stylistics) and social purposes (e.g., Finnemann, 2005; Jensen, 2010; Lüders, 2008).[1] For instance, television as a medium involves a physical device (the television set), characterized by audiovisual means of communication, as discursively manifest in different genres, including entertainment and news genres. With digital media, software enters the equation as an intermediary between medium and genre, disturbing both concepts, because software is tied both to medium and genre, and thereby complicates the distinction between them. In a sense, software is a material component of digital technology. It has properties upon which communicative practices are contingent, and may be programmed as invariant features in specific devices dedicated to specific purposes (e.g., a digital camera) (Finnemann, 2005: 162). However, regarding the internet as a multipurpose or meta-medium (Finnemann, 2005: 165, Jensen, 2010: 69–70, 100), as well as social media in particular, the software dimension is not invariant, but offers the user configuration options at the discursive level. On a blog, you can add or deselect specific interactive features, such as the comment function and thereby customize the software in use. Furthermore, at the interface level, software manifests as (typically interactive) communicative functionalities that are inseparable from genre formation at a discursive level of actual communicative practices and patterns. The mastery and ability to exploit the interactive potential embedded at the software level of social media is a necessary prerequisite for posting content, or responding to other users' contributions on Twitter or a blog, for example, and thereby enter the communicative negotiation of genre. Because of this interference of software with the discursive elements in actual use, in the analysis of social media as communicative genres it is crucial to include the software dimension and its enabling and constraining capacities for communication.

LOCATING GENRE BETWEEN MEDIA AND TEXTS

The concept of genre as used here to conceptualize social media is elastic and multidimensional; it includes differentiations at the software level and at a functional level, for instance (Finnemann, 2005: 163–165). At the software level, genres, including online chat, blogs, social network sites, microblogs, and other types of social media may be distinguished on the basis of their communicative characteristics and interactive functions. Each of these software genres may include functional genres, characterized by specific communicative purposes and social uses at various levels of specificity. As a software genre, the blog, for example, contains a wealth of functional sub-genres that may be classified according to content, directionality of communication, and style, including the personal blog, the corporate blog, and so forth (Lomborg, 2009). The higher level category of 'social media' is understood as a continuously evolving system of interrelated and interdependent communicative genres—as sketched in the beginning of this chapter. The elasticity of the concept of genre is necessary for relating genre to a broad range of texts, because it allows for systematization, by grouping similar texts at different levels of similarity. However, elasticity may also weaken the conceptual usefulness of genre, because it makes it difficult to localize the genre level in concrete analyses. For purposes of clarity, the present analysis operates at a functional genre level, unless otherwise stated in the text.

According to Yates and Orlikowski (1992: 310), genre analysis struggles with two main inconsistencies: The first concerns the *level of abstraction* of the concept of genre. Studies of digital communication often confound 'media' with 'genre,' and there is no conceptual agreement as to what is media and what is genre (Yates & Orlikowski, 1992: 303; also Bhatia, 1996). This inconsistency is directly linked to the problem posed by the interposition of software between medium and genre. For instance, in keeping with the concept of genre I propose here, Herring, Scheidt, Wright, and Bonus (2005) consider the blog a genre, whereas Lüders, Prøitz, and Rasmussen (2010) describe the blog as a medium containing various genres, including the diary blog, for example. In her conceptualization of personal media, Lüders (2008) labels the blog a 'media form,' or a subtype of digital media that lies between the media and the genre levels. The second inconsistency concerns the *normative scope* of the concept of genre, that is, how extensively must norms be recognized, for the recurrent communicative situation to qualify as a genre (Yates & Orlikowski, 1992: 304)? How much room is there for internal variation? Conceptualizing and analyzing social media as genres therefore requires some basic clarification concerning the differentiation and interrelationships between the levels of media, genre, and text.

Arguing for the necessity of separating medium and genre in the analysis of social media, and using blogs as an example, Lüders and colleagues conclude that genres should be located below the software level:

> [. . .] blogs might more conveniently be seen as a *medium,* based upon specified software and templates, on user-friendly updating functions, and with possibilities for comments and presentation of comments in reversed order. Independently of these technical features, different blogs apply different conventions and meet different expectations. To define a genre according to its technological features reduces its important conventional dimensions. (Lüders et al., 2010: 952)

This move clearly separates medium—understood in terms of technical-material features—from genre, understood in terms of communicative conventions and expectations. Hence, genres come into play in Lüders' and colleagues analysis as subcategories of blogs—although the criteria for establishing these subcategories remain unclear. However, the main drawback to their conceptual separation is that by locating genre below the software level, Lüders and colleagues (2010) downplay the fact that the 'technological' features—meaning communicative characteristics, such as reverse chronology, threaded communication, archives, and commenting options—that make the blog recognizable as a blog, are, in fact, socially negotiated, and therefore variable, rather than fixed. These communicative characteristics have not all been common to blogging since its emergence in the mid- to late 1990s, but have gradually come together to constitute the genre (Blood, 2005; Rettberg, 2008). Indeed, this is an example of communicative expectations and conventions of a genre operating at a software level. With changes in software, the discursive functionalities, conventions, and social purposes of a given social media genre may also evolve through usage patterns over time. Additionally, despite the common understanding of blogs as dialogic and bidirectional, not all blogs have commenting functions, for instance, but they are still based on blogging software, and commonly recognized as blogs.

In contrast, if we take Herring and colleagues' perspective, also on defining blogs, there is a similar lack of nuance in the understanding of the interplay between media, communicative functionalities embedded in the software, and communicative practices of users in shaping the blog as a genre over time, albeit here, the defining problem is reversed. Herring and colleagues (2005) define the blog solely from a software perspective, as a genre of CMC: a frequently modified web page in which dated entries are listed in reverse chronological sequence. This definition simply ignores the communicative practices, expectations, and social purposes that constitute the genre at a given point in time. Apart from not being exhaustive at a software level, this technical definition of genre also seems to lose sight of any relevant distinction between medium and genre. As a further note concerning the software level, some of the communicative characteristics associated with blogs, such as reverse chronology as a temporal organizing principle, are also characteristic of other genres within the social media landscape, including Twitter, and various forms of newsfeeds on social network sites. In these other services, reverse chronology as a particular software element is embedded in a different configuration programmed into the software. Accordingly, what constitutes a blog, in relation to other software genres, is the specific configuration of communicative characteristics that have become conventionalized for blogs, and make blogs socially recognizable and distinct from other genres.

To avoid definitional deficits, and to retain the relevance of distinguishing between media and genre, we may want to consider the blog and other types of social media, as expressed through the medium of the internet, as overarching software genres with subgenres—negotiated, variable, and possibly changing over time (Lomborg, 2009). Such subgenres may be closely related in terms of social purposes, or primarily resemble each other through the communicative characteristics that have come to conventionally define the blog.

Media may contain genres, and media often play a significant role in the recurrent situation from which a genre arises (Yates & Orlikowski, 1992: 310). The internet and the mobile phone are media or meta-media, which contain a wealth of genres (text message, phone call, homepage, email, blog, social network site, online chat, etc.). These genres are often primarily tied to the internet (homepage, blog, online chat, etc.) or the mobile phone (text message, telephone call), but in principle, the uses of the various genres are independent of media platforms. In the past few years we have seen an increase in social media genres functioning across media platforms. Social network sites, image-sharing and microblogging services are used both on web and mobile applications and are thus framed in the interplay between the internet and the mobile phone as communication media.

The notion that genres are influenced by media platforms and technologies (including the physical architecture of the platform) is not new, although genre studies often lack an elaborate sensibility to the influence of the mediation on the genre. For instance, television has specific capacities to influence the news genre, because it is an audio-visual medium, typically situated in living rooms in people's homes. This allows for specific modes of address, and expands the expressive register of the news genre. However, with the interposition of software between media platform and genre in digital media, a new dimension is added to the adjustment and development of genres.

As described in the introduction to this chapter, genre differentiation within the social media landscape rests on a socially shaped evolutionary process in which emergent genres are negotiated at the intersection of existing genres (digital genres, as well as those associated with print and electronic media technologies, for instance; Lüders et al., 2010; Miller &

Shepherd, 2004), and the communicative potential and constraints offered by digital media. Compared to other media technologies, the span of communicative potential is quite broad, because digital media technology, at the software level is extremely variable (e.g., Finnemann, 2005: 154–160). Developers (and sometimes technologically skilled users) explore these communicative potentials and constraints, to design and launch new software and new services, and to expand and transform existing genres. Ordinary users explore the communicative potentials too, in and through their communicative practices and interactions with peers, within and across different genres. With regard to more fundamental genre adjustments, Twitter is a particularly vivid example of the social shaping of genres, and genre change from the bottom up. As an example of the microblogging genre, Twitter was originally designed as a communicative network through which individuals could tweet short blurbs about what was on their minds, with other users reading them—it was not really designed for conversation. However, users themselves began to have conversations, and to disseminate each other's tweets, resulting in the addressivity function of the @ sign, and the RT (retweet) function becoming embedded in the design over time (boyd, Golder, & Lotan, 2010). By making changes at the software level, Twitter has sought to adapt the service to the users' needs and practices.

From an everyday perspective, however, ordinary users' sensemaking and negotiations of genre in social media take place at a textual level, that is, within the mostly unproblematic and commonsense communicative practice, enabled and constrained by the technological framework of the genre at hand. Coding and programming is limited in ordinary users' social media practices, simply because it requires exceptional technological skills and a lot of work to, say, use the API of Facebook to program a casual gaming application for Facebook. Furthermore, such fundamental developments, additions to, or reorganizations of the technological features of a genre (e.g., development of a new application for Twitter on iPhone) may involve a significantly longer time frame than the simpler, more situated challenges of genre conventions, through content contribution in a specific text in a given context, at a given point in time. Text, here, is understood broadly as communicative practice, that is, users' actual discursive (written, aural, visual, multimodal) contributions within a given social media service.

At a functional genre level, genre constitution entails a continuous effort and negotiation of relevant skills and knowledge through communicative practice, manifested in specific texts. According to Yates and Orlikowski (1992), the constitution of a genre (or subgenre, for that matter) is only realized insofar as the communicative practices, conventions, and expectations linked to the genre are socially shared and recognized within a group of users, and recurrently expressed as text. Consequently, with regard to its normative scope, genre constitution is a collaborative accomplishment, although individuals or relatively small groups of people may play leading roles in shaping the genre. Because social recognition plays such a vital part, 'doing' genre is, in a sense, a negotiation of membership in the communicative circuit of a genre. To be accepted within a given network of users engaged in, and connected to a specific genre, it is necessary to demonstrate an understanding and knowledge of how the genre works, which behaviors and skills are considered appropriate and relevant to the genre. In short: to enter the negotiation of a genre, one must be capable of enacting the genre competently, according to already established conventions. Once accepted as a competent user of the genre, the individual may contribute to its reshaping and evolution. Bakhtin writes that genres must be mastered to be manipulated freely (1986: 80). Therefore, genre development always rests on and refers to already established genre conventions and expectations.

Genres are developed through the transgression of existing genre conventions in concrete communicative practice. Genres are abstract categories or prototypes that are expressed in actual text, but a text is never a pure instance of a genre. Any given blog or online chat is a bearer of genre traits, and therefore a situated expressions of the genre, but local communicative practices also constitute a blog as a unique, emergent text. Different texts within a genre offer diverse interpretations of the genre, owing to local contingencies such as the individual participants' social or psychological trajectories, experiences, and expectations, and the relationship among the communicating parties. In social media, ordinary users are the drivers of genre transgression and development. By experimenting with different content, forms, and stylistic-expressive means, ordinary users play a very active part in shaping, interpreting, and developing a genre over time.

GENRE AND CMC

The argument that genre is becoming increasingly relevant as a useful concept for grasping the myriad of online communication forms is not entirely new, but has been raised sporadically in the field of CMC since the public breakthrough of the internet (e.g., Erickson, 2000; Yates & Orlikowski, 1992; Yates & Sumner, 1997). Yet, genre analysis has not gained much traction in the study of online communication.

There is some related work on genres and CMC, regarding both conceptual and analytical frameworks for digital genre analysis (e.g., Bauman, 1999; Erickson, 2000; Yates & Sumner, 1997), and concrete analyses of digital genres such as email (e.g., Yates & Orlikowski, 1992), homepages (e.g., Askehave & Nielsen, 2005; Crowston & Williams, 2000), blogs (e.g., Miller & Shepherd, 2004; Herring et al., 2005; for a detailed review, see Lomborg, 2009), and mobile communication (e.g., Erjavec & Kovačič, 2009; Ling, Julsrud, & Yttri, 2005).

Most of the studies of genre in CMC are grounded in either functional linguistic genre theory (Bhatia, 1996; Swales, 1990) or rhetorical genre theory (Bazerman, 1988; Miller, 1984), and draw on classic text analysis methods. Despite a theoretical emphasis on studying genre as social action that accomplishes certain communicative purposes and functions for the communicators, these studies rarely take the genre analysis beyond a classificatory level that describes a given genre and its subgenres, based on form and content. Exceptions include Miller and Shepherd (2004), Lüders and colleagues (2010), and Giltrow and Stein's (2009) anthology on genres and the internet, all presenting historical perspectives in which the analyses focus on explaining emergent genres by connecting them to their antecedents, such as the personal blog as a reframing of the diary.

A focus on textual classification is not necessarily problematic, but it misses the wider potential of genre analysis in explaining how genres are constituted, negotiated, stabilized, and destabilized in the communicative process. Focusing specifically on discussions of the blog as a genre, boyd (2006a) contests the analytical value of (content-based) genre classifications, such as describing blogs as extended diary-writing or as journalism. By using these content labels, she argues, the analytic gaze is blurred and constrained, resulting in a lack of sensitivity to the wealth of practices and social functions that may characterize blogging. Classification simply reduces complexity too much. As a top-down approach, classification entails analyzing and inferring on the premise of existing genres, thereby potentially failing to account for any distinctly new traits that could be constitutive of new genres, and that could be inferred from the grounded analysis of actual communicative practice. Genre analysis based purely on classification might create an inappropriately static description of genre; it loses sight of the dynamic aspects and situated uses of a given genre at a given time, including the specific social accomplishments entailed in a given enactment of a genre. Instead of classification, genre analysis should focus on what genres do, and how they are socially negotiated in actual communicative practice.

FUNCTIONAL GENRE THEORY

Genre analysis is an interdisciplinary approach that has been developed, and is quite influential in several research fields, among them—and for the present purpose, most importantly—rhetoric, applied linguistics, and media studies. In these three fields, a functional perspective of genre has become influential, one that shifts the focus of genre analysis from content/form-based description and classification, to an understanding of genre in terms of function and purpose. There is considerable overlap between the different strands of genre theory, especially in the linguistic and rhetorical approaches to genre (Bhatia, 1996). This overlap is also evident in most of the cited studies of digital media genres, which combine various genre theory approaches. In this section, I briefly sketch some of the chief components of the above-mentioned three strands of genre theory, to map out similarities and differences between the guiding principles in genre analysis.

The common basis for *applied linguistics genre studies* is the study of situated linguistic behavior in institutional—for example academic, educational, or other professional—settings (Bhatia, 1996: 40). The applied linguistics approach to genre is primarily associated with the works of John Swales (1990), whose definition of genre emphasizes the communicative purpose as a guiding principle for the genre:

> A genre comprises a class of communicative events, the members of which share some set of communicative purposes. These purposes are recognized by the expert members of the parent discourse community and thereby constitute the rationale for the genre. This rationale shapes the schematic structure of the discourse and influences and constrains choice of content and style. (Swales, 1990: 58)

The emphasis on communicative purpose, or why people in a discourse community use language as they do, for Swales entails an analytic focus on the detailed use of language in terms of linguistic style and content. By examining these textual traits, or 'move-structures,' as Swales calls them, the communicative purpose or goal of the genre is uncovered.

The model of genre analysis proposed by Swales has been used and elaborated by Askehave and Nielsen (2005) in their analysis of corporate websites, in which they identify basic communicative characteristics and their strategic purposes. In their socio-linguistic study of communication in a computer conferencing system for distance learning, Yates and Sumner (1997) classify the communication according to communicative purpose and move-structure, and use this to discuss the shaping and fixity of digital genres.

A somewhat parallel development in *rhetorical genre analysis* is marked by a seminal and highly influential essay by Carolyn Miller (1984), suggesting that genre should be seen as social action. Miller builds on the works of Alfred Schutz, and specifically the idea that humans act on the basis of their understanding of a situation. Understanding, in turn, is generated by a process of typification, or categorization, in which humans establish recurrence and similarity between events (Miller, 1984: 156). Genre can be considered one such recurrent pattern:

> Genre refers to a conventional category of discourse based in large-scale typification of rhetorical action; as action, it acquires meaning from situation and from the social context in which that situation arose. (Miller, 1984: 163)

With this definition of genre as typified communicative action in recurrent situations (Yates & Orlikowski, 1992: 299), Miller emphasizes the social context in which the genre it put to use as important for understanding the social action that it accomplishes. The situated action that the genre accomplishes is highlighted as the guiding principle, implying that genres must be analyzed from the bottom up, according to the communicative purpose and rhetorical situation in which they occur. This is very similar to Swales' focus on communicative purpose, a similarity that is further underlined by Miller, who argues that the content and form (including the structural and linguistic features and the medium (Yates & Orlikowski, 1992: 301)) of a given genre reflect the situated action it accomplishes. However, whereas for Swales communicative purpose is framed as individual intention and function, from Miller's perspective, purpose—or 'social motive' as she calls it—is instead an objectified social need (Miller, 1984: 163). Hence, the genre's communicative purpose in Miller's genre theory is, in a sense, socially negotiated. Along these lines, she further contends that a genre is a rhetorical means for mediating between private intentions and social exigency (the objectified social need); it connects the private with the public, the unique with the recurrent (Miller, 1984: 163). Elaborating this point, Berkenkotter and Huckin (1993) suggest viewing genre as situated cognition, tying together individual understandings with the social situation. This perspective is developed in Chapter 3.

A core component of rhetorical genre theory is an emphasis on dynamic or mutable aspects of genre. Linking Miller's concept of genre to the process of structuration, Yates and Orlikowski (1992) stress that genres evolve over time, owing to the mutual influence of the institutionalized practices, and individual actions and interpretations of the genre. 'A particular instance of a genre need not draw on all the rules constituting the genre' (Yates & Orlikowski, 1992: 302): it suffices that the communicating parties recognize it as an instance of a specific genre. By enacting the genre only partly in compliance with the genre rules, the genre is challenged, and thus must be renegotiated.

Yates and Orlikowski (1992) used Miller's rhetorical concept of genre to study the evolution of the memo in organizational communication, focusing particularly on the role of email in shaping the memo genre. Their study is pioneering and widely cited in the academic literature on digital genres, as they were among the first to conceptualize recurrent electronic communication practices in terms of genre.

The notion of genre in *media studies* has its roots in literary and film studies (Bakhtin, 1986; Neale, 1980; Todorov, 1990), and has been cultivated in the study of television program genres. Whereas the linguistic and rhetorical approaches to genre are primarily concerned with the communicative purpose or social action of the author or rhetoric as manifested in communication, in media studies the core achievement of the concept of genre is the idea that genres are understood as systems of orientations, expectations, and conventions that circulate among producers and audiences through mass media texts (e.g., Neale, 1980: 19, Tolson, 1996: 92). Consequently, the scope of genre analysis is broadened to encompass not only the study of textual types, but also frameworks of production and interpretation (Andersen,

1994: 10–11). The central element is the idea of genre as a relatively stable 'horizon of expectations,' understood as assumptions or genre knowledge guiding the recipient's making sense of a given text, and a specific production model guiding the sender (Palmer, 1990: 11–13). Familiarity with, and ability to distinguish a variety of genres is a necessary communicative skill for the media user. Accordingly, genre may be thought of as a tacit contract or a conventional relationship among producer, text, and recipient, which ensures mutual understanding in the communication process (Mikkelsen, 1994: 55, Neale, 1980: 19).

Genre knowledge is a precondition for (successful) text production and text-processing because it reduces communicative complexity and contingency and delimits the interpretive space (Andersen, 1994: 18). Furthermore, in keeping with Miller's dynamic and negotiated concept of genre, genres constrain communication and regulate behavior (Livingstone, 2008: 396) and are also dynamic, shaped through interaction, and changing over time, as new texts within a genre reframe or challenge the genre conventions (Neale, 1980: 48–50; Palmer, 1990: 14). To illustrate this, we may consider an individual blog as a) an instance of the blog genre that is inscribed into the general dynamics of blogging, and thus adheres to socially defined norms and practices surrounding blogging; and b) a subjective interpretation of the blog genre, shaped by the blogger and his or her readers. In other words, the individual blog is shaped by already established conventions of the blog genre, *and* contributes to the continuous shaping of the genre, creation of subgenres, and so on.

Palmer (1990) argues that genres cannot be unequivocally defined, because they are dynamic social processes, and refer to multiple dimensions within and outside the text. Within the text, genre may be manifest at the levels of content, style, and as a communicative or compositional structure. To this, Andersen (1994) adds a pragmatic dimension—how genre is used, and what the genre conventions accomplish for the user in a given usage context. This is similar to what is seen in Miller's (1984) approach. The pragmatic dimension thus reaches beyond the text itself, and inscribes production and reception in their contexts of use. With genres conceptualized as sensemaking devices and horizons of expectations in the communication process, the pragmatic dimension becomes the overarching principle in the genre analysis.

Operating with a functional concept of genre, the linguistic, rhetorical, and media studies approaches to genre share a focus on studying the communicative purpose as manifest in genre conventions of form, style, and content, in recurrent communicative situations or texts. Textual analysis thus plays a pivotal role in genre studies. With the inclusion of production models guiding text production, and horizons of expectations guiding text interpretation in the concept of genre, media studies broaden the methodological and analytic scope of genre analysis, by explicitly identifying elements outside the text as starting points for understanding how genres work, and what they accomplish for the communicating parties. Thus, in a media studies perspective, genre analysis may include production and reception studies, using classic sociological methods such as participant observation and interviews with media professionals and audiences (e.g., Bruun, 2010; Frandsen & Bruun, 2005; Ytreberg, 2000).

The functional concept of genre has primarily been used to study written documents (e.g., the memo, the business letter) and television formats (e.g., talk shows, news, soap operas) and to some extent in media studies, their reception. Written documents and television formats are institutionalized forms of communication, insofar as the text is a fixed and bounded product, usually produced by a professional author, and received by an audience. With social media, these conditions change. Ordinary users increasingly become producers, texts are constantly modified and expanded, and the separation of audience and producers becomes increasingly obsolete. This raises the question of whether the functional concept of genre must be reformulated— theoretically and methodologically—in the study of social media. Arguing that the concept of genre is still highly relevant and analytically useful, in the next section I discuss and accommodate the genre perspective to the study of social media as communicative genres.

CHALLENGING GENRE ANALYSIS

What happens to genre theory when the analytic object changes? What challenges and opportunities do social media bring to classic genre theory? Beginning with a revision of the producer-text-audience model, social media may be described according to their distinction from forms of mass and broadcast communication, and in terms of a number of key characteristics.

First, whereas in mass media there is an unequal or asymmetric communicative relationship between producer and audience, because the communication is unidirectional (i.e. one way, from producer to audience), the internet and mobile phone involve a greater potential for *symmetrical communicative relations* among the interacting parties. Producers have a less privileged position in the communicative process because text production is often collaborative and conversational in nature. Moreover, the networked interactional structure that forms the basis of many of the currently flourishing social media means that users communicate directly with one another, instead of through an intermediary agent (e.g., via a blog or a chat room, as opposed to a newspaper, in which reader commentaries are selected and edited by a moderator or gatekeeper). Bruns' (2008) concept of 'produsage' and the associated collapse of the producer and user into a joint category, 'produsers,' even suggest that in social media, users are always also producers. However, despite a strong focus on individual user agency in social media, this agency is of course to a great extent framed by the institutions and companies who provide social media services and used them to mine user data for their own purposes (e.g., Bechmann & Lomborg, 2013; van Dijck, 2009).

Second, social media constitute a *deinstitutionalized* or *deprofessionalized* space (Lüders, 2008), because ordinary users and media professionals alike have equal, easy access to the means of digital production and distribution of content. For instance, blogging software from various companies is available for free, and blogging is thus accessible to everyone who wants to contribute. The flip side of this is that social media require more effort from the user to flourish and are dependent on popularity among and participation of users in the production and filtering of content. Having ordinary users contribute content implies that they, too, set the criteria of what is topically relevant in social media. This has sparked an enormous amount of content, reflecting the personal, everyday lives and moods of users, their daily efforts to coordinate social activities, and a vast amount of informal small talk, alongside more information-oriented media uses. Hence, social media make the lives of ordinary people the center of attention.

Third, social media, and the internet more generally, entail a *destabilization of the text* or media product as epitomized in the concept of 'produsage' (Bruns, 2008: 21). In other words, texts are emergent and continuously revised and may change their course (thematic scope, style, form) over time as different users leave their footprints on them. Consequently, it may be more suitable to simply conceive of the online text as mediated social interaction or conversation, in which the users' interests, understandings, and values are actualized, negotiated, reproduced, and transformed, to make sense of the situation and attune users to one another.

These intrinsic characteristics and dynamics of social media have significant consequences for the communicative environment. They potentially render genres much more dynamic and unstable, when compared to a mass media environment. The initiative concerning genre renewal in mass media is left to a fairly small group of professionals (e.g., business leaders, filmmakers, or television producers) who share a certain mindset. This shared mindset may result in mass media productions being more likely to reproduce than innovate genre. Furthermore, the communicating parties (author[s] and audience) are usually separated by time and space, rendering immediate and direct feedback on the text impossible. Considering this in connection with the primacy of commercial logic in mass media, with regard to retaining audiences (for either public service legitimacy or advertising revenue), institutional media outlets may be inclined to 'play it safe,' and serve familiar products to their mainstream audiences. Consequently, the institutionalized production patterns and the separation of senders and audiences in time and space may significantly slow down genre development. However, this principal presumption must be examined through empirical analysis.

In contrast, social media genres may be expected to exhibit more dynamic and unstable genre patterns, because a larger and more diverse number of producers and audiences are in direct dialogue, making feedback instantaneous, especially in synchronous, short-form genres such as micro-blogs or online chat. As a consequence of the direct feedback structure online, genres are likely to be organized in a more ad-hoc manner, as the horizons of expectations of the users as producers may be constantly challenged, reproduced, and adjusted through interaction with fellow users. Again, the argument here is a theoretical one that must be tested through empirical analysis. Additionally, because communication in many social media genres is embedded in practices of network creation and maintenance, the dynamics of networking influence genre development. The network structure may involve less tightly knit norms among a fixed set of participants, and thus engender greater genre instability, but the dependence on connecting with others through networks may also generate pressure to conform. Whether the network structure is a stabilizing or destabilizing factor for genre cannot be answered solely through theoretical discussion, but must rest on empirical analyses of the actual dynamics related to the networks active in the expression and negotiation of a given genre.

When the ordinary (prod)user, rather than media institution, defines the genre conventions, this has the potential to create more ambiguity, more variation, and less stability in the expression of a given genre; the wealth of subgenres and hybrids within the blog genre illustrates this (Lüders, 2008: 688). Furthermore, genre overlaps, combinations, and mergers may be more common. For instance, Twitter and other microblogging services combine core features from social network sites (articulation of networks of friends or followers) with elements of blogging (e.g., author-centeredness, reverse chronology). Genre mixing is also widespread within individual texts: for example, a specific blog may combine political statements and arguments with notes on the author's private life (Lomborg, 2009). Along similar lines, users often simultaneously communicate through multiple genres with the same people (e.g., Rainie & Wellman, 2012), implying, perhaps, that genre norms linked to, for instance, conversations in a microblog migrate to text messages or other social media. Another example of the intersection of separate genre circuits is the practice of auto-updating, which involves interlinking one's Twitter, and Facebook accounts, for instance, so that new posts in one appear automatically in the others.

The dynamism of social media is perhaps most evident in the almost incessant emergence of new services that enter the genre system, and have the potential to destabilize existing genres. The advent of the microblog (Twitter, and the Facebook status update in particular), for instance, initially destabilized the blog. Its short form involved easier and less time-consuming communication than the often-lengthy postings prevalent in blogs, and microblogs quickly gained popularity. This led some media commentators to proclaim the death of the blog—outstripped by a simpler and faster genre. This claim was overly dramatic, but when new genres acquire a foothold, the functions and social uses of existing genres within the genre system of social media are readjusted, and their purposes redefined.

GENRE ANALYSIS AS A FRAMEWORK FOR
SOCIAL MEDIA STUDIES

In this chapter, I have sketched a quite chaotic communicative environment in which social media are seen as genres in constant flux. Paradoxically, this is the reason that genres and genre knowledge are still extremely important orientation and sensemaking devices for users: they frame communication with certain conventions and expectations, and thus provide a sense of 'fixity' (Lüders et al., 2010; Yates & Sumner, 1997). Arguably, genre analysis is highly relevant and useful for understanding how users navigate social media.

Rather than reject genre theory in the study of social media, I suggest that it may be attuned to this field by moving the pragmatic dimension already emphasized by Miller (1984) and Andersen (1994) to the center of genre analysis, and by incorporating sensitivity to enactment and interactional dynamics as an important aspect of the negotiation of genre (Yates & Orlikowski, 1992). The concept of horizons of expectations distributed among producers and recipients already entails possibilities for the formulation of a pragmatic concept of genre. It bears a strong resemblance to the micro-sociological concept of 'frames,' denoting how people behave in social situations, based on their previous experiences, as indicated, but not elaborated on by Palmer (1990: 12–13) and Frandsen and Bruun (2005), among others. Miller's (1984) understanding of genre as social action expresses a similar inclination toward social interaction, in that she likens rhetorical genres to mundane behavioral routines. Furthermore, Helles (2009), drawing on Miller (1984), and Yates and Orlikowski (1992), has discussed genres as interactional scripts. Genre analysis would benefit from being drawn in a more interactionist direction. Enhanced emphasis on the pragmatic dimension of genre analysis, including interaction dynamics and negotiations of meaning, attunes genre analysis to the interactional and networked logic of social media.

A genre analysis of social media must take as its starting point the communicative practices that characterize (a) specific instance(s) of the genre. That is to say, classic textual analysis remains central to genre analysis. However, methodologically and analytically, this creates a range of new possibilities for genre analysis. If genre is enacted through social interaction, this implies that genre may be studied and analyzed within a pragmatic framework focused on how users 'do' genre. That is, how do users accomplish meaningful communication by bringing interactional norms, conventions, and genre knowledge into play in the communicative process? How do they demonstrate genre competence?

What may a more interactionally attuned genre analysis look like? I have identified four interrelated dimensions of genre—composition, content, style, and pragmatic function (Andersen, 1994)—to analyze how the participants make sense of their communicative practices on social media.

Analyses at the *compositional level* would include two elements. One element is an examination of the network composition, structures of participation, and activity levels in concrete instances of social media to yield an initial understanding of the relationship between the individual author (i.e. the user contributing content by writing a blog or maintaining a Facebook profile) and the networked audience, as participants in situated, communicative networks, in which the social media genre is enacted and negotiated. The second element is an analysis of the social organization of communicative practices on social media, including how participants engage in ongoing communicative structuring of their interactions, according to a set of genre conventions and expectations (e.g., concerning frequency, responsiveness, reciprocity, etc.). This would also include participants' management of the spatio-temporal conditions and the networked structures of (participation in) social media.

An analysis of the *thematic orientations* would explore the predominant topics of communication and the associated relevance structures as negotiated and regulated by patterns of responsiveness. This would unveil the norms of appropriate content, including how participants balance the personal experience and perspective from which social media are used, with a sensitivity to general relevance, privacy protection, and a wish to connect with, and engage the audience in conversation.

An examination of the *stylistic traits* of communication on social media would address the specific tone that participants must master in order to enact the genre competently, and be recognized and validated by fellow participants as relevant peers and members, in the ongoing negotiations of genre.

Identifying recurrent practices according to composition, thematic and stylistic traits in social media is a starting point for studying the communicative functionalities and social practices that characterize the uses of a specific genre, and make it distinct from other genres. This provides important insights for the *pragmatic dimension* of genre, that is, for what underlying social purposes or motives the genre caters.

Moving beyond textual analysis of communicative practices on social media may expand the analysis of the pragmatic functions and significance that users ascribe to a genre in everyday life. A clarification of the notion of genre as a cognitive tool for organizing experience elicits a deeper understanding of how the use of a genre connects with—and is embedded in—broader patterns of meaning in participants' everyday lives, including how 'doing' genre contributes to sensemaking of the self and social worlds we inhabit. The next chapter expounds on how genre functions as a sensemaking device in everyday communicative practice.

CHAPTER SUMMARY

Social media may be conceptualized as communicative genres negotiated at the intersection of the enabling and constraining capacities of software, and the actual unfolding of communicative practice. To analyze social media, I have devised a pragmatic approach to genre analysis, aimed at documenting broader patterns of interaction in social media, and the social purposes they accomplish. Addressing participants' genre knowledge and expectations, a central analytical task is the identification of interactional skills necessary for engaging in meaningful communication on social media. What types of knowledge are considered important in a given genre, what are the basic components of this knowledge, and to what degree are genre knowledge and expectations shared and agreed upon? How do participants' practices stabilize and destabilize genre knowledge and patterns over time? In addition, how is the skilled enactment of genres of social media related to other activities, experiences, and meanings of the everyday? These are key questions for beginning to explore how engagement with social media is rendered significant as a communicative condition in contemporary society.

NOTE

1. To be sure, media are not solely defined by their material properties. For instance, Finnemann defines media as physically organized matter that is used for symbolic purposes (2005: 89).

3   Genre as a Cognitive Category for Making Sense of the Ordinary

In the introduction to the previous chapter, I briefly connected genre to cognitive processes with the idea that genres are devices for orienting and making sense of everyday life. In this chapter, I develop this claim in detail, by examining the cognitive underpinnings of genre as a sensemaking device. Here, cognition is broadly understood as encompassing emotional and bodily aspects, as well as processes of acquiring and using knowledge to navigate everyday life (cf. Hagen, 1998: 60). This chapter focuses on the relation between cognition, in terms of socially negotiated and mentally anchored categories of classification and systematization of experiences in the social world, and actual, practical, instances of sensemaking in everyday life. Sensemaking denotes the process through which individuals actively construct events and experiences as meaningful, usually by ensuring a pattern fit between event and cognitive categories, that is, a confirmation of expectations (Weick, 1995: 4).

In media studies, there is a strong tradition of qualitative research on media audiences and their reception of media texts. Audience studies cover a range of theoretical approaches with roots in the humanities as well as social sciences, including cultural studies, literary criticism, media ethnography, and reception analysis, which may be distinguished by their conceptualization of the relation between the text and recipient (Schrøder, Drotner, Kline, & Murray, 2003). For instance, literary criticism emphasizes and studies the textual traits and structures as they condition the process of reception, whereas media ethnography is rather uninterested in the medium and the text, and gives weight to the audience and the social activities that evolve around the use of media in various everyday life contexts. The trade-off between focusing on text or context is fundamental to audience studies—and widely debated (e.g., Ang, 1996; Hermes, 1993).

In reception analysis, the text and the activity of the audience are regarded as equally important objects of study, and those involved in this line of research are particularly interested in sensemaking processes in the meeting between text and audience. A few Scandinavian studies that have a close affinity with reception analysis and use the concept of genre may be labeled socio-cognitive reception studies (Bruun, 2004; Höijer, 1992; Jensen, 1998).

These studies address the reception of television and conceptualize the sense-making process as a socio-cognitive activity. Common to these studies of sensemaking of television genres are their theoretical roots in schema theory, a cognitive psychology theory of how humans process information about the social world.

I begin my examination of the relationship between cognition and sense-making with a literature review and discussion of socio-cognitive reception studies, because these—like my study—use genre as an analytic concept to balance a strong media and textual anchoring with an elaborate under-standing of the media user's active, meaning-producing engagement with media texts. I problematize these studies on two grounds: a) their concep-tual balancing of the psychological and the social aspects of cognition, and b) their difficulties in operationalizing the cognitive component in empiri-cal research designs. To address these shortcomings, I elaborate the meta-theoretical foundations of a more sociologically oriented, socio-cognitive approach to communication and media use, inspired by pragmatic theories in the social-psychological domain. On this basis, I formulate some method-ological premises for the empirical study of how ordinary users make sense of social media as communicative genres in everyday life, by invoking genre knowledge and establishing shared understandings of the communicative situation with other users, and inscribe social media use in broader contexts of meaning.

SCHEMA THEORY AND MEDIA RECEPTION

Socio-cognitive reception studies address the psychosocial processes of the recipient in relation to the media text, and how the activation of specific cognitive schemas influences the recipient's making sense of the text. The studies use the qualitative, in-depth interview with the individual television viewer to generate data on these sensemaking processes. Höijer defines cog-nition as 'the imaginative and conceptual world that an individual mentally builds up on the basis of his or her socio-cultural experiences and uses to form interpretive models for new experiences' (Höijer, 1998: 73). A central aspect of this theory of cognition is the concept of 'mental schemas', that is, psychological structures that shape our perceptions, interpretations, and sensemaking processes, in relation to our experiences.[1] These schemas are tools for processing information and reducing complexity, thereby helping us navigate everyday life (Höijer, 1992). This conception of cognition implies a separation of psychological processes and social processes, although they are connected. The concrete acts of perception and interpretation are men-tal processes exclusively accessible to the individual, although the cogni-tive schemes guiding these acts are shaped by, and shape our experiences in the social world. However, Höijer seems slightly inconsistent on this point. She also argues that schemas are sometimes shared among individuals in socially constituted groups, thereby forming 'interpretive communities' (Höijer, 1992: 286). How is such 'sharedness' possible, if cognitive processes of interpretation are inherently mental and individual?

There seems to be some ambiguity concerning theoretical conceptions of the role of the social in cognitive processes within the schema theory approach to reception. Waldahl (1998), for instance, takes a strong mentalist stance, and barely considers the social in his theory of media effects. He relates schemas to long-term memory, and considers them information-processing tools for organizing the stimuli that individuals perceive in their environments (Waldahl, 1998: 41–45). Bruun (2004) and Jensen (1998) seem to place a somewhat greater emphasis on the social, in their understanding of socio-cognitive processes of sensemaking. Bruun (2004) softens the distinction between the mental and the social by arguing that schemas are both individually anchored and collectively shared (Bruun, 2004: 74–80), but she still maintains that sensemaking is an individual activity influenced by societal conditions (Bruun, 2004: 75). Jensen, while not explicitly discussing the theory, seems to take the social perspective further, by emphasizing meaning as socially produced (Jensen, 1998: 58). This social production of meaning is revealed in so-called 'super-themes,' general understandings and assumptions that respondents draw upon when making sense of televised news. Jensen writes that 'super-themes are not merely abstract cognitive categories, but are rooted in a specific cultural and historical context as well as in particular events in the news thematizing this context' (Jensen, 1998: 50). In other words, the socio-cognitive activity of sensemaking is not considered a purely individual activity, but a social process, and meaning is not isolated in the individual mind, but is anchored in culture and societal discourses. Hagen (1998) argues for the need for a more cultural and historical focus in socio-cognitive reception theory, and subscribes to an even stronger socio-cultural orientation in her discussion of schema theory. Hence, Hagen and Jensen both recognize the importance of context for the sensemaking of media texts. However, none of these scholars provides concrete directions as to how schemas may be shared and socially anchored, or as to how context may be systematically included in the socio-cognitive analysis of media use.

Another ambiguity becomes apparent when looking at the use of schema theory in empirical studies, that is, whether schema theory should be considered a meta-theoretical framework, or an operational theory. Whereas Jensen and Bruun, studying televised news and daytime talk shows, respectively, leave social schemas in the background of their analyses, they do use them actively, to generate the central analytical themes of their studies. Jensen focuses on cultural themes apparent in reception experiences and sensemaking, and Bruun investigates genre knowledge and expectations as schemas to be described. Höijer looks more explicitly for activated schemas, thereby placing cognitive schemas at the center of her methodology. I find it useful to outline her empirical studies in more detail, because a discussion of the operational difficulties of schema theory in reception research provides important insights into the critical discussion of the schema theory perspective, and a reformulation of the socio-cognitive approach to reception studies of genres.

Höijer explores individual sensemaking of various television genres in two different studies. The first study is guided by the hypothesis that genre influences the degree of textual 'openness' to the interpretation of television programs (Höijer, 1991). The second study explores how different schemas are actualized, and what kinds of experience and knowledge from the personal lives of audiences are brought into play in the reception situation (Höijer, 1992). She investigates this by exploring audiences' streams of thought after screening texts, and these streams of thought are revealed through in-depth interviews that ask respondents questions such as: 'What did you think of?' 'What does it remind you of?' (Höijer, 1992: 293). The first study measures the degree of textual openness by counting the number of thoughts generated by a particular television clip, and by coding the different types of thought (Höijer, 1991: 32–40). The results suggest that televised fiction triggers more thoughts than do factual genres, leading Höijer to claim that fictional texts are more open to interpretation than factual texts (Höijer, 1991: 54). Furthermore, different textual genres generate different types of thought—hence, different genres initiate different psychological processes (Höijer, 1991: 60–68). In the second study, Höijer demonstrates that television audiences draw on experience from their everyday lives when making sense of screened television clips. She claims that this reveals how different cognitive schemas (relating to occupational spheres, leisure and family activities, media consumption, etc.) are activated in the reception situation, guiding the interpretation of the text (Höijer, 1992: 294–299).

SCHEMA THEORY PROBLEMATIZED

Höijer's empirical studies of the schemas at work in text reception indicate a fundamental operational problem with the cognitive component in reception analysis. Although Höijer's study documents that textual genres influence the recipient's processes of sensemaking, it does not provide empirical insights into how sensemaking is a *socio*-cognitive process. The results do not tell us much about how experience and interpretations are constructed, informed by, and constituted as *socially shared knowledge*, and in what *contexts* of use they are meaningful. Instead, the study simply confirms that the individual recipient processes *texts* by activating various cognitive schemas.

Schema theory has a strong affinity with the information-processing paradigm of cognitive psychology, with its theoretical focus on memory and comprehension studies (for a review see Matlin, 2005: 274–290), and a heritage of neurobiological theory (Bruun, 2004: 75; Augoustinos & Walker, 1995: 33). Based on the idea that cognitive schemas are fundamental to human thinking, it is assumed that facts about human experience, understood in terms of the functioning and content of cognitive schemas, may be discovered through research (Augoustinos & Walker, 1995: 262). Thus, schemas are studied as rather static mental structures. This implied ontological and epistemological realism is to some extent reflected in socio-cognitive reception studies, perhaps most clearly in Waldahl's (1998) theoretical contribution to schema theory and Höijer's (1991, 1992) empirical studies, in the way she explicitly seeks and identifies activated schemas in the reception situation. Jensen (1998), Hagen (1998), and Bruun (2004) seem to combine realist ontology with a more constructivist epistemology, hence their greater emphasis on the social in their conceptions of cognition. This epistemological stance is much more in tune with the conceptual framework of genres as socially negotiated, and thus dynamic cognitive tools for organizing experience.

From a reception analysis perspective, one could argue that schema theory is too rigid to be applied usefully (Augoustinos & Walker, 1995: 165). The strong focus on cognitive structures and information processing makes schema theory unsuitable for addressing some rather central questions in reception studies, including the quality of the reception experience, and audiences' socially situated interpretations of texts. In a sense, we learn more about the content of the individual recipient's schemas, and how they influence comprehension of texts, than about how making sense of texts is socially shaped, how interpretations and experiences are shared between people, and how they relate to, and are used in everyday life. In other words, schema theory analysis of media reception reduces the richness of the reception experience, and loses sight of its social context. The analytic emphasis on and claim relating to the content of mental schemas in Höijer's studies might be attributed to her very specific aim of documenting the activation of schemas, and it is evident that when applied directly in analysis, socio-cognitive schema theory tends to produce rather simplistic insights. Cognitive theory—whether schema theory or other approaches—seems better suited as a meta-theoretical framework that needs to be coupled with more specific theory, for example, genre theory, as in Bruun's work (2004), and perhaps other methods, to produce rich analytic insights. Höijer's more recent work acknowledges this need to combine schema theory with more operational theory (Höijer, 1998, 2007).

Regarding the question of method, it may be argued that schema theory approaches to media reception subscribe to a quite individualistic approach to understanding the social world, and the socio-cognitive processes of sensemaking (Augoustinos & Walker, 1995: 165). This emphasis on the individual is common to the empirical socio-cognitive reception studies discussed. In their empirical work, the primary method for collecting data on socio-cognitive processes in relation to media texts is the individual, in-depth interview, following a screening of the text. Accordingly, the individual, psychological processes in the reception situation are the main units of analysis, and the social dimensions of reception are inferred from the individual-level data, for instance, in the form of historically and culturally anchored 'super-themes' (Jensen, 1998), social distinctions, intersubjectively shared norms of self-disclosure and intimacy (Bruun, 2004), and as concrete connections to the everyday lives of the audiences (Höijer, 1992).[2] It is not necessarily problematic to 'see the social through the individual,' but this individual-psychological approach to socio-cognitive processes can fruitfully be supplemented by a stronger emphasis on the social aspect in research design and empirical analyses.

The understanding of media use implied in socio-cognitive reception theory of sensemaking, as an individual recipient's engagement with a fixed and pre-produced text, is of limited value, particularly when dealing with social media. Not only do social media entail a destabilization of text and a blurring of production and reception, they also challenge the individualistic approach to media use because social media are defined by invitations to interact and connect with others by contributing content. Consequently, the engagement with social media is inadequately described as an individual's isolated consumption of a text. A rethinking of socio-cognitive activity, emphasizing its social dimensions, not only in theory but also in methodological orientation, arguably offers a better fit for studying sensemaking and genre in social media.

Finally, being primarily concerned with the relationship between text and audience, the notion of *context* to some extent disappears in socio-cognitive reception theory. Context is, at best, treated in terms of the accumulated experience that an individual 'stores' in the cognitive schemas, as seen with Höijer's (1992) and Jensen's (1998) studies, but it is not explicitly and systematically dealt with in empirical socio-cognitive analysis of media reception. This implies a lack of sensitivity to the social situation in which text reception, sensemaking, takes place. Yet, the social situation plays a crucial role for the concept of genre as a cognitive tool for organizing experience. Genres are actualized and practiced based on participants' negotiated understanding of the communicative situation. In other words, understanding the context in which the genre unfolds is essential to understanding the experiential significance and value that participants ascribe to the use of the genre in their everyday lives. To examine the *pragmatic dimension* of genre more systematically and fully, context must be reflected in the analysis.

RETHINKING COGNITION FOR GENRE ANALYSIS: A PRAGMATIC APPROACH

Following the discussion unfolded so far, one might ask: Should the socio-cognitive perspective be abandoned altogether, in qualitative studies of media reception and genre? If a focus on cognition implies an individualistic approach to socio-cognitive processes in a social world, and the framework is difficult to operationalize profitably, how can it enrich the study of making sense of media use? I retain cognition—or rather socio-cognition—as a central concept, because it allows for a bridging of the psychological and the social aspects of media use. This is particularly relevant when studying social media as genres used by the individual to engage in social interaction with peers. It may further contribute to unpacking and explaining the dynamics of genre, including how individuals acquire genre knowledge, and how distinct genres of online communication emerge and stabilize over time. That is, how genres come to manifest themselves as recurrent situations that regulate participants' communicative practices.

However, it is necessary to reconceptualize cognition and sensemaking in media use, in order to usefully incorporate the social dimension, to steer the socio-cognitive approach around the problems of individualism and operationalization. Zerubavel (1997: 5–7) suggests that cognition may be researched at three different levels: a universal level, addressing how human beings think and process information (e.g., through mental schemas); an individual level, dealing with the unique experience and knowledge of the individual; and a social level, researching knowledge and experience as common to specific groups, institutions, types of situations, and so forth. Although schema theory per se does not exclude the study of the context-specific (the individual and social elements of cognition), in practice, the emphasis in schema theory—as we have seen with Höijer's work—often is on the universal elements of cognition (Wertsch, 1991: 19; also Matlin, 2005), including the human capacity for information processing, comprehension, and recollection (Höijer, 1991), or on the individual elements, such as a person's unique schemas with regard to occupation, family life, and so forth (Höijer, 1992).

In this section, I discuss and qualify the contributions of a *social* perspective on cognitive processes as a meta-theoretical framework for the genre analysis of social media. The point of departure for this discussion is a patchwork of related social-psychology and sociological theories of cognition and sensemaking that share a pragmatic foundation (Berkenkotter & Huckin, 1993). Thinking of sensemaking along pragmatic lines is characteristic of a broad range of theoretical approaches in several disciplines, including social representations theory, socio-cultural theory, and the critically oriented, discursive psychology in the social-psychological domain, distributed cognition in human-computer interaction, situated cognition in educational research, interactionist microsociology, and conversation analysis, among any of which there is often little contact or cross-fertilization. Despite differing in focus and being rooted in different research disciplines, the basic theoretical threads of sensemaking and cognition in these theories are woven around the fundamental pragmatic assumption that meaning is communicatively grounded. Hence, it is intersubjectively anchored and situated in instances of communication. With this fundamental premise, it is possible to formulate an alternative to the cognitivist schema theory, namely, a more pragmatic approach to cognition. This corresponds with the genre perspective on social media, and the notion that social media is a communicative condition with social consequences for how everyday life is organized and conducted.

To develop a pragmatic approach to cognition and sensemaking in everyday life as a basis for the present purpose, I wove together two complementary approaches, namely social representations theory and ethnomethodological theory, addressing sensemaking in terms of the cognition/communication nexus, from a theoretical and a methodological standpoint, respectively. Both approaches are particularly compatible with the genre perspective, and the interest in ordinary people's social media practices.

The Social Underpinnings of Cognition

The theory of social representations, most notably developed in the works of the French social psychologist Serge Moscovici, offers a way to balance the psychological and the social in socio-cognitive theory (Moscovici, 2001). Drawing insights from socio-cultural theory, phenomenological sociology, and Russian formalism, social representations theory formulates a social-psychological theory of knowledge and sensemaking that departs from the cognitivist information-processing paradigm, schema theory included. Information-processing theories, it is argued, imply a fundamental—and false—Cartesian split between thought and action, between knowledge and those producing knowledge in a given socio-historical context (Jovchelovitch, 2007: 1–2).

Thus, social representations theory is not concerned with an individual's mental capacity for information processing, but with the representations, or knowledge, of the world that humans produce through cognitive and communicative activity. The point of departure is that knowledge is socially constructed, and that thinking is merely reproduction or elaboration of what others have thought or said before us (Moscovici, 2001: 24). The social representation is thus a dialogic form, generated in the interrelations between self and other (Bakhtin, 1986: 69; Markova, 2003). The central task of social representations theory is to deal with these social underpinnings of our cognitive activity and frameworks of sensemaking, and the concept of social representations is defined as:

> [. . .] a system of values, ideas and practices with a twofold function: first, to establish an order which will enable individuals to orient themselves in their material and social world and to master it; and secondly to enable communication to take place among members of a community by providing them with a code for social exchange and a code for naming and classifying unambiguously the various aspects of their worlds and their individual and group history. (Moscovici, 1973: xiii, cited from Moscovici, 2001: 12)

In other words, social representations support processes of sensemaking by providing individuals and groups with an orientation in the social world, and a common ground for communication.

Whereas the first element of this definition, 'social representations,' resembles the idea of schemas as psychologically grounded orienting devices, it is the second element that is distinct and key to the approach advanced here: namely, social representations as intertwined with communicative processes. Underlying this definition is an assumption that without *some* shared knowledge, interaction is impossible: that people share at least an idea of what the interaction is about, how to interact, the interaction partner(s), and so on, and that these ideas are continuously drawn upon, negotiated, and adjusted as the interaction unfolds, thereby providing a framework for making sense of the situation. Accordingly, social representations condition the sensemaking processes of interacting individuals and groups (Moscovici, 2001: 20–26). At the same time, social representations are created by groups and individuals in the course of communication, and once created, have a life of their own, merge with other representations, and so on (Moscovici, 2001: 27). Social representations typically operate in a commonsense or practical manner (Moscovici, 1994). According to Moscovici, the shared knowledge presupposed in interaction is often layered as practical or 'tacit' knowledge (Polanyi, 1967). The social representations held by individuals and groups are *enacted* in their practices, and therefore people are often unaware of the social representations they hold.

One might argue that there is a conservative bias in social representations theory: How can we theorize changes in the experiential patterns, behavior, and cognitive structures of individuals and groups, if change relies on reconfigurations of existing social representations initiated by social interactions? To avoid the fallacy of reducing the (re)production of social representations to something purely social, I want to emphasize the contribution of the individual to the construction of social representations. Part of the cognitive activity is psychological, and relates to individual thoughts, emotions, and previous experiences, accumulated outside the communicative situation. How are social representations shaped by individual knowledge and thinking? The main function of social representations for the individual is to 'make the unfamiliar familiar' (Moscovici, 2001: 37), and Moscovici describes the processes in which social representations become practical knowledge as processes of anchoring and objectification, a nod to Berger and Luckmann's *The Social Construction of Reality* (1967), in which the concepts of anchoring and objectification are developed to describe how socially constructed knowledge becomes so conventionalized over time, that it is accepted as objective and unproblematic fact. Anchoring and objectification may be conceived of as the inner psychological and outer negotiated and conventionalized dimensions of cognition, respectively.

Experiences in the social world are internalized through anchoring processes, whereby they are categorized in relation to the individual's previous knowledge and experience, and confirm, reshape, and challenge the social representations that the individual already holds. Consequently, the individual's social representations are influenced by his or her unique experiences and personal history and acquire a unique, individual shading. Anchored knowledge constrains future encounters with a given social phenomenon by eliciting expectations, appropriate behaviors, and so forth. The process of objectification means that when anchored knowledge remains unchallenged over the course of time, and through interactions with others, it is reproduced, gradually becoming unproblematic fact, layered as tacit, commonsense knowledge among groups of people in given contexts (Moscovici, 2001: 41–54).

In sum, social representations are both knowledge anchored in individuals and groups, *and* objectified social phenomena that exist outside the mind, in societal institutions, group processes, and interpersonal communication, as distributed knowledge structures reflected in discourse and interactional practice.

In relation to media, one such objectified or institutionalized knowledge structure is that of genre. Translating social representations theory to the relationship between genre as a cognitive orientation frame with a slightly different shading from individual to individual, and a cultural product manifest in text, genre knowledge is a precondition to (successful) text production and text processing, because—at a more abstract level—social representations facilitate communication by functioning as orienting devices for the parties involved in communication. Processes of anchoring and objectification in the recurrent enactment of the genre contribute to explaining how genres are rendered stable or destabilized through communicative practice. Thus, with social representations theory, genre may be understood as a socially distributed and situated cognitive structure that is oriented to, drawn upon, and reworked, when making sense of media and texts.

The process of making the unfamiliar familiar in social representations theory underlines how an individual's genre knowledge does not emerge from a vacuum, but from the mobilization, reworking, and adjustment of existing knowledge and previous experience, as well as from the recurrent interaction with other (more established) practitioners of the genre. When encountering and enacting a new genre (e.g., learning how to blog), participants invoke genre knowledge and practices from other types of media use and conversation, to render this unfamiliar type of conversation familiar (Orlikowski & Yates, 1994), or develop new representations altogether. Hence, with the processes of anchoring and objectification, social representations theory offers a conceptualization of the development and individual acquisition of genre competence and knowledge.

The stated goal of social representations theory is to reinstate the *social* as the main unit of analysis in social psychology, by identifying the project of the social-psychological discipline as the study of how social representations are produced, negotiated, institutionalized, and challenged in ordinary people's sensemaking activities in everyday life (Moscovici, 2001: 27; Moscovici, 1994). This means viewing individuals and groups as active producers, thinkers, and communicators of representations, when they make sense of their experiences (Moscovici, 2001: 29–30). For the study of genre as a specific social representation, this implies that genre surfaces and must be studied in its empirical enactment, by analyzing naturally occurring instances of the genre, with a specific focus on processes of joint sensemaking, that is, the negotiation of the conventions, functions, and meanings ascribed to a genre, in and through social interaction (Moscovici, 1994: 164–165).

Social representations theory provides the meta-theoretical foundation for an exploration of cognitive processes, because they are evident, socially distributed, and invoked as underlying patterns of reasoning in interaction and communication—they are not solely individual mental constructs. However, the theory offers very little analytic guidance on how to study these socio-cognitive activities. Therefore, it needs to be linked with operational theory to be analytically useful (Augoustinos & Walker, 1995).

Cognition and Communicative Practice in Everyday Life

With the actual processes of sensemaking identified as key to the study of social representations, and social representations being embedded in practical knowledge, it is natural to look for methodological and analytical inspiration in those strands of micro-sociological theory that focus specifically on describing the unproblematic character of everyday life, and make tacit, presupposed knowledge explicit through analysis. Specifically, I draw ideas from ethnomethodology (Cicourel, 1973; Garfinkel, 1967), and its offspring, conversation analysis (Atkinson & Heritage, 1984; Sacks, 1992), in which the common key question is how processes of interaction are organized to produce meaning and social order, thereby making everyday life manageable and more commonsense. Conversation analysis builds on the theoretical foundation of ethnomethodology, but differs somewhat in analytic scope. Whereas ethnomethodology has a broad practice orientation, conversation analysis has a more limited analytical scope that focuses specifically on the structural (temporal, sequential, etc.) organization of discourse at a micro-level.

Like social representations theory, ethnomethodology is inspired by Schutz's phenomenological sociology of everyday life, and its notion of commonsense or practical knowledge as the primary mode of experiencing and interacting in the social world (Schutz, 1971: 7–19). Thus, ethnomethodology is an inquiry into the 'methods' that ordinary people use to render their everyday lives orderly and intelligible (Garfinkel, 1967: 36–37; also Cicourel, 1973). The aspects of common sense that interest scholars in ethnomethodology are those that enable skilled practitioners to perform their ordinary activities in ways that are recognizably appropriate, rational, intelligible, proper, correct, or reasonable for all practical purposes (Coulter, 1979: 21).

What makes the contribution of ethnomethodological inquiry important to the present framework for understanding genres as sensemaking devices is its sensitivity to the micro-dynamics of interaction, for example, the dimensions of composition, theme, and stylistic norms of social media as described in Chapter 2. Ethnomethodology provides analytic tools for describing *how* different social representations, that is, understandings pertaining to a given genre, are drawn upon and reworked in interaction, how communication enables people to accomplish certain actions in an orderly way, and how we ascribe meaning to ourselves as individuals and groups, and to the social world, through communicative practices (Potter & Wetherell, 1987: 33–38).

Despite the fact that only Cicourel (1973) explicitly uses the concept of cognition as part of a theoretical framework, ethnomethodological thought shares the effort to bridge cognition and action with social representations theory (Heritage, 1984: 306–307). It reworks ideas of cognition by arguing that cognition is not *reflected in* interaction and communication, it is *embodied in* people's interactional practices, in their active constructions of, and orientations with regard to experience (Potter, 2006; Sacks, 1984). People's practical organization of their activities and interactions is simply understood as situated expressions of cognitive processes that enable them to make and share the sense of things (Edwards, 1997).

A basic premise of meaningful social interaction is the participants' procedural demonstration of mutual understanding and shared interactional competence. Although intersubjective understanding might not actually be established, participants must assume and display such a shared understanding, in order to produce and interpret actions, and continue an uncomplicated course of interaction (Cicourel, 1973: 52–53). Hence, participants collaboratively create interactional coherence to make conversation meaningful. Moreover, a central tenet is that members of a group share interactional competence, norms, and expectations that enable them to produce appropriate actions, and to interpret the actions of others, by cuing the interaction partners towards certain implicit meanings. It is the researcher's task to render visible 'the commonsense understandings and procedures people use to shape their conduct in particular interactional settings' (Garcia & Jacobs, 1999: 342; also Cicourel, 1973: 63–67).

As suggested in Chapter 2, with the genre perspective, we can consider social media to be interactional settings, the social organization of which are collaboratively constituted and negotiated through the communicative practices of users. Thus, the primary objects of study are the characteristics and micro-dynamics of sensemaking in naturally occurring, everyday interaction among peers (Heritage, 1984: 238–240; Sacks, 1984). This involves an analytic focus on how practical, normative conventions are socio-cognitive resources that create a common ground for interaction and communion, and thereby establish sense and orderliness in daily activities. Ethnomethodology argues that these implicit understandings and expectations mainly become visible when they are breached, that is, when a shock or unexpected behavior shakes the course of interaction (Garfinkel, 1967; Weick, 1995: 85). In such instances, it becomes relevant to scrutinize each other's intentions, assumptions, and so on (Coulter, 1979: 42–43).[3]

The ethnomethodological emphasis on the micro-level analysis of ordinary—commonsense—activities marks a difference in how studies of social representations have traditionally been conducted. Potter and Edwards (1999) criticize social representations studies for being uninterested in microanalyses of conversation. Certainly, social representations studies have tended to focus on collective representations of health and illness, the diffusion of psychoanalytic representations into society, ideology, and intergroup attitudes and conflict, for example, as manifested in societal discourses (Jodelet, 1991; Moscovici, 1976; for an in-depth review, see Augoustinos & Walker, 1995: 142–155). However, as previously demonstrated, and acknowledged by Potter and Edwards (1999), social representations theory does not reject a focus on micro-interactional processes in principle—on the contrary, it implicitly encourages research into communicative practices, because these are central to the construction of representations. Accordingly, conversation analysis and ethnomethodology are not only compatible with social representations theory, they also complement it by creating new research foci, and by introducing microanalytic ideas and perspectives to the study of social representations. Moscovici, acknowledging this affinity to ethnomethodology, does, however, voice a slight concern with regard to ethnomethodological analysis, which, he argues, is too narrowly focused on describing conventions and norms as they become visible in breaches. To him, ethnomethodology neglects the tying of descriptive analysis of norms and conventions to underlying patterns, that is, the social representations on which they rest (Moscovici, 2001: 65). Arguably, ethnomethodology, and conversation analysis in particular, has tended to so emphasize behavioral dynamics in analysis, that the motifs and functions of communication are rendered insignificant.

STUDYING SENSEMAKING IN EVERYDAY LIFE: METHODOLOGICAL NOTES FOR A GENRE STUDY

I have now sketched the underlying theoretical framework for a pragmatic conceptualization of genres as socio-cognitive devices for sensemaking in everyday life.

First, sensemaking is fundamentally a *communicative activity*. Communication is to be understood in its broadest sense, as including not only conversation, but also nonverbal social interaction, whether technologically mediated or not. Sensemaking is the social organization of events and experiences as meaningful in their practical unfolding. Echoing Bakhtin's (1986) dialogical conception of the utterance, and more broadly, language and text, communication, whether one-way, or multidirectional and conversational, is dialogic by nature—it is functional, purposeful, and directed. According to Bakhtin, any speaker presumes, orients him- or herself to an audience, and anticipates a response (Bakhtin, 1986: 69–72); any speaker is always a respondent to previous utterances in a chain of communicative exchanges. The listener, in turn, is not a passive recipient, but is actively engaged and responsive, whether directly, with a reply, or indirectly, interpreting, relating to, and perhaps learning from the speaker's utterance. The utterance is filled with dialogic overtones, writes Bakhtin (1986: 92), including cues in composition and style that invoke genre knowledge and guide listeners towards certain intended meanings and purposes of communication. To make sense of the utterance, the listener must continuously and actively attend to these cues. Hence, sensemaking occurs at the point of contact between two or more individuals in a given context (also Wertsch, 1991: 52). The idea of sensemaking as an ongoing collaborative accomplishment in communication, a process of negotiation and recursive creation of coherence, resonates with the ethnomethodological observation concerning the conundrum of intersubjectivity, described above. Cicourel argues that, whereas participants in communication can never be certain that they do in fact share an understanding of the situation, they must assume and display such an intersubjectivity or reciprocity of perspectives, if the interaction is not to break down (Cicourel, 1973: 52–54). This implies that sensemaking is not merely an individual task of cognitively perceiving and comprehending a given situation, but endogenous to the social organization of communicative practices, and therefore intersubjectively anchored. In social media, sensemaking is thus part and parcel of the textualized interactions among participants.

Second, sensemaking is *situated,* context-dependent, and embedded in specific 'discourse communities,' that is, groups that share interpretive procedures and normative orientations within a social situation (cf. Swales, 1990). With reference to Berkenkotter and Huckin (1993), genre knowledge is a form of situated cognition enabling sensemaking: the participants who are able to enact a social situation competently are those who have acquired and mobilized the relevant knowledge and communicative skills. Enactments of genre in social media are embedded in networks of participants who, to some extent, share an understanding of the genre and its purposes. At the same time, each participant brings unique meanings to the ongoing negotiation of genre (cf. Moscovici, 2001: 168). Furthermore, other groups or clusters may conceive of the genre in different ways, thereby bringing different norms and expectations into play.

The context or social situation provides interlocutors with cues to frame and guide their interaction (Cicourel, 1973). Therefore, sensemaking must be analyzed in its practical unfolding in social interaction among specific groups of individuals in given settings. In social media, for instance, the software of a genre is a contextual factor, enabling and constraining the sensemaking process. The communicative functionalities and constraints built into software and interface must therefore be reflected in the analysis of interactional practices, dynamics, and purposes of social media, to provide a fuller analysis of situated genre negotiation. Another contextual factor is the broader everyday activities and life circumstances of each social media user.

Situatedness underlines the necessity of empirically studying sensemaking and genre. As Heritage argues, 'knowledge which is used in everyday settings cannot be analyzed independently of the courses of action through which it is acted upon, maintained and validated' (1987: 266). Interpretive procedures, meanings, and social order emerge and develop in the course of interaction: they are not static, nor do they exist prior to interaction (Cicourel, 1973: 28). Therefore, only by looking at the actual enactments of genre in social media can we study sensemaking at work in social media use. That is, we must examine how social media are actively constructed in practice, by people in specific situations, and what meanings they ascribe to it. Implicit in this argument is a call for the analysis of sensemaking to not only include empirical data, but also to let it drive a close analysis from the bottom up.

Third, and related to the previous point: Despite the emphasis on studying situated practice, this does not mean that genre analysis cannot make claims beyond the situated instance of genre. Given that genre is a cognitive orienting and sensemaking device, evoked in and through communicative practice, the concrete instances of a given genre are *both unique and indexical of a more general genre pattern* (Coulter, 1979: 24). Sensemaking relies on both situated cues and general assumptions and expectations (Weick, 1995: 13). Thus, genre arguably reconciles the dualism between structure and agency, in identifying structure as not external to human action, but embedded, generated, negotiated, adjusted, and developed in an iterative oscillation between stability and change. In other words, genre establishes links between situations, and makes situated practices useful entry points for grasping broader social understandings of given communicative phenomena.

With regard to social media, the individual user actively takes part in the sensemaking processes by interacting with other users, thereby contributing to the ongoing development of text. Additionally, the textually negotiated genre conventions, and relations to others, contribute to shaping individual sensemaking in relation to both the concrete text, and the genre as a cognitive category and future sensemaking device. The posts and comments of users in social media may therefore be seen as textual traces of psychosocial processes, which are fundamentally about making sense of the self and social reality through ongoing negotiations with others, about the meanings and social purposes of the genres at hand.

Together, these methodological premises necessitate a qualitative methodology that allows for in-depth analysis of concrete instances of genre enactment in social media. While retaining sensitivity to the richness of unique, situated enactments of a given genre, genre analysis is inherently pattern seeking, that is, it strives to identify recurring elements and conventions across individual genre enactments (Bhatia, 1993: 40). To balance the sensitivity of the micro-dynamics of concrete interactions with the broader scope of genre analysis in the research design, I have conducted three consecutive, empirical, multi-case studies of personal blogs, Twitter, and Facebook in everyday life. Each of these case studies identifies genre patterns and variations within and across individual cases of social media use. Each of the case studies have served to explore the potential and limitations of a genre analysis, and establish a foundation for larger-scale empirical studies based on the framework of genre.

METHODS AND DATA

Using the experiences and practices of social media users as a baseline for understanding social media as a communicative phenomenon, I rely on two data sources for the case studies: web archives of naturally occurring communication between participants on the selected social media and qualitative interviews with the authors, whose blogs, Twitter, and Facebook profiles were part of the study. Whereas the textual archives aim to capture genre negotiation in communicative practice, the individual interviews seek to explore personal histories, routines, and reflections concerning the use of social media. The inclusion of interviews is methodologically important, as an attempt to balance the individual and social dimensions of sensemaking within the genres being studied. Complementing and contextualizing the social dimension captured by the web archives, the interviews generate data on the study participants' individually anchored expectations, and the personal significance and function of social media in their daily lives. The interviews depict the online activities from another, more explicitly interpretive and reflexive perspective, and complement the 'practices data' from the archives, by creating a space for the negotiation of different types of member accounts relating to social media as a communicative condition in everyday life.

The research design combining textual material with interviews in the analysis is, in a sense, classic to media reception studies. However, the use of web archives also represents new developments of the methodological toolbox of audience studies. These are discussed in more detail in Lomborg (2012b). Using web archives to study the textualized communicative practices of users on social media intersects with two core methodological approaches in audience studies: (1) *textual analysis* of meaning as embedded in circuits of production, text, and reception; and (2) *media ethnography* with its detailed accounts of people's contextualized practices of interaction and engagement with media and with fellow users.

Compared to the ethnographer's often-participatory engagement in the field of research, web archiving is an unobtrusive method that generates fine-grained data on communicative practice without interfering with participants and their ongoing activities during the process of data collection. Moreover, because of its unobtrusiveness, web archives allows the researcher to maintain a distance and unfamiliarity with participants' practices that is needed to question the participants' taken-for-granted, habitual ways of using social media, and thus to understand genre negotiation as a practical matter.

Web archives of social media lend themselves particularly well to close-up textual analysis of genre negotiations as sensemaking in communicative practice. Recognizing that social media texts may be conceived of as instances of interpersonal communication provides significant opportunities for expanding the methodological toolbox of textual and genre analysis in the direction of micro-sociological methods. As developed in the upcoming analysis chapters of this book, the pragmatic genre analysis framework for studying social media appropriates analytical concepts such as turn-taking, interactional coherence and facework, which have their origins in ethnomethodological and discourse analyses of interpersonal communication, to the study of communicative practice in social media.

CHAPTER SUMMARY

At its basics, communication is the practical means for navigating everyday life in a meaningful and problem-free manner. Through a diverse set of communicative practices—coordinating work tasks, talking through the day's activities around the dinner table, small talking on social media, etc.—our taken-for-granted assumptions and well-established knowledge of social situations, and the social world at large, are enacted, negotiated, and sometimes challenged and readjusted.

In this chapter, I have re-developed the framework of genre as a theoretical platform for conceptualizing and analyzing such sensemaking activities in everyday life. This involves a foundational discussion in audience studies of how meaning is generated in the intersections of media texts, individual recipients, and social groups. Based on socio-cognitive and pragmatic theories of human experience, we may characterize genre as an experiential, cognitive construct for making sense of the social world—one that is most often deployed skillfully and effortlessly in everyday communication. The use of social media is one communicative activity, one example of genre enactment, among many others that shape the social fabric of meaning in ordinary, daily life.

NOTES

1. Schema theory was originally developed by the educational psychologist Richard C. Anderson (Anderson, 1978; Anderson & Pearson, 1984). The concept of schemas originates in the philosophy of Kant (1929), in memory studies (Bartlett, 1932), and the developmental psychology of Piaget (1952).
2. These studies do not thematize television viewing as a social activity, which is quite remarkable, since at the time the studies were conducted, the importance

of the social, for example, family interaction in front of the television set, had been richly documented in a number of media-ethnography studies (e.g., Lull, 1980; Silverstone, 1994).

3. Garfinkel's foundational work in ethnomethodology (1967) is renowned because of his so-called breaching experiments, in which Garfinkel and his students sought to uncover implicit and commonsense knowledge by violating the commonly accepted social norms in various situations.

4   Negotiating the Personal Blog

Blogs were chosen as the first case study of social media as communicative genres. In the context of social media, blogging is a comparably 'old' phenomenon, dating back to the late 1990s. The user base of blogs in Denmark is relatively stable, grows at a slow pace, and, at least in terms of reading, blogging is relatively mainstream in Denmark. GemiusAudience, which logs Danes' internet traffic, consistently reports that about 800,000 users, or about 25 percent of the internet population, occasionally view blogs, and thus are at least somewhat familiar with the genre. According to Statistics Denmark's 2009 annual report on the Danes and the internet, 18 percent of Danes have contributed content to blogs, in the form of written posts or uploaded images (Danmarks Statistik, 2009: 17).[1] The Danish blogosphere was estimated to comprise about 90,000 blogs at the beginning of 2008, and 130,000 in early 2009, the period during which the data were collected (Lomborg, 2011). At an international level, Technorati (www.technorati.com), a US-based blog aggregation service and search engine, has consistently tracked well over one hundred million blogs globally since 2008. Hence, blogging appears to be a relatively well-established and mature genre. For this reason, the analysis of blogs was a natural starting point for testing and developing the framework of genre: some kind of common understanding of the genre and its norms was likely to have crystallized—and perhaps stabilized.

At the same time, blogs constitute a case in which the communication is not based on already established relationships from other spheres of the users' everyday lives, but at least partially on connections between likeminded strangers who share a certain interest. In such instances, where users do not know (what to expect from) each other in advance, genre negotiations and social meanings conveyed through communication must be expected to appear more explicitly than in communicative exchanges between friends, family members, colleagues, and so forth, who are assumed to share common ground from the outset.

In this chapter, I examine how the personal blog genre is enacted and continuously negotiated in and through the participants' communicative practices on personal blogs. I analyze the resources, expectations, and conventions that participants voice and use to orient themselves in their interactions, with a specific view to what these genre conventions help the participants to accomplish, in terms of making their blogs significant and meaningful in everyday life.

My argument proceeds by combining the four dimensions—composition, theme, style, and pragmatic functions– in the analysis of the personal blog within the framework of genre. In the first section, I provide a structural analysis of the composition of the networks that are articulated through the activities on the personal blog. This provides an important entry point for grasping the relationship between the blogger and his or her networked audience as participants in the situated negotiation of the personal blog genre. As argued in Chapter 2, any enactment of a genre is only valid and relevant insofar as others recognize the enactment as an instance of the genre. In blogs, this recognition is chiefly manifested in the connectivity of an individual blog to other blogs. In the second section, I focus specifically on the compositional genre conventions and dynamics as expressed in communicative practice, by examining the social organization of the blog conversations, and the ongoing negotiation of thematic relevance on personal blogs. I begin to tie these communicative conventions to pragmatic functions of creating presence and communion. In the third section, I examine look at how bloggers learn to enact the genre competently, and are recognized by fellow bloggers as relevant peers, or members, in the ongoing negotiation of the personal blog genre. I link this idea of membership in the genre circuit to blogging sociality and relational development, to investigate further the pragmatic function and significance of blogging activities in the everyday lives of the participants. Finally, I specifically examine diversity within the personal blog genre, by analyzing the sampled blogs as distinct topical and stylistic formations that adopt and express the personal blog genre in unique ways.

EMPIRICAL METHODOLOGY AND SAMPLING

Empirical studies of genre negotiation in the everyday use of social media have their focal point in the actual, situated, interactional practices: practices of producing and uploading content, and responding to other users' contributions. This is where genre negotiations, including relevant genre knowledge and appropriate behavior, are made visible in communication on social media. Accordingly, the analysis of genre negotiation is primarily focused on those users who actively enact the genre, whether by blogging, tweeting, or commenting on other users' posts. The lurkers, who only read but never comment, do not directly contribute to genre negotiation, because they do not voice their understanding of the genre to fellow users. Lurkers do, however, contribute indirectly, in that by reading a blog, they become visible in the blog's viewing statistics, or as 'quiet' followers of a given Twitter or Facebook profile, thereby likely contributing to motivating the author's ongoing contributions. Therefore, the lurkers may be included in a genre analysis to some extent, in terms of the author's conception of his or her audience.

Given these parameters, relevant cases for the empirical study of genre were limited to active blogs, and Twitter and Facebook profiles that are—to a greater or lesser extent—interlinked, and display conversations with other users, assuming that this interlinking and interaction gives access to direct negotiations of the genres. Moreover, following the interest in how ordinary users become producers of social media in everyday life, I started the systematic search for relevant cases from the fundamental criterion that the sampled users write as private individuals, not professionals.

Any individual case exhibits general qualities as well as unique expressions of the genre, so the number of cases needed to develop theory of genre negotiation on social media should be established with a careful consideration to information richness, that is, saturation and complementarity (Kuzel, 1999). In each of the three case studies, I worked in depth with multiple cases, to ensure variation in the situated expressions of the three genres. The number of cases is limited—three blogs, and six Twitter and Facebook profiles—to make the data sets manageable for close analysis, including balancing the sensitivity of case-specific dynamics with the analysis of cross-case genre patterns. The small number of cases allowed me to explore the complexities and ambiguities of the practical enactments of genre in the cases, from which to develop saturated and refined theoretical insights (Yin, 1994: 30). The theoretical and empirical findings may then be tested in larger-scale empirical studies in future studies. Given the small number of cases, the case studies are intended neither to identify causal relationships and infer statistical generalizations about the users, nor to support firm conclusions about blogs, or Twitter and Facebook as such.

I followed the same purposive sampling strategy for each case study to obtain comparable, yet varied and rich data. The blog study was set up as a longitudinal study, with communicative practice data collected over a 6-month period for each case, because I wanted ensure rich, in-depth data on genre negotiation, adjustment, stabilization, and possibly challenges and transformations in the interactions between authors and commenters over time. Assuming from the outset that the blog was a relatively well-established genre, the relatively long time span of six month was chosen in an attempt to explore possible changes and ambiguities in genre expression, and thereby document the degree of the blog's stability.

To identify relevant cases in the blog study, I developed a typological framework to classify subgenres of blogs according to three dimensions: content (ranging from a highly personal to a topical orientation), style (ranging from confessional and intimate to an objective tone), and directionality (i.e., whether the blog is primarily used for self-expression with no dialogue between author and readers, or it is highly conversational and densely networked; for a more elaborate explanation, see Lomborg, 2009).

The typological framework served as a tool for the purposive sampling of different kinds of blogs for the study, and as a means of balancing homogeneity and heterogeneity in the sample. Furthermore, I selected blogs that had existed for a minimum of 6 months, assuming that these would provide data on well-established practices and routines, and an integration of the blogging activities in the authors' everyday lives. In a Danish context, blog use declines with age, although older Danes are far from absent on blogs. There are no systematic differences in terms of sex and education and the likelihood of using blogs (cf. Lomborg, 2011), but I tried to ensure some variance in age and sex because these parameters have previously been shown to produce differences in blog behavior (Herring & Paolillo, 2006). The blogs were archived using a software script for the interaction analysis software TATIANA (Dyke, Lund, & Girardot, 2009), which collected and displayed blog communications as well as relevant meta-data (usernames, date, and time stamps, etc.) in a textual archive.

The three blogs included in the blog study are different types of personal blogs. They mainly consist of written text, supplemented by illustrative photos taken by the authors. The content ranges from highly intimate accounts of the authors' everyday lives to descriptions of their hobbies; the posts are at times written as confessions, at others, with humor and ironic distance; the three blogs also vary in the number of comments they normally receive. Two of them are written by women, 'Maggie' and 'Elise,'[2] and these two bloggers are part of a broader network of Danish female bloggers, and frequently contribute to one another's blogs. Maggie, a woman in her late thirties, blogs about her daily life as a Danish expatriate in a European metropolis. She launched the blog in 2007. Elise, a woman in her late fifties, has kept her blog since mid-2005 and mainly blogs about her daily experiences and personal interests. The third blog, in existence since 2007, is authored by a 30-year-old man, 'Ben,' and is part of another network of blogs that focuses on cycling and mountain biking. In contrast to Maggie and Elise's focuses on everyday life, Ben's blog is a 'topically oriented' blog about a hobby: his passion for and experiences of cycling.

THREE BLOGS AND THEIR NETWORKS

The blogosphere is structured as a widely dispersed, permeable, and highly dynamic network that the individual internet user is free to join and leave. The network is made up of those who keep blogs, those who contribute actively to others' blogs by posting comments, and those who choose to read blogs, but never contribute content, and thus remain fairly invisible in the network. Some participate on a regular basis, others more sporadically. The blogosphere may therefore be considered a loosely connected structure with more densely knit clusters or subgroups forming around particular themes and interests, and through which the participants link and interact.

In Maggie and Elise's blog network, the participants are typically strangers to each other at the outset, but some develop close personal friendships over time. In Ben's blog network, some of the fellow bloggers are his training partners, so he knows them from other (cycling) contexts, and knew many of them before starting his blog. Ben's blog has also facilitated new friendships with others (previously strangers to him) interested in cycling. However, in contrast to the women's blog network, which is based solely in the blogging activities, the bike blog activities supplement other activities that connect people in the cycling network, for example, interaction at races and training sessions, where most of the participants meet. As will be evident later in the analysis, this has consequences for the enactment of the personal blog as a genre, and for the meanings attached to blogging in everyday life.

A blog involves an ongoing articulation, management, and negotiation of relationships between the blog author and audience through blogrolls, links, and comments. This explicit articulation of the networks to which a blogger belongs provides a useful entry point for studying some of the structural components and social dynamics of the genre. In this section, I analyze how networks of affiliation are articulated and negotiated in the blog, by providing structural descriptions of the networks and interactional activities characterizing each of the three blogs.

Blogrolls and the Public Articulation of Relationships

Rettberg (2008: 76) and boyd (2007) both identify blogging as a public articulation of relationships, emphasizing the importance of the public display of one's network relationships in blogrolls and so on. My data support blogging as publicly articulated relationships, albeit with some modifications to the original argument. Relationships are not just on display on the blogs, they are continuously negotiated—affirmed and developed—in and through the linking practices, blog conversations, and other conversational activities in which the parties engage. Furthermore, the idea of relationships on display indicates a kind of superficiality that seems incompatible with the data, which show that blogging participants seem to experience their relationships as valuable, friendly, and sometimes deep and personal—especially the relationships that are not developed on the blogs alone.

The blogroll, the list of blogs that is conventionally placed in the right column of the blog to indicate a blog's connection to others blogs, rests on an expectation of mutuality. It is common, when a blogger links to a fellow blogger, for that link to be reciprocated by the other blogger. This norm appears to be particularly important for Elise, who describes her blogroll as a snapshot of those with whom she is currently interacting.

> I keep it relatively ajour, in the sense that if I don't have contact with people for a while, they are eliminated. There are some instances where it [the contact] is sporadic, and then I feel that if there is a month without resonance, I delete them. (Elise)

It will be evident throughout the analysis that every aspect of Elise's blogging activity is imbued with this principle of resonance and mutuality. If there is no resonance, she contends, 'then, in my opinion, it is uninteresting' (Elise). The same is largely true of Maggie, who is member of the same blog network as Elise, and who describes her blogroll as indicating the blogs that she visits on a regular basis and posts comments to. There is a certain fluctuation in the blogroll: new bloggers are found through existing networks and added, whereas others are deleted, depending on the mutual, continued interest. Hence, for Maggie and Elise, the blogroll fulfills a role beyond the mere public display of relationships—it is part of an ongoing negotiation of relationships with fellow bloggers with whom they experience a connection.

In contrast to the women's blogrolls, Ben's blogroll does not reflect the blogs he *reads,* but the network of bloggers that he *knows* from the Danish amateur cycling scene. The cycling community is his primary blog audience, as he is part of a cycling and mountain biking blog network. For Ben, then, the blogroll functions as a public articulation of relationships. In the interview, Ben asserts that he ought to keep the blogroll more up to date and delete those blogs that he finds annoying or that are updated too rarely. Accordingly, the blogs in his blogroll have no specific relevance to his blogging practices as a means for signifying and negotiating affiliation with fellow bloggers—the blogroll merely lists a set of pre-established connections to biking enthusiasts who also happen to blog. Keeping a blogroll is not compulsory, but a genre convention that bloggers generally adhere to, although they ascribe different meanings to it.

International studies have found a similar ambiguity in the meanings that participants attach to their online connections on various social media, and in various contexts of use (e.g., boyd, 2006b; Fono & Raynes-Goldie, 2005). This indicates a need to nuance the one-dimensional notion of 'friendship' often ascribed to the networked relationships in social media (also, Baym, 2010: 145–146).

Elise's Blog

Maggie and Elise are both parts of a densely knit, primarily Danish cluster of about 200 to 250 personal bloggers. This particular cluster is highly conversational, as evidenced by people's habitual commenting on each other's posts, a practice that is quite unusual. In general, most blogs receive few, if any, comments. There is a certain degree of asymmetry in the blogosphere, in that some blogs (a minority) receive considerable attention from readers and commenters, whereas the vast majority has very limited audiences. This is also characteristic of the cluster to which Elise and Maggie's blogs belong.

As one of the oldest and best-known blogs in the cluster, Elise's blog is a central node of activity. During the period from March through August

2008, during which I archived her blog, Elise wrote 393 posts, which received 8567 comments in total—on average, about 22 comments per post (posts received from zero to 90 comments in the archived period). As is evident from the number of posts, Elise blogs very frequently, usually two or three times a day. Most of the blogs in the cluster are not as densely connected as Elise's blog. Informal observation of the cluster suggests that the norm is for an individual blog to connect, through links on the blogroll and comments, with a subset of blogs, perhaps 20 to 30, so that smaller groupings are formed within the cluster, typically around a common theme (e.g., books, knitting, food, psychology, and spirituality). Thus, each blog has its own unique set of relationships. Elise's blog is one of few blogs in this cluster that is connected to most of the other blogs through mutual links in the blogrolls and commenting activity.

However, being so well connected does not mean that Elise keeps in touch equally with everybody in her network. During the archived 6-month period, 167 different readers left comments on her blog, including the 'anonymous' category of readers, which is likely to include more than one person. This is a quite large commenting audience, compared to that of the other blogs in the network, and it probably reflects the blog's large audience of about 250 unique visitors per day, according to Elise's blog statistics. Most comments are left by fellow Danish and Scandinavian bloggers, with only 28 commenters not leaving links to a blog. Although they may have blogs, most likely they do not, because linking one's comments to one's blog is a well-established convention that aids the author in identifying conversation partners in the blogosphere. The finding that most of the commenters are themselves bloggers is consistent with findings in other studies of blog-commenting behavior (Furukawa, Matsuo, Ohmukai, Uchiyama, & Mitsuru, 2007).

Figure 4.1 below displays the actively contributing network on Elise's blog. The vast majority—87 percent—of the commenters are women, and only six male bloggers appear regularly in the commentary threads, indicating an almost exclusively female blog cluster. Whereas some of the commenters leave a comment only once or a few times during the period studied, more than half of Elise's commenters are loyal, in the sense that they return to her blog and leave comments several times. Still, the distribution of contributions among commenters on the blog is uneven. The ten most active contributors post about two-thirds of the comments. Elise's own share of these comments is 47.7 percent. The more a given participant interacts with Elise on her blog, the thicker is the tie connecting them in Figure 4.1.

As Figure 4.1 indicates, the main contributors comprise a very stable group of about 20 to 25 fellow bloggers, all of whom who leave comments on a nearly daily basis, and who may be considered the most important and influential peers in the negotiations of the personal blog genre, as expressed on Elise's blog.

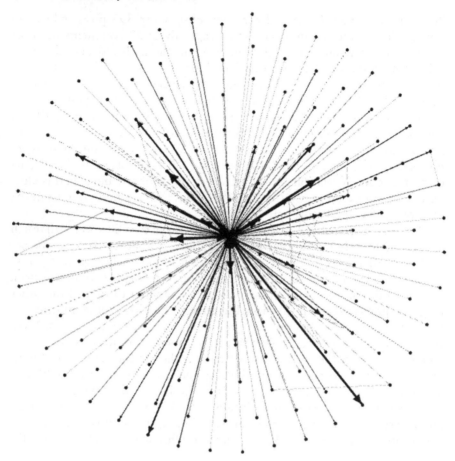

Figure 4.1 Elise's personal network

Maggie's Blog

In March through August 2008, the period during which Maggie's blog was archived, Maggie wrote 156 posts, which received 1918 comments. The posts were fairly equally distributed across the 6 months, with an average of 26 posts per month. Although Maggie posts regularly, typically 4 days a week (sometimes more than one post per day), she is a far less active blogger than Elise is. Typically, Maggie's posts receive between 5 and 15 comments, and the number of comments per post during the archived period ranges from zero to 35, with an average of about 12 comments per post—still a considerable number of comments. According to Maggie, the blog has about 90 readers per day, but she cannot tell from her blog statistics whether this number reflects unique users, or the total number of visits per day: Readers who visit more than once a day may be counted every time they access the blog. Thus, her readership may be much smaller.

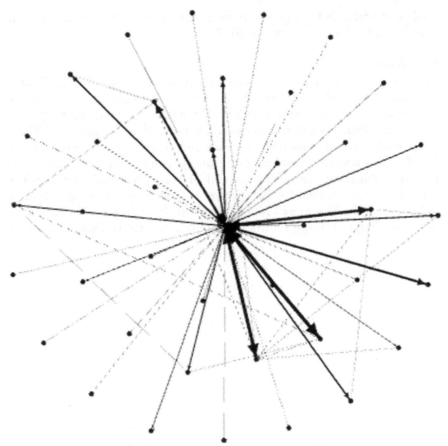

Figure 4.2 Maggie's personal network

Compared to Elise's blog, Maggie's blog represents the average blog in the cluster, with a much shorter blogroll indicating links to fellow bloggers, and significantly fewer commenters. Figure 4.2 displays Maggie's personal network, as indicated by the commenting patterns on her blog. During the registered period, Maggie had 39 commenters—most of whom left comments on several occasions. Apart from Maggie's mother, who occasionally leaves a comment, almost all the comments are left by fellow Danish bloggers. The majority of commenters are women—there are only three male bloggers who appear regularly in the commentary threads.

Although most of the participants comment more than once or twice, six participants are particularly active, and generate almost 70 percent of the contributions. Maggie alone authors 37.9 percent of the comments, that is, more than one third. During the archiving period, the most active commenters all leave comments on an almost daily basis. With this commenting pattern, Maggie's blog resembles Elise's blog, although the activity is more modest in scale, and the group of core participants is much smaller. The cluster is still vibrant as of spring 2013.

Ben's Blog

The data on Ben's blog were collected from October 2008 through March 2009, and during the archiving period, Ben wrote 46 posts, which received 278 comments, equivalent to roughly six comments per post (ranging from zero to 25). Hence, Ben's blog is much less active than Maggie's and Elise's blogs, both in terms of posting frequency and number of comments. During October, November, December, and January, Ben's posting frequency was relatively stable, with between seven and 11 posts per month, but in February and March, the intervals between posts grew longer, eventually leading to his closing the blog in mid-March. Ben had about 100 to 150 readers per day, according to his blog statistics—placing him between Maggie and Elise

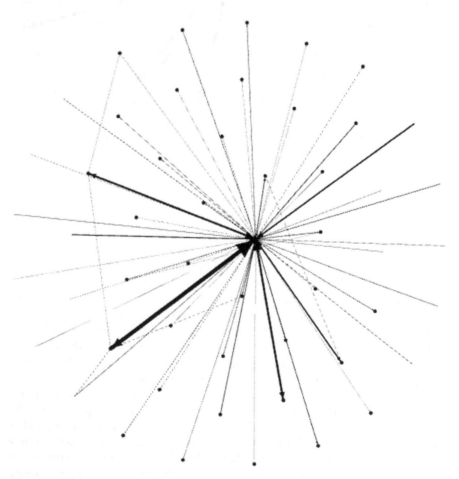

Figure 4.3 Ben's personal network

in terms of audience size. The large readership combined with a low level of commenting activity identifies Ben's blog as less driven by conversation than the other two blogs. Despite variations in interactional activity in the three blogs, it is evident from the numbers that at least some regular conversation is taking place. As mentioned briefly, Ben's blog is part of a primarily male blog cluster, centered on a common interest in cycling and racing, in which he is densely connected to fellow bloggers through the blogroll and, to some extent, the commentary threads. In his blogroll, Ben links to about 30 fellow bloggers, all in the cycling network. Ben's exit from the blog cluster led to the closing down of several of the bike blogs whose authors were active on Ben's blog. Yet, in spring 2013, some of the cycling blogs still appear to be active.

As displayed in Figure 4.3, there were 44 commenters on Ben's blog during the data collection period, including the 'anonymous' category, which is likely to contain more than one person. The vast majority of commenters are male, suggesting that male bloggers attract a male audience, whereas female bloggers like Maggie and Elise attract female readers. Despite posting less frequently than the two female bloggers in the study, and receiving far fewer comments, with 44 commenters, Ben's commenting audience is quite large, larger than Maggie's is. However, Ben's commenters are also less loyal than Elise's and Maggie's commenters are: over half comment only once or twice. In a manner similar to that found with the two other blogs, a small group of core members generates most of the activity on the blog. The six most active participants author 72 percent of the comments in the archive: Ben himself posts 32 percent of the comments.

Networks and Negotiations of Genre

The unequal distribution of contributions among commenters on the blogs is not surprising. Although embedded in multiple groupings within densely knit clusters of blogs, participants manage their engagement through a stronger affiliation to a relatively small group of important peers.

The distribution of comments indicates two important issues in blogging. First, participation structures may vary, depending on the character of the blog network. The strong commitment to regular and continued participation in Maggie and Elise's blogs may indicate a fairly strong sense of cohesion and community surrounding these blogs, and the cluster in which they are embedded. In Ben's blog, most contributors—even those who contribute the most—participate very inconsistently. The loose participation structure in his blog might indicate that the participants are less committed to each other, compared to the participants in the women's blog network. However, as will be evident throughout the analysis, this is not the case. The loose participation structure simply reflects the fact that the blog is not the main expression of the cycling community. At its center is the interest in cycling, so the daily or weekly training sessions and the races, where riders meet and talk, constitute its primary expression.

Secondly, the distribution of participation indicates that blogging activity and socializing are centered on a group of insiders, and thus are essentially about membership. Previous research on groups has found that the frequency of interaction is a key feature in groups developing interdependence, emotional attachment, and intersubjectively shared understandings over time—in short, group identification (Markovsky & Lawler, 1994; Paxton & Moody, 2003). In internet research, Baym's analysis of an online newsgroup confirms the notion that the more people participate in the online interaction, the more invested they become in the group (Baym, 2000: 143–147). Baym further suggests that those who participate most by frequently, writing and commenting on posts, become central actors in defining the rules, norms, and perceptions that characterize the group. From a genre perspective, the practices and normative orientations of these core participants are essential to understanding the intersubjective meanings negotiated through enactment of the genre.

THE SOCIAL ORGANIZATION OF BLOG CONVERSATIONS

One of the basic arguments presented on sensemaking in Chapter 3 was that, in order to interact meaningfully, interlocutors must procedurally demonstrate mutual understanding and shared interactional competence, that is, they must negotiate a shared understanding of the genre. Although participants in interaction cannot be sure that mutual understanding is established, they must assume and display such an intersubjective understanding, to produce, monitor, and interpret their own and one another's actions (Cicourel, 1973). Accordingly, to make conversation meaningful, interlocutors procedurally and collaboratively create interactional coherence in and through their interactional practices. The process of creating interactional coherence is particularly challenging in blogs, owing to the spatio-temporal disruption of communication.

In this section, I examine the communicative structuring of conversation in the posts and comments on the blog, by analyzing how interactional coherence and meaning are collaboratively accomplished in practice by bloggers and commenters. This involves investigating how the participants actively and collaboratively organize and make sense of blogging as a communicative genre, by orienting themselves to and enacting specific—and often implicit—communicative abilities and expectations linked to blogging. I further discuss what this social organizing accomplishes for them, in terms of facilitating relationships through the blog.

Turn-Taking and the Accomplishment of Interactional Coherence

The basic units of interaction are 'turns,' defined as everything a participant writes before sending a message (e.g., a post or a comment in a blog) (Harrison,

2008). Turns are typically organized in 'adjacency pairs,' that is, two consecutive utterances that form a relatively ordered interaction sequence (Silverman, 1998: 105). Oral interaction, such as telephone conversations and face-to-face encounters, is sequentially organized, so that every turn relates to the previous. The same is true of asynchronous, written forms of one-to-one dialogue, such as letter writing, text messaging, and, to some extent, email. The blog is also asynchronous, and the software allows for multilogue among several interlocutors, as well as multiple, simultaneous dialogues. This complicates the social organization of blog conversations, as the turn-taking system in blogs is not necessarily unilinear and sequential (Herring, 1999a).

In blogs, conversations are organized in threads, and the sequential order is disrupted, as contributions appear in the order they are written and submitted. This linear order does not necessarily reflect the adjacent structure of conversation that makes it meaningful, as turns that relate to each other may be interrupted by an intervening turn that is part of an entirely different adjacency pair, and therefore pragmatically irrelevant (Garcia & Jacobs, 1999). Consider the following interaction sequence in the commentary thread following a post in which Elise expresses her concern for a fellow blogger, whose blog has suddenly been removed.[3]

> Kristin: Yup, you worry straight away when there are changes on a blog . . . I don't really know how to interpret this . . .
>
> Tina: I was surprised too. But I'm sure there's a technical explanation. Maybe Sarah is changing blog platform or changing her layout or something like that.
>
> Hope so.
>
> Elise: Kristin, I don't know either—but hope we get the mystery cleared up with this missing person alert.
>
> Elise: Tina, I hope so too . . . Sometimes people can't be bothered to blog, for a time anyway. If that's the reason, it's best to post a notice.
>
> Nadine: She's promised to email me an explanation. It says on the blog now that she has closed it. I was very sad, because I find that blog very inspiring [. . .]
>
> Elise: Nadine, I was sorry too that Sarah decided to shut down her blog—I think she's an inspiring person too.

Parts of the commentary thread display a coherent, sequential organization of the conversation. For example, the comment from Nadine is immediately followed by a response from Elise. However, the thread also illustrates how adjacency pairs are not necessarily sequentially linked: For example, the adjacency pair 'Kristin's comment—Elise's response comment' is interrupted by a pragmatically irrelevant comment by Tina.

Although blog conversations are in principle multi-party, because anyone may contribute, read, and respond to other people's contributions, this interaction sequence illustrates one of the striking tendencies in the data material: that conversations are primarily between the author and one commenter at a time, making the conversation *dyadic*. The typical structure of interaction in the data is a post that 'opens' the conversation, a commenter's response to the post, and the author's response to the commenter, which functions as a closing act in the conversation. This pattern is repeated in the next thread, often with the same participants.[4] Generally, blog threads are active until the next post is published, with the majority of comments being submitted within the first two days after a blog post. On Ben's blog, commenting is not necessarily as concentrated in the first days after a post, but is sometimes spread over a week or more. This may be attributed to Ben's less frequent posting.

Conversational exchange sequences following the dyadic 'post-comment-response comment' structure often overlap, as is the case with the conversations between Elise, on the one hand, and Kristin and Tina, respectively, on the other (Garcia & Jacobs, 1999). It is evident from many of the readers' comments that they have read not only Elise's post but also the previous comments. However, they still direct their comments at the author, and thus only indirectly to the group as a whole. The blog author is clearly the center of attention in the interaction on her blog, because the conversational exchanges follow the one-to-one interactional structure.

In addition to the dyadic structure of the conversations, participants in the blog conversations *identify themselves by name* when posting comments. There are very few 'anonymous' comments, and these most often come from a regular participant who forgot to put his or her name in the comment, and then immediately corrects it with an additional comment in the thread. When responding to the comments, the blog author mentions the person she is addressing by starting her response comment with this person's name. For instance, in the excerpt above, Elise starts a response with 'Kristin, . . .', to link her response to the comment left by Kristin. Naming, as a direct form of addressivity, is almost indispensable on the blogs.

The recurrent practices of dyadic structuring and naming connect turns and may be considered a means of maintaining a sense of orderliness and interactional coherence in the conversations. These practices constitute the backbone of the social organization and structuring of blog conversations. They compensate for the lack of temporal and spatial simultaneity in interaction, and make turn-taking coherent. This is a prerequisite for creating intersubjectivity, and, by extension, for genre negotiation among the participants.

Practices of naming have also been found in other studies of online communication. For instance, Honeycutt and Herring (2009) found a similar practice of addressivity to be widespread in Twitter exchanges, Werry (1996) documented it in Internet Relay Chat, and Harrison found naming central to creating coherence in listserv discussions (Harrison, 2008). This indicates that naming is not distinct to blogging as a genre, but is rather an institutionalized feature of online communication in general.

Apart from serving as a structuring mechanism in the blog conversations, dyadic sequencing and naming serve the vital functions of 'personalizing' the communication on the blog, despite the spatio-temporal dispersion of the participants. Through the enactment of one-to-one encounters, participants identify and recognize one another as relevant peers, or members, in the network, thereby enabling both author and commenters to locate themselves in a distributed and, at least in the case of Elise and Maggie's blogs, often quite anonymous network of strangers who simply met online owing to shared interests (or mere coincidence).

Expectations of Frequency, and the Accomplishment of Social Presence

The recurrent, interactional 'post-comment-response comment' structure indicates that some institutionalized genre expectations and conventions are tied to interaction in the two blog clusters in which the blogs included in this study are embedded. What does this structure achieve in interaction, and what does it indicate about blogging as a communicative genre?

According to Licoppe (2004: 135), physically absent parties gain presence through multiplying their interaction gestures. Following this argument, one major accomplishment of the conversational structure on the blog is the creation of a sense of social presence—the author and readers' demonstration of mutuality and continuous engagement over time. By this means, blogging becomes a joint project, rather than just the author's project, causing the conversational structure to play a vital part in keeping the blog cluster vibrant, and creating cohesion among participants. In this section, I explore a central challenge to blogs, namely, how participants may create a sense of mutual social presence and engagement, despite the lack of physical co-presence and temporal synchronicity. I will show that they do this by adhering to a set of conventions concerning frequency and responsiveness, articulated in both the blog interactions and the interviews. In this process of creating a sense of mutual social presence, phatic elements in communication play a vital role as presence markers.

I define 'sense of social presence' as a measure of social connectivity, that is, as referring to the extent to which participants in communication are mutually oriented toward each other, whether in synchronous or asynchronous forms of communication (Zhao and Elesh, 2008; also Baym, 2010: 52). A sense of presence among interactants is accomplished differently in various media and genres. For instance, Horton and Wohl's seminal essay on parasocial interaction, describes presence as invoked on television by the presenter through a direct mode of address, facing the camera, and thus the viewer, to simulate eye contact, and an informal speech style 'as if he were conversing personally and privately' with the audience (Horton and Wohl, 1956: 215). This simulation of mutual orientation obscures the fact that communication is unidirectional, without the possibility of feedback during the course of interaction, owing to the specific form of mediation that characterizes television. Similarly, Milne (2010) describes how interlocutors in epistolary practices may signify and imagine a sense of presence, for instance, through discursive acts of embodiment in letter writing. Tying letter-based communication to a constant tension between the actual absence, and a profound need for presence in the written, personal exchanges, Milne produces an evocative account of how, by inscribing the body and the immediate situational context of the writer in the communication, the letter evokes in the reader the sense of having been physically present at the time the letter was written. This establishes an imagined sense of presence and intimacy (Milne, 2010: 53–58). Indeed, different media offer different means for establishing a sense of social presence, and the practices in blogging follow specific, unique pathways for creating mutual social presence between authors and readers.

Blogs are often defined formally in the literature as 'frequently modified web pages in which dated entries are listed in reverse chronological sequence'(Herring et al., 2005: 142). Although my analysis does not question that frequent updating is characteristic of the blog genre, it clearly suggests that the updating frequency is a *negotiated convention and expectation,* not a formalized feature. Herring and colleagues' (2005) above-quoted definition of the blog as a genre conflates the software and practice levels of analysis, by listing frequent updating alongside communicative features that are built into the software, such as reverse chronology and date stamps. As I will demonstrate in this section, frequent contributions through posts and comments are genre conventions driven by the mutual expectations of bloggers and their readers, and linked to the desire to achieve a sense of social presence.

Social presence in blogging is most simply demonstrated by frequent interaction. Despite variation in blogging frequency among the three participants, it seems that a certain frequency and continuity are important to the blog genre—both when posting and when commenting. For instance, at a time when Ben has been silent for 11 days, one of his readers writes in the most recent thread:

> Charlie: Hi Ben. Hope everything is ok.? Am I the only one who is thinking that it has become a little silent on your blog? You have also disappeared from f-book, and are you no longer the administrator for Team L? All the best (from a Jutland that is just sinking more and more into darkness without your positive input . . .)

Albeit perhaps a bit sarcastically, Charlie wonders why Ben has not been blogging, and indicates that he misses the updates that his posts usually provide. Similarly, as we saw with the previous excerpt from Elise's blog, fellow bloggers express concern when one of the blogs in the network unexpectedly disappears. In this context, Elise notes that when a blog is silent or removed, 'it is best to post a notice' in advance. Furthermore, when a blogger posts an update after a period of silence, it is common for readers to express excitement for the fact that the blog is 'alive.' In short, readers anticipate and look forward to new posts. This further suggests that the relationship among bloggers and readers is vulnerable—when the relationship is solely based on the blog, it must be kept alive by frequent updating.

As we have seen, Elise herself posts very frequently, and because she starts her day early, readers may expect at least one new post from her, if they visit Elise's blog when they turn on their computers in the morning. Whereas the other bloggers post less frequently, there seems to be a general agreement that bloggers should post at regular intervals, so that the readers know when to expect a new post. Ben argues that bloggers should demonstrate continued presence by posting continuously and at a stable frequency because he finds it annoying when people only post status updates once a month: 'I want the things that are current here and now. I don't want all these "summing up" posts' (Ben).

Ben is the least frequent poster of the three bloggers, and he asserts that he sometimes lacks inspiration for blogging. This blogging fatigue and lack of inspiration appear to be common in blogging, and—as eventually is the case with Ben—it often leads people to close down their blogs. To compensate for running low on inspiration and ideas, Ben sometimes pre-fabricates posts for later publication, and he writes what he calls 'filler' posts to create continuity, and meet the expectation of frequent posting. Hence, despite his struggle to adhere to the norm, Ben—as do the other bloggers—orients himself to the expectation of frequent and continuous posting.

Nardi, Schiano, and Gumbrecht (2004) found that readers and their expectations are often what keep a blog alive, in part because readership motivates blogging, in part because readership imposes a certain pressure on bloggers to continue, 'so as not to disappoint their audience' (Nardi et al., 2004: 224; for a similar argument, see Baumer et al., 2008). With regard to this, Ben claims that a main motivation for his continued blogging is that the blog has become a benchmark in the biking community. In a sense, then, bloggers and readers are mutually enforcing, urging each other to continue interacting through their posting, reading, and commenting activities. One might even suggest that this mutual constitution reflects a sort of contract of participation that characterizes the blog as a genre—blogging conversations only remain vibrant through the mutual commitment of authors and readers/commenters to sustain their engagement, and to meet one another's expectations.

Another central practice in the achievement of continued social presence is the reading of other bloggers' posts, and leaving comments. Visiting other blogs is a source of inspiration and new knowledge. For Elise, Ben, and Maggie, and for many of their readers, reading other blogs is an almost-daily routine. Whereas for Maggie and Elise commenting is central to their daily visits to their favorite blogs, Ben rarely comments on other blogs. These differences reflect the general interactional practices in the two blogging networks to which they belong—commenting is widespread among the women, but scarcer among the male cyclists. It is likely that commenting is more crucial in the women's network, because the interaction is almost entirely embedded in the blogging activities, whereas Ben and his readers see each other regularly, and are therefore less dependent on the blog to express mutual presence and negotiate their relationships. In the women's network, commenting is a method of demonstrating mutual engagement, and overcoming the spatio-temporal disruption of their conversations and relationships. According to Maggie, a comment on a blog is a way for her to mark her awareness of the other. By commenting, 'you have shown the person that you have read her post and thought about it' (Maggie). Accordingly, the act of commenting has a distinctly phatic function, regardless of its content; that is, it indicates social presence, and by this means confirms the existence of a social relationship between the commenter and the author.

Finally, social presence is accomplished through the author's response comments. Responding to comments seems to be a quite institutionalized practice. As Maggie elaborates: 'I have never felt it was not appropriate to respond' (Maggie). She and Elise consider responding to comments imperative, a view apparently shared by many other participants in their blog network, given the commenting activity in the network. Ben also prefers to respond to the comments he receives, but does not feel obligated. What is interesting in this connection is that response comments are not only given when the commenter has created a slot for the author to comment back (e.g., by asking a follow-up question to the post), but are also prevalent in sequences that are, in a sense, already closed. The following example is taken from a post in which Ben describes and comments on how the lead mountain biker collapsed completely during a race at the world championships:

Peter: I don't think I've ever seen a man SO cold, its mad, yeah, it should just be me ;o)??Peter.

Michael: Shocking. But you have to say that he made it good again at OL.

Jones: Aw . . . that is really sad to see.

Ben: YES SIR . . . when you really do have to fall, so be sure to do it in style :-)!

In this interaction sequence, commenters merely confirm what Ben has already described in his blog post, but nonetheless, Ben replies, by confirming once again what both he and the commenters have noted. This practical convention of responding even if there is no immediate reason to do so indicates that response comments serve a function not only in relation to creating structural coherence in conversation. The convention of always responding to comments is a way for the author to express appreciation of the comment, to signal responsiveness, and to indicate that she is still available for conversation (Herring, 1999a).

Comments are the main vehicles for creating what Elise calls *resonance*, in the sense that commenting plays a pivotal role in finding and confirming mutual interests that extend the conversation over time. The practical accomplishment embedded in the interactional 'post-comment-response comment' structure is a recursive creation of mutuality, responsiveness, understanding, recognition, and social presence. Participating in the women's blog cluster means taking part in each other's daily lives by posting, reading, and commenting. This indicates that, for bloggers, enacting the genre may facilitate rich, meaningful social experiences that are principally sustained by the continued mutual commitment of author and readers.

This commitment to continued interaction also seems to be reflected in a post in which Maggie blogs about being unable to participate in the conversations on a daily basis, owing to work deadlines and an upcoming vacation.

> It is actually rather hard to be a weekend-blogger all of a sudden . . . but it just can't be anything other than that for the present! I need to do a whole lot of work before the holiday—and as I mentioned, the holiday feeling is just now beginning to make itself felt.

> It is a lot to be able to catch up on 5 days' absence from the blog. . . . sniff! And then the ensuing 15–16 days without any certain access to the blog—In any case, holidays are holy! I will not go around looking for a PC—I see quite enough of them every day.

With this post, Maggie signals to her readers and fellow bloggers that she finds it hard to be away from the blog. This suggests that blogging is an integral part of Maggie's daily life—her relationships with fellow bloggers are felt and experienced not only when she is engaged in blogging in front of the screen, but also extend into other spheres of activity, corresponding to what Chayko (2002) has described as 'sociomental connections.' The following exchange in the commenting section of Maggie's blog post (above) indicates that being unable to participate, even for a short while, means that bloggers and readers miss each other's company.

> Paul: I suddenly realized that I would miss you whilst you are gone. It is a little strange . . . I really hope that just once in a while you might find the opportunity and time to write a few lines in the blog. [. . .]

> MAGGIE: Paul—that is really sweet . . . and it makes me happy here in my on-off blog time! Very happy! I have seen that you have written several blog posts but I need to be fresh and awake tomorrow to be

able to comment on them as they deserve ;-) But I'll most likely find a PC whilst there—even though I won't let myself be controlled by that—after all, holidays are holidays ;-)

This sequence does indicate that Maggie and Paul are connected, but the expression of their connectedness is remarkably emotional. It may be that the spatio-temporal distance those participants must overcome in blogging leads them to overarticulate their relationship. After all, blogging is not so important that Maggie will spend time hunting for a PC to stay tuned while travelling.

In a similar vein, being without internet connection makes Elise feel 'amputated,' because she cannot blog and read emails. Hence, in Maggie and Elise's cases, it seems that being away from their blogs leads to their feeling disconnected from the social relationships and communicative exchanges it involves. Accordingly, being prevented from participating is not only experienced as missing out on interesting posts and interactions, but as neglecting one's commitment to being available for company and conversation with fellow bloggers. Blogging may thus be regarded as a joint project in which individual participants have obligations towards the others.

The daily exchange of comments by some of the participants, especially on Elise and Maggie's blogs, develops and strengthens this relationship over time. Because the most active participants visit and comment on each other's blogs on a daily basis, they gradually develop personal relationships and group cohesion. The continuous social presence thus functions as a phatic marker, enabling participants to create and maintain rather close relationships in a networked space, the blogosphere, which in principle is not very personal.

FRAMING CONVERSATION AND
NEGOTIATING TOPICAL RELEVANCE

In addition to establishing responsiveness and social presence, participants engage in practices that create topical coherence and relevance in the blog conversation. Blogging software supports topical coherence through the threaded structure of blog communication, which ensures that contributions concerning a specific topic are grouped together (Herring, 1999a). The data further suggests that topical coherence and relevance within a thread is an interactional accomplishment, in that participants exhibit significant collaborative effort to keep conversations on track, and ensure alignment and mutual understanding in the development of the topic.

According to Herring (1999a), CMC is generally vulnerable to topical decay and digressions, which threaten the interactional coherence. Contrary to Herring's predictions, digressions are quite infrequent in the data. The commenting sections display very little topical development and digression in the blog conversations, with participants often merely confirming viewpoints and experiences that have been articulated in the blog post. In this section, I analyze framing conventions and rights, focusing on how the core practices of blogging and commenting allow participants to reach an agreement regarding what constitute relevant topics for conversation.

A basic premise of blogs is that they are author-driven. Personal blogs are initiated and motivated by the author's personal interests and experiences. In most blogs, including the three blogs included in this study, the author presents him- or herself on the blog's front page. This provides (new) readers with an indication of what they may expect to find on the blog. The blog author's posts frame the interaction, by initiating a conversation and setting a particular topic or set of topics as its starting point(s). Conversations in the commentary threads are then tied to specific blog posts. This means that the blog author has a certain degree of control. Ben describes his preference for blogging, in contrast to online discussion forums: 'I think what I really like is that I can control everything in here. I decide how I'm portrayed. I decide what photos to bring'(Ben).

The data reveals what appears to be a deep respect for the author's framing of the conversation, in that comments address the issues raised in the posts, and often discuss them with their point of departure in the author's perspective. Typically, a commenter will note something from the post, and tie it to his or her own thoughts and experiences. Occasionally, someone posts a comment that is topically irrelevant, such as when participants use the comment section in Ben's blog to coordinate a training session with him. Such digressions are rare in the material. There is a tendency to stay on topic, and accept the topics of conversation suggested by the author. This practice of complying with the author is also constituted in the discursive style of the blog, which is defined by the posts setting the tone for the subsequent comments. This is particularly striking in posts that 'breach' the normally quite informal tone of the blogs. For instance, when Maggie blogs about missing her father, the tone of the comments becomes more serious to express respect for Maggie's loss. Similarly, smileys are omitted in the comments, and the tone becomes less playful, when Elise blogs about people with disabilities or political issues. Therefore, blogging seems to demand sensitivity and ongoing adjustment to the author's state of mind. Thus, an asymmetrical relationship seems to exist between participants in a blog, given that the readers contribute by taking the author's perspective, and 'thinking' from the standpoint of the author (Thorseth, 2008: 229; also Lomborg, 2012a).

Despite the author's privileged position in a blog, readers and commenters may influence the author's framing in numerous ways. First, commenters may seek to influence directly, by requesting, or expressing expectations of posts. This occurs regularly in the data sets. For instance, a reader encourages Ben to review a new bicycle, something Ben then agrees to do. Similarly, when Maggie mentions an upcoming date on her blog, a recurrent commenter writes that she is waiting in anticipation for a follow-up post. Such expressions of expectation may be considered reader efforts to enter the negotiation of what would be relevant topics to post on the blog. However, on Maggie's blog, direct expressions of expectations for up-coming posts are often followed by a disclaimer, such as Amanda's 'I didn't mean to pry' in an exchange about a dinner Maggie had with a male friend, or Paul's reaction to Maggie's reflections about changing career and home base: 'I am extremely curious. What? Where? When? How? But I won't ask.' Both are examples of the reader politely indicating that although a certain topic would interest him or her, Maggie is not obligated to meet the request. Again, this demonstrates that the author has a privileged position with regard to the right to frame blog content, and decide what is relevant.

Second, readers and commenters may indirectly influence blog content by their mere readership and participation structure. In the interviews, both Elise and Ben talk about how they use blog statistics to keep track of the traffic on their blogs, sometimes basing their ideas of what to blog about and when to do it, on these statistics. For example, Elise notes: 'I would like to blog more about flea markets, how wonderful they are [. . .] but I constrain myself a bit' (Elise). Sensing that flea markets apparently do not interest her readers, Elise tries to tone down this interest on the blog. In this way, Elise adjusts the blog content to her perception of the audience's expectations and interests. By 'hiding' aspects of herself that are less attractive to her audience, she hopes to keep the audience committed. Maggie claims to be less interested in her statistics, but she does admit that she notices if a post receives very few comments. Accordingly, bloggers seem to be very aware of their audiences.

Third, and correspondingly, readers may negotiate relevant topics with the author, by making or withholding comments. By making the effort to post a comment, the reader indicates that a post is relevant and interesting. It is likely that many comments to particular posts encourage more posting about the same types of issues. If a post receives few comments, or if the tone of the comments is negative, it is likely that the author will be less inclined to post something similar, so the reader may influence the framing of conversation through the simple acts of reading and commenting. Consequently, over time, some topics become more central, whereas others become peripheral. Indeed, the thematic orientation is narrowed in scope, so that only topics that are commonly deemed interesting are covered.

Blogging, then, implies an informal and subtle contract between readers and authors, regarding what to blog about, making it difficult to blog about other topics. The influence of reader expectations and interaction regarding what content is deemed relevant indicates that interaction has a conservative effect on the blog content, and, ultimately, on the dynamics of the blog genre. The inertia in thematic orientation is self-perpetuating. As some themes feature more prominently, and are thus tagged more often, the ranking of a blog is boosted in searches for these particular themes. In turn, the blog is more likely to attract new readers interested in these already-established themes than readers with other interests. Hence, there is some path dependency in the blog, owing to the network; that is, the future expansion and development of the blog network in which Elise's blog, for example, is embedded is contingent upon the preferences and interests of the blog's current network of affiliation. Consequently, the continuous negotiation and adjustment of the blog theme seems to lead to a stabilization of appropriate topics within each specific blog, over time. Of course, who has the upper hand in this negotiation may vary, depending on the author's appreciation of comments and feedback.

In conclusion, the framing of the conversation in personal blogging may be considered a collaborative accomplishment in which author and readers are mutually enforcing. Nardi et al. (2004) stress the mere presence of the readership, rather than its active engagement with the blogger through comments, as the main contribution of the blog's audience to the constitution of the genre. Consequently, the blog is seen as broadcast with limited interactivity and responsiveness. My analyses modify this, by demonstrating that even though the author is by far the most active contributor to the framing of the communication, the conversation becomes coherent and meaningful for the participants, in the negotiation of relevance between author and readers, and the procedural unfolding of interaction. However, it is possible that the readers are granted a special role and power in the ongoing negotiation in my analysis, vis-à-vis Nardi et al. (2004), simply because my data are collected from blogs with relatively extensive commenting.

General Observations on Topics of Relevance: What Generates Activity on the Blogs?

There is a striking similarity between the three blogs in terms of the relationship between the type of content posted, and the number of comments a given post receives. In general, intimate and self-disclosing posts, such as those dealing with family relations, personal dilemmas and conflicts, and confessions of private thoughts and emotions, receive many comments. This holds true for all three blogs and suggests that readers enjoy posts that reveal something personal about the author. Furthermore, there are many comments to Ben's posts about bike races in which many of the readers participate. Finally, activity tends to be high when the bloggers post about blogging. The large number of comments on posts about bike races and blog-related issues indicates an eagerness to contribute when the topic is an activity or experience bloggers have in common. Given the high activity around the participants' shared experiences, a genre convention appears to be that blogging is primarily kept vibrant through the sharing of personal reflections, and converging around topics of common interest.

However, the data is contradictory, especially when it comes to Elise and Maggie's blogs. A few posts about 'blog rallies' (i.e., meet-ups for bloggers) on Elise's blog show very little response, for instance, and, generally, when personal posts are mere stories from their everyday lives (e.g., when Maggie and Elise blog about going for a walk, reading a good book, and other daily activities), they get very little response. Conversely, there are highly topically focused and less intimate posts that get many comments. Hence, it is not reasonable to draw firm conclusions about when activity levels are high—and what participants consider the most important topics of the personal blog genre.

Though it seems that certain types of content are considered more relevant and appropriate to the blog, it is not an imperative rule. The lack of clear patterns relating to activity-generating content, especially in the two women's blogs, suggests that other conditions and conventions might be more important for genre expression on the blog. I suggest that one such condition is the ordinariness and daily routine of blogging. When participation follows no strong pattern concerning content, it might indicate that the object of the blog conversation is not what is talked about, but is instead related to the experience of togetherness, and the possibilities created by blogging, for maintaining daily contact among peers and being part of each other's daily lives.

BLOGGING AND SOCIALITY IN EVERYDAY LIFE

The data indicate that a sense of unity and friendship may blossom around blogging, through social presence, mutuality, and intersubjectivity, despite the fact that bloggers and their readers are spatio-temporally dispersed and often do not know each other in advance. Elise explains that, to a great extent, what has made the blog fun and worthwhile for her is the way it has facilitated connectivity: 'It is a great part of my life [. . .] it got more and more fun as I began to develop relationships with people' (Elise). Therefore, how relationships are established and maintained, and the meanings bloggers assign to them seem key to understanding what makes blogging a significant activity and experience in the everyday lives of the participants.

In this section, I home in on what participants accomplish in terms of membership, social inclusion, and peer relationships in blogs by enacting the genre competently, to explore the pragmatic uses and meanings of blogging practices in their everyday lives. I ask what it means to competently enact the personal blog, as a prerequisite for entering a collaborative negotiation of the genre.

Using Blogs in Everyday Life

Being online appears to be an integral part of the three bloggers' daily lives. This is reflected in the 'rhythm' of the three blogs.

Maggie posts throughout the week, estimating that she spends approximately one hour per day on blogging, primarily during breaks at work. She writes more posts and comments between 6 am and 9 am, and during the afternoon between 3 pm and 6 pm, indicating that she blogs in the morning when drinking her coffee, and during her breaks, if she needs a bit of distraction in the afternoon. Other participants on her blog explicitly state in their comments that they use blogging in the same way, as a break from everyday and work life.

As previously mentioned, Elise is very active on her blog in the morning. She typically posts before 9 am, or between 3 pm and 6 pm, whereas she is less likely to make new blog posts during her workday. This is similar to Maggie. However, she posts many comments to her own and others' blogs when at work. 'I have a job that involves quite a lot of waiting time, so I can use this time for visiting blogs and have ideas for posts to blog during work, without neglecting my work. I have to sit and monitor stuff, so I'm already in front of the computer' (Elise). The analysis of the temporal distribution of contributions by the other participants on Maggie and Elise's blogs confirms this daily routine of visiting blogs. The active periods vary with participants, but generally, comments are fairly equally distributed, both throughout the week and throughout the day, from 6 am to 9 pm.

The daily rhythm of Ben's blogging differs a bit from Elise and Maggie's. He posts and comments throughout the day, but is considerably more active between 3 pm and 9 pm. To a large extent, comments from others follow the same pattern. Whereas the distribution of comments throughout the day indicates some blog activity at work, the frequent use of the afternoon and early evening seems to imply that blog activity, in comparison to that of the women's blog network, is skewed towards the participants' leisure time.

Overall, considering the consistent activity throughout the waking hours, blogging seems highly entangled and incorporated into the participants' everyday lives, both as a break from work-related tasks, and at home, as an enjoyable leisure activity in its own right.

As we have seen, the three bloggers read blogs on a daily basis, and keep track of many blogs. Despite this, none of them uses newsreaders with RSS aggregators to keep track of new posts on the blogs that they read, although such software offer automatic monitoring of new posts to read, collected in a newsfeed in the newsreader, with headlines and links to the new content. Instead, the participants consult the blogs directly every time, either using their own blogroll as the entry point, or, as in Ben's case, opening all his bookmarked blogs in a folder in his browser. For Ben, a teaser as provided by a headline in a newsreader is unsatisfactory.

> I have a folder where I open all the blogs at once [. . .] It is stupid, actually, because most of the time, there is nothing new on them. I just like the routine of clicking in, just to get my half hour, clicking and looking. (Ben)

Whereas the practice of visiting blogs directly is more time-consuming and often in vain, it serves the vital function of giving the three study participants a break when they need one during the day. Along those lines, Elise explains that she has actively chosen not to use RSS feeds, to not feel obligated to visit a blog at a certain time, suggesting that blog reading should be motivated by a personal need and availability, not by a compulsion to keep up with other bloggers' activities in real time. In sum, for the participants, blogging has become an ordinary activity in everyday life, but it also provides a 'break from the everyday' (Maggie). They immerse themselves in blogs when they feel like it, on their own terms, and in the time slots that become available during the course of their daily activities.

Blogging Competently: Becoming a Blogger

The three bloggers studied have been actively and consistently involved in blogging for lengthy periods—Elise since mid-2005, the two others since early 2007. Elise and Ben were introduced to blogging by their partners, who were already active bloggers. Maggie accidentally 'fell over' blogging when searching for a recipe and found one on a well-known Danish blog that is linked to the network of blogs in which Maggie's blog is now embedded.

> I visited it [the blog] over a couple of months, and one day I left a comment [. . .] stating that I had been there and found the recipe I was looking for, and so on. And then I returned, and I could see that she had responded to my comment, which roused my curiosity regarding what that was all about. (Maggie)

Soon after this experience, Maggie started her own blog. When she launched her blog, her initial purpose was to communicate with her family in Denmark, so they could relate to her daily life. Hence, the blog was—and still is—a means of remaining connected with her loved ones, despite living·abroad. However, Maggie explains that as she started to explore other blogs and leave comments, these bloggers began to comment on Maggie's blog, which soon became linked to a larger blog network of primarily Danish female bloggers. According to Maggie, this has changed the blog a bit, and reflects its current state: the posts are shorter, and the blog is updated more frequently, as she suddenly caters to multiple audiences: her family in Denmark, which she wants to keep updated and, mainly, the fellow bloggers with whom she interacts on a daily basis in the blogosphere. The development of Maggie's blog is a good example of how the blog is 'a living thing' (Elise) that changes over time, and how the awareness of the audience plays a role in this continuous refinement of the individual blog's interpretation of the personal blog genre.

Bloggers develop genre competence by reading other blogs and finding inspiration to improve their own blogging. As Berkenkotter and Huckin (1993: 483–486) argue, mastering a genre comes with active participation, including imitation and correction from others. Ben, for instance, describes how he tries to put effort into the visual expression of his blog, by posting photos that offer cues to the theme of the blog post, adjusting the design, and so forth, because he, as a reader, likes when other bloggers do this.

Along similar lines, an important criterion for navigating the personal blog genre competently is to learn how to enact the genre through writing interesting, and appropriate blog posts. Adjusting his or her writing over time is one way for the blogger to develop and consolidate genre competence. When asked to describe high quality in blogging, participants emphasize brevity, a clear focus, and an engaging, relevant story.

> You have to try to grab people's attention, if it is possible to make a good, captivating story. If you don't grab their attention quickly, they will leave without reading to the end. (Elise)

It is custom in both blog networks to include a photo in the blog post, usually one that reflects and connects with the topic, to 'spice it up' and thereby enhance the reading experience. Furthermore, the good blog post is preferably told from a personal angle that participants may recognize, and with which they may identify. As Maggie phrases it, the good posts are those 'that give me something to think about, or that reveal something about the person' (Maggie). At the same time, the three bloggers distance themselves from blogs that are navel gazing, or describe the banalities of everyday life, so although a personal angle is, in principle, an important quality, it must not override the general relevance. The blog post should both embrace and transgress the personal. Elise contends that, in comparison with a personal letter, the blog post is more topically focused, and typically addresses only one theme. However, across blog posts, a certain degree of topical variation is an important quality. These largely agreed-upon genre qualities are implicit to blogging, argues Elise: 'It is not really something you think about. It becomes routine, you just do it' (Elise).

Being able to enact the personal blog genre competently by writing relevant, inspiring, and personal blog posts is a prerequisite for gaining access to, and being recognized as a relevant interaction partner in a given blog cluster. Although commenting on others' blogs is widely acknowledged as a useful strategy for attracting readers to one's own blog, because it makes the commenter more visible in the blog network, it is not enough to result in inclusion, in the sense of the other bloggers reciprocating the attention. In a thread on Elise's blog where Elise takes up the theme of blogging and commenting, and in which 73 comments are posted, the participants agree that blogging and commenting should not be focused on getting attention, but instead on the writer's own pleasure in blogging. For instance, Jen asserts in a comment, 'the blogger cannot demand anything. I comment on very few of the posts I read. I do try to utter a sound when something engages me.' Similarly, Greta writes, 'comments are written when I have something to say. Hope the same is the case on my own blog.' Both Maggie and Ben describe a similar practice of commenting when a blog post is inspiring and thought through, although Maggie adds that she also comments on the blogs for which she feels a close affinity. However, at least for the blogger at the periphery of the network, receiving comments is an extra bonus that functions as recognition of the blogger. The blogger cannot demand this attention. Instead, she must earn it, by keeping the readers interested.

Establishing and Developing Relationships

In a post celebrating the anniversary of her blog, Maggie writes:

> In the middle of a busy time—and with decreased blog activity—today is still a birthday . . . 1 year since I started my blog.

> Little did I know what it would lead to . . . as my very first post testified! I had become inspired by others—one person in particular! But didn't think that I had terribly relevant stuff to say or write about.

> I also visited other blogs—I wondered about the comments. . . . I thought that these people must know each other on a personal basis, in order to leave comments for one another? One fine day I took the leap—I left a comment with a COMPLETE STRANGER!!!! It was almost boundary breaking for me—a relatively shy creature by nature. I was so surprised when I got a response—and the larger it became when my blog got visitors. . .and comments. . .

> All of a sudden, there were more comments, then there were also personal emails. [. . .]

> New blogs, new acquaintances, and new experiences are still being added to the picture . . . even though my participation is minimal at the moment. But even so, I do wonder how others are getting on. . . . and a mail during a blog vacuum says a lot!!!!

In this excerpt, Maggie describes how she initially thought that all the other bloggers knew each other, and felt like an outsider. She elaborates in the interview: 'When I saw the comments that they posted to each other, I thought they must be old friends, they must go way back, because it sounded so very perceptive' (Maggie). In the commentary thread following Maggie's post, her readers echo this initial impression of bloggers, as well as the experience of developing deep and meaningful relationships over time. For Maggie, it is through comments, in particular, that bloggers come to know each other: 'It makes a big difference whether you read their posts or their comments. Often, in the comments you learn more about the person' (Maggie).

This, again, suggests that conversational activities play pivotal roles in developing relationships—they make the blog communication personal, and it is through ongoing conversation that participants become perceptive and knowledgeable insiders in the network of peers.

This evolving process of building relationships through continued participation in blogs is similar to what Baym describes in her analysis of online community and the threaded discussions in a Usenet newsgroup: People begin by reading other people's conversations (lurking), then enter the conversation themselves (as newbies), and slowly learn the conventions and rules of participation (becoming full members), and over time friendships develop with fellow participants (Baym, 2000: 119–120). Hence, this relational development over time is certainly not unique to blogs.

On Elise and Maggie's blogs, it is common practice, when a new reader 'unlurks' and submits her first comment, for the blog author to welcome her in a response comment, thereby demonstrating awareness that a new potential member has entered the network. For instance, when a reader unlurks in a thread, Maggie applauds by responding that it is 'lovely when readers unlurk,' thereby implicitly sanctioning and accepting her participation—and at the same time signaling that she would like to know more about her readers. Similarly, Elise is quite eager to know who her readers are. Apart from greeting new commenters on the blog, she follows the blog's statistics closely, including studying the locations of the IP addresses of visitors, and she explicitly encourages readers to 'unlurk.' 'A couple of times I have asked on the blog, 'who ARE all of you who read along'?' (Elise). Upon welcoming new readers, Elise often visits their blogs as well. In short, she prefers to know her visitors, and 'putting a face' on the audience gives her a better idea of whom she attracts to the blog, and how they might relate to each other.

Whereas it may be quite simple to be welcomed in the blogging network, it seems that there are still degrees of participation and closeness. As an outsider or newbie, much of what is said seems like inside talk—participants talk perceptively and knowledgeably about their lives, tastes, and so forth, and thereby demonstrate shared knowledge and understanding. On Ben's blog, for instance, knowledgeability mainly means being familiar with cycling, as participants use esoteric terms about gear and biking teams that are unfamiliar to those who are not cycling enthusiasts. Furthermore, many of the bloggers have inside jokes that they continuously refer to when interacting. In sum, some of the exchanges on a blog may be quite difficult to decipher for an outsider, or even a newbie, because they address an already familiar audience, and presume some degree of knowledge on the part of the reader (Nardi et al., 2004).

Being a full member in a blog cluster requires such inside knowledge and perceptiveness—something that is built over time through continuous participation and mutual social presence. As a newbie, not only does one have to learn the conventions of participation and the blog as a genre, one must also build knowledge about the other participants, their interests, and blogging activities. With regard to this, Herring (1999a) notes that CMC has an advantage over oral communication, in that the conversation is to some extent persistent, because textual records of the conversation may be archived. Typically, blogs have archives of blog posts and commentary threads, so in principle, participants may go back and read the history of the blog, learn how the conversations have developed, and so forth. As Herring (1999a) argues, this persistence of conversation in blogs may aid newbies to cognitively manage the interaction, because they can catch up on the shared knowledge that insiders have accumulated over time.

Among those who are regulars or core members of the blogging network, there are indications of a greater degree of closeness between the most active participants, particularly on the women's blogs. Not only do they refer knowledgeably to each other's interests and blog posts, they also discursively mark their groupness by using inclusive discourse. For instance, concerning Maggie's post about an upcoming date, Molly comments, 'we are all with you,' and others follow up with similar remarks in the thread. Additionally, Elise refers to 'our Molly' in a comment to a post where Maggie blogs about a gift that Molly has sent her. Finally, participants regularly talk about the blog network as the 'blog friends,' indicating that their relations are of a friendly character. This discursive articulation of the group is one of the core practices that establishes and maintains relationships and a sense of 'groupness.' Keyton (1999), for instance, argues that 'relational communication'—'verbal and non-verbal messages that create the social fabric of the group'—creates bonds among members (Keyton, 1999: 192). Furthermore, Brewer and Gardner (1996) found that when a 'we' discourse is prominent in a group, the members are more likely to activate relational or collective identities. Extending this, the use of 'we' by the blog participants may be seen to function as discursive priming for group identification (also, Chayko, 2002: 102–107).

Through the clear discursive marking of the group's insiders, perceptiveness among them, and, thus, inclusivity in a given cluster, the outside also becomes visible. Indeed, implicit meanings of exchanges may only be grasped by the skilled, long-term participant, indicating a certain degree of exclusivity within the blog clusters, which might make it difficult for others to enter the conversation. On the one hand, Ben criticizes fellow bike bloggers for writing only with a niche audience of fellow cycling enthusiasts in mind. Against this background, Ben distinguishes himself as a blogger striving to blog in a nonexclusive manner. 'If you open up a little, other people have the opportunity to get something out of it every time, then you [they] don't have to sit and read all the posts from way back' (Ben). On the other hand, Ben does acknowledge that it may sometimes be difficult to avoid writing with a certain degree of tacit perceptiveness, when communicating with those participants he knows very well.

Expanding the Relationship by Adding Contact Points

The development of blogger relationships is not restricted to the blogs. Numerous examples in the data indicate that interactions migrate to other communicative genres, for example email, telephone, letters and gifts, Facebook, postcards, and even face-to-face encounters. In the interview, Maggie agrees that relationships grow stronger and more intimate when the conversation is not restricted to the blog, but may unfold on a one-to-one basis through email and telephone calls. Similarly, Ben contends that of those he has met on the blog, some have become more like friends with whom he has contact through Facebook, text messages, email, and face-to-face encounters.

Several studies have similarly documented the connection between relationship formation and the use of multiple communication media. For instance, in social network analysis, Haythornthwaite (2000, 2005) has developed—and found support for—the idea of 'media multiplexity,' suggesting that people who are strongly connected communicate frequently, and use multiple media to do so (Haythornthwaite, 2005: 130). In other words, Haythornthwaite argues that the more media used to communicate, the stronger the tie between the communicators. Moreover, in a study of distance learners, Haythornthwaite (2000) found that being strongly tied to specific others in a given social network enhances not only the individual's sense of belonging to the network as a whole, but also the perception of the social network as a cohesive group. This resonates with online community studies that suggest that offline encounters between community members enhance the experience of community among attending members (e.g., Nardi et al., 2004, Sessions, 2010).

Whereas meeting face-to-face is quite normal and commonplace for the members of the cycling blog cluster in which Ben participates, meeting fellow bloggers face-to-face is not an everyday happening for most bloggers. However, in the women's blog network, core participants such as Elise have initiated face-to-face meetings with fellow bloggers, 'blog rallies,' which take place every couple of months. These meetings seem to have further enriched the blog-based relations for those who have attended. According to Maggie, who has attended one of these blog rallies, meeting her peers in person strengthens the relationships, and creates a greater engagement and commitment to blogging. Elise confirms this experience of blog rallies as enriching the blogging experience, stating that 'it really adds something extra to meet people in reality, it does. Because you cannot present the entire person in what you write on the blog' (Elise).

Considering that the bloggers' experience and relationships are enriched and strengthened by other forms of contact than the blog, most notably the face-to-face meetings, a relevant question is why blogging activities remain important to them. Why continue the effort of maintaining and developing relations through a blog, when participants have other, apparently more personal and intimate venues for conversation? First, as argued by Elise, blogging provides a convenient, distributed platform for keeping daily contact with a large number of people, accessible whenever it fits into the daily schedule of the individual participant:

> It is easier to build an expanded network this way than in real life, I think. Because close friendships, that is about. . . well you might see each other once a month or every other month, and then it is not so intimate. Here, there is perhaps almost daily contact, so something really intimate can come out if it, and friendships. (Elise)

Compared to, say, one-to-one communication (e.g., personal email, phone calls, and text messages) and synchronous forms of communication in which multiple parties may participate simultaneously (such as online chat or face-to-face encounters) the blog is very flexible. Along similar lines, for Maggie, who lives abroad and thus only rarely has the opportunity to meet blogging peers, blogging enables 'interaction with Danes, which I appreciate a lot because I don't have it here' (Maggie). Blogging, then, takes on a specific situational relevance in Maggie's case, because it allows her to maintain a daily connection to her Danish roots (for a similar argument, see Bakardjieva, 2005: 128). In addition, Maggie suggests that the effort already put into the blog would make it difficult to abandon blogging altogether. It is something she has created, her 'own little baby' (Maggie), indicating an attachment to the activity of blogging in itself, not only to the people she has met through the blog.

Leaving the Blog

In contrast to the two women, who continue to value their blogging activities, Ben chose to leave his blog at the end of the study period. As we have already seen, Ben had for some time struggled a bit with his blogging, lacking inspiration, and so forth. In his farewell salute on the blog, he writes:

> As if it was a funeral for an old friend, it is with sadness that, after two years and 330 blog posts [. . .], I have decided to call it a day—for now at least.

> This decision has been on its way for quite some time. At times I've felt like a burnt out artist, who has begun to lack words and repeat himself, and at the same time I think there have been bigger and bigger gaps between the good stories, which earlier on, made the blog alive and interesting.

In the post, Ben further explains to the readers what he has gotten out of the blog: expressing his passion for cycling, and getting to know others. He concludes by thanking the readers for following his blog. Ben has less at stake than Maggie and Elise would, if they considered leaving their blogs. Whereas for the women, especially Maggie, who lives abroad, a farewell to blogging would probably mean losing daily contact with people with whom she has become friends, Ben's exit from the blog network is not a breaking-off of contact with his fellow bloggers, because he sees many of them at training sessions and races. Thus, quitting the blog does not imply quitting the cycling community. Perhaps because of this, his readers react with understanding to Ben's farewell to blogging. Yet, some express disappointment, and some think that others in the network will follow (which, indeed, some have). The post in which he announces his quitting has received more comments (19 in total) than any other post on Ben's blog. In a sense, then, in this thread, the community of the bike bloggers suddenly becomes visible, with the 'loss' of a core member.

Ben's decision to stop blogging had been underway for quite a while, following changing circumstances in his everyday life: he had become a father. As Helles (2010) argues, fundamental personal changes such as entering a different life phase, likely leads individuals to reassess their existing habits, and rearrange priorities and media preferences. Following this line of argument, Ben's farewell to keeping a blog might be seen as a natural consequence of having less time for himself, and prioritizing his family.

LOCAL MANAGEMENT OF THE GENRE: CONTENT AND CONVERSATIONAL STYLE

In the previous sections, I intentionally focused on common traits across blogs, to present the commonly accepted knowledge and functions of the personal blog. I have yet to present in greater detail how local norms and blogging practices, as expressed in the individual blogger's enactment of the genre, contribute to constituting and negotiating the personal blog as a genre. Although a number of socially accepted and reified conventions exist, the personal blog is no monolithic genre, but has a variety of expressions.

I have briefly indicated that the social relationships in the three blog networks have different conditions. In this final section, I explore how the personal blog as a genre, and the expressions of sociality associated with the genre, are locally negotiated and anchored in the specific blogs. I do this by analyzing the three blogs separately, as texts in their own right, with unique shadings of the personal blog genre. I emphasize how the blogs differ, in order to explore the variety and richness of the personal blog genre. Consequently, in this section the blogs may appear more different from one another than they actually are.

The three bloggers all self-identify as personal bloggers, writing with their personal experiences as their points of departure. However, from a textual perspective, the three blogs differ in content and style. Maggie's blog is what might be labeled a prototypical personal blog, in that she mostly writes about matters of personal interest and private character, in a rather intimate and self-disclosing fashion (Lomborg, 2009). Ben's blog is primarily topic-driven, in that it covers several themes related to cycling: training, diet, cycling gear, and reports of races. The tone is personal, yet typically, the posts are written with humor and an ironic distance from Ben's cycling experiences. Elise's blog is located somewhere in between—less focused on personal confession, more topic-driven, but still with the author disclosing personal values and experiences through the topics discussed. Despite difference in thematic and stylistic modes of expression, there is overlap between, and variation within the blogs, making in difficult, at best, to categorize them unambiguously. Ben's cycling blog is sometimes rather confessional and intimate, for example, when he posts about becoming a father, and about his decision to close the blog. Conversely, Maggie's blog is sometimes topic-driven, for example, when she blogs about her passion for travel, art exhibitions, and books. The shifting content reflects the norm of varying content from post to post. The way in which topics are discussed and the tone of the blogs are also quite varied, partly owing to the influence of content on discursive style. The analyses will demonstrate how these differences in content and style relate to core functions of the daily exchanges on the blog, and the meanings ascribed to the blog as a social space. Specifically, I outline the three blogs with different thematic and stylistic characteristics, according to a continuum, ranging from highly personal to topical content, on the one hand, and from the highly confessional and intimate, to a more objective and impersonal style, on the other hand.

Maggie's Blog: Everyday Togetherness, Support, and Recognition

Reporting her day-to-day activities as well as reflections of her work and private life on her blog, Maggie blogs from a highly personal and confessional perspective. In this sense, her blog bears some resemblance to a diary. This seems to spark a friendly ambience on the blog, one that is supported by the conversational style. In conversation analysis, it has been well documented that there is a general preference for agreement in interaction (Pomerantz, 1984). With the data from Maggie's blog, the preference for agreement seems to hold. A majority of contributions to the conversations involve confirmation, recognition, and alignment with the author's viewpoints and experiences. Accordingly, Maggie's blog does not generate dispute, but constitutes a cozy and friendly social space. The constant confirmation and alignment challenge some previous findings from studies of CMC. For instance, Kendall (2005) found participants reluctant to engage in this confirmatory behavior in online chat and MUDs, because they found it 'noisy' and unnecessary. Similarly, despite finding that newsgroup participants adhered to an ethic of friendliness themselves, Baym (2000: 138) found that the participants considered members' failure to contribute new information or ideas in their comments a waste of bandwidth. A possible explanation of this discrepancy is that, in contrast to online chat, MUDs, and newsgroups as genres, the blog is a space hosted by an individual participant, the blogger. Thus, the communicative space is arguably more personal, leading visitors to this space to invoke norms of politeness and alignment to a greater extent.

In Maggie's blog, there are few instances of disagreement, typically in connection with less intimate posts in which Maggie expresses her opinion about some subject. Disagreements are characterized by the involved parties collaborating to mitigate any possible offence and conflict such disagreement may cause. A principal method in this category is *repair work*, that is, an active, collaborative effort by the participants to save each other's face,[5] self-correct, or even apologize for disagreeing (Garcia & Jacobs, 1999).

One of Maggie's most active commenters, Paul, is more often implicated in disagreement and debate on Maggie's blog—for example, he puts the conversational conventions on Maggie's blog to the test by engaging in political discussion, and discussions about cultural taste with Maggie. Consider the following example, in which Maggie and Paul discuss an apparently controversial book.

Paul said: I am surprised that you read Elisabeth Gilbert—there is one place where we don't share the same taste! I am looking forward to hearing what you think about The Yacoubian Building. I am also in the middle of a cozy reading weekend, but I have planned to read some other books. But now I feel a little tempted to follow your example. I'll have to think about that. . . . .

MAGGIE: Paul, I hope, that it all meets all regulations for how it should be . . . will be crossing my fingers. I don't know much about Gilbert's book—other than the thought of travelling appealed to me. I have read just 50 pages in The Yacoubian Building—and it is fantastic! I am really interested in hearing what you think of it . . . but you would understand that ;-)

Paul: I have heard a lot about Gilbert's book and it is apparently quite religious- it is not something for me. It is one of Oprah's favorite books!

MAGGIE: Oops—I didn't know that . . . it was a bit of an impulse buy! But I have to see about that . . . it doesn't seem to come near my taste!

Paul: Ok, I was also a little surprised when I saw that on your photo. It is about the author's way 'to God'. She travels round the world, but finally discovers that god is always with her! The point is that, you should pray to god, then you'll have a good life. In any case, that was how Oprah reviewed the book. Eat, pray, love = prerequisite for a good life. ??Enjoy it!

Despite disagreement, Maggie and Paul make a collaborative effort to ensure mutual adjustment of opinion, and not threaten each other with loss of face. When Paul first criticizes Maggie's book choice, he does so by stating that her choice surprises him. Thus, he indirectly says that he normally thinks Maggie has good taste in books. He further wraps the critique in their common experience of another book, *The Yacoubian Building*, which they both like. Hence, he disagrees by emphasizing something Paul and Maggie share. In her first response, Maggie explains she does not know much about the book, except that it is about travel, and that she hopes for the best. This move deflects Paul's skepticism, defends her book choice by downplaying her knowledge about the book, and ultimately is face-saving for her. It is particularly noteworthy that it is actually Paul who creates the slot for Maggie's self-repair, through his initial expression of surprise at her book choice. Consequently, saving Maggie's face is a collaborative accomplishment. Maggie further reaffirms the good tone, by responding concerning their common excitement about *The Yacoubian Building*. In the next turn, Paul challenges Maggie's book choice again, by revealing what he dislikes about it—it is religious, and Oprah likes it. This is apparently not a quality mark for Paul—and this threatens Maggie with loss of face. With her almost apologetic 'Ooops—I didn't know that' Maggie aligns herself with Paul, and acknowledges that it may be a book that does not sound like something she would enjoy, and that it was an impulse buy. This way, she positions herself as 'innocent' regarding her book choice, to demonstrate that her good taste is still intact. Paul concludes the exchange by acknowledging Maggie's disclaimer concerning the book, and confirming that it does not fit his picture of Maggie and her taste. In sum, through their collaboration and mutual adjustment, Maggie and Paul manage to build a sort of alignment, despite their initial disagreement, thereby mitigating the possible offence, loss of face, and threat to their relationship that disagreement could cause.

The preference for agreement in Maggie's blog contrasts somewhat with Maggie's account in the interview, of why blogging is interesting.

> It is interesting, not to be reconfirmed, when people write something back to you, but because people challenge you on some issues, on your thoughts and opinions. . . sometimes it will all be all banal, but at other times it will be more substantial, where you get a dialogue going that teaches you something about that person, but where you are also forced to disclose your own viewpoints. (Maggie)

Here, Maggie argues that disagreement is good, even central to her experience of blogging, because it is through differences of opinion and experience that bloggers get to know each other better. It appears that it is not the disagreement in itself, but the outcome of it, that Maggie applauds. In this light, it is a bit surprising that disagreement is so rare, and Maggie's account in the interview might be taken as representing an ideal of blogging as a space for debate. It is also possible that Maggie and her peers do not experience their conversations as being as consensual as they seem from an outsider's analytical perspective.

The consensual nature of conversation in Maggie's blog gives the impression of a social space that is fairly controlled by the author—it is a 'protected space' (Gumbrecht, 2005) with an asymmetrical distribution of communication rights. The strong tendency to create and sustain consensus is likely a consequence of Maggie's blog being about her personal experiences, a quite intimate topic, about which Maggie is presumably the most knowledgeable. If people were to express disagreement, it would not only be a threat to Maggie's face, but might even be considered a personal attack. In light of this, disagreement is better expressed across blogs, than within the personal blog. One might find that there is disagreement between participants, but it is manifested by other bloggers in the network writing about other things, and providing other perspectives and opinions on their own blogs, in which they meet the same acceptance and recognition as they give Maggie in hers.

Herring (1999a) compares multiparty interaction with a noisy cocktail party, but in the case of Maggie's blog, blogging seems more like a private dinner party, where participants' interaction is framed by a host-guest relationship. The politeness and strong preference for agreement in conversations on Maggie's blog achieve a friendly atmosphere that encourages private talk and social support among participants, and is respectful to the host. The host-guest relationship is also evident in participants' discursive framing of blogging activities—they talk about 'visiting' each other's blogs and about 'coming over.' Hence, the blog comes to represent the author's home, and the invitation to read is an invitation to experience and participate in each other's private lives. Thus, the conversation is sociable, yet quite intimate, in that it is carried out in a sphere that participants discursively construct as highly personal.

Elise's Blog: Collaborative Storytelling and Resonance

In thematic orientation, Elise's blog is less about the author's personal experiences and everyday life than Maggie's blog. The topics chosen for blog posts tend to be of a more general character (e.g., nature, health, aging, food), albeit with a personal angle and viewpoint, something that probably has to do with Elise catering to a very large audience. She describes her blog as

> . . . 'feel good', but with an educational element of 'eat well', 'care for your body', 'be good to each other'. I would say, love between people, right, in a broad sense, that is it, that is what matters in life, right. You don't write that, but it can exist between the lines [. . .]. It is no problem to find a lot of things we don't have in common, but I don't see any reason for it. I don't engage in political discussions, or anything like that. (Elise)

Thus, Elise finds it important for the content to be generally relevant, and not only meaningful to herself. She strives to post content that enables her to connect with her readers, and 'hit their antennae' (Elise). Elise keeps records with ideas for future blog posts, and asserts that the blog is always in the back of her mind. For instance, she likes taking photographs, and with the blog, her photos have a specific purpose, namely to illustrate her writing and underline their general relevance. This systematization of her blog production indicates a very strong commitment to her audience. Furthermore, with Elise's professional background in radio production, it is tempting to describe her approach to generating ideas and giving them a generally relevant framing as journalistic, something that she does not deny when asked in the interview.

I have previously indicated that the key purpose of Elise's blog is to create resonance. Consistent with this idea, Elise often asks readers directly to share their habits, tastes, and preferences (e.g., regarding food, local newspapers, whether they are orderly or messy, or type A and B persons) in her blog posts, and this generates much activity on the blog. Hence, the readers of the blog seem to enjoy Elise's encouragement to share details about themselves. Elise's frequent encouragement of her readers to share their own stories, by ending her posts with a question to the readers, epitomizes this notion of resonance as being essential to Elise's blog. To further foster resonance, Elise thanks commenters for sharing their experiences, thoughts, and emotions. In this way, the author seeks to recognize the perspectives of readers in the conversation, and thus legitimizes their unique contributions. Through the comments responding to the question, the threads on the blog often develop as a sort of collaborative storytelling, emphasizing the conversation as a collaborative effort and accomplishment, an exchange of perspectives (Thorseth, 2008).

Despite this emphasis on taking each other's experiences and viewpoints into consideration, the collaborative effort rarely creates topical development, as we have already seen. Typically, commenters simply demonstrate the similarity of their experiences to those of Elise, often in the form of phatic markers like 'me too,' also prevalent in Maggie's blog, again invoking the idea of a host-guest-relationship. In this way, the experiences shared are established as common to the group of bloggers. However, efforts are made to take on a plurality of perspectives in the conversation on Elise's blog, and to make room for debate, to expand the author's initial experience, and learn something from each other. For instance, in a thread about the dilemma of euthanasia, a diverse range of opinions and insights are shared in a sober tone, and several of the contributors to the thread claim to be enlightened by the comments of one of Elise's readers, who is a nurse, and thus has professional expertise regarding the subject.

There are several other instances where the blog debates various issues, such as elderly Danes moving to southern Europe to the enjoy the good life, the TV show *X Factor*, the need for national policies for a healthy lifestyle, people with disabilities, and work environments and professional recognition. In all these threads, a spirit of exchange and openness to different viewpoints is nurtured. The debate often unfolds with more direct statements of disagreement, when compared to Maggie's blog, and with different—perhaps less careful—attention to facework and repair, to mitigate possible offense and soften disagreement. Consider the following exchange from the thread about policies to support a healthy lifestyle, in which Elise has declared herself supportive of more regulation:

Jane: I don't go along with that. Okay—maybe for a minority. Maybe one or two need to be deprived of the possibility of going wrong—but if so, I think it's because deep down they were ready to change. I believe abstention is a conscious decision. [. . .]

For me the problem here is that we forget about ethics—we forget that we can't define the good life for someone else. An alcoholic will find his liquor if he needs it—even if he has to travel to the moon and back. [. . .]

Elise: Jane, of course we can find an ethical problem here, if we really want to. But unfortunately experience shows that it doesn't help very much to leave this as a private matter, what we expose our bodies to. On the contrary, the record shows that restrictions help. [. . .] For years we made fun of 'Prohibition Sweden' and their Systembolag shops. But still, there are fewer alcoholics in Sweden than there are here. You can call it an attack on privacy, but is it fair that the right to self-determination should have economic consequences for all other citizens, in the form of costly treatment, which could have been avoided? Is that ethical? I don't think it is.

Thanks for your thoughts, Jane.

Sarah: Thanks for this post. I'm with Jane. For me, conscious choice is the way, just as responsibility in life is our own. I don't believe in bans—I believe in becoming more aware. We all know that change only comes about with the will to change. For me, the best possible thing is when someone shows us the way by force of example, and that doesn't include bans. Carry on having a wonderful day. Sarah

Elise: Sarah, thanks for your comment, and a great day to you too. Hope you get to sit outside and enjoy the weather!

If you guys have the time, [an expert] explains in the article why she thinks laws are the answer. It's an easy read. [. . .]

Jane: We don't have to agree—or see things through the same eyes :-)

It's good when a post like this forces you to take a position. We get to know ourselves, and each other, more clearly—and maybe make some others think too . . . :-)

Now I have to fetch not one, but two kids who, naturally, got what they need today—and now they'll nag me for PlayStation time—but will have to put up with an ice-cream on the balcony!

Elise: Jane, no, it's great to exchange ideas and perspectives. And this was a well written article which energized me. Now you go and have a good time with those kids :-)

I have only included part of the exchange here, and between turns in the discussion between Jane and Elise, others intervene with arguments supporting both positions. Although an analysis of the argumentation strategies and positions for and against regulation of individual health would be interesting in itself, my aim here is not to decompose the discussion along these lines. Instead, I consider it crucial to highlight the conversational style, demonstrating that a sober debate is indeed possible, and regarded as relevant by participants in the personal blog.

Rather than concurring with Elise's initially stated opinion in the blog post, Jane opposes it quite bluntly in her first comment, making no effort to soften her disagreement with Elise, who in turn, follows with a confirmation of their disagreement, by providing additional argumentative fuel to the discussion (e.g., Is it reasonable that others must pay for a smoker's treatment, etc.?). There is no mutual adjustment in this exchange, in contrast to Maggie and Paul's subtle, face-maintaining moves, which were analyzed in the previous section. Instead, Elise legitimizes their disagreement and Jane's argument, by thanking her for her contribution, while at the same time reinforcing and providing additional argumentation for her position on the subject. This legitimizing action is repeated with Sarah, who, in her contribution, chooses to align herself with Jane—in opposition to Elise. Later in the thread, after a few exchanges, Jane closes the debate at her end by smoothing out the disagreement, thanking Elise for raising the issue, asserting that disagreement is good, and acknowledging that the debate has been an interesting opportunity for her to consider her own stance. Elise then confirms that the exchange of viewpoints was interesting, and wishes Jane a happy day. With these final turns, the two women reassure each other that their disagreement was 'nothing personal,' and thus not a threat to their relationship, before continuing along their individual courses for the day.

Arguably, the reason debate thrives on Elise's blog, at least in some instances, is attributable to the themes addressed. The predominance of themes of general interest on the blog simply makes disagreement less threatening to the author's (or a commenter's) face. If the topic of conversation is of a less personal nature, it is easier to navigate and develop the conversation, to contribute different viewpoints and thereby enrich and nuance one another's knowledge and reflections on the topic at hand. The participants may more readily express and accept disagreement on general topics, because it does not threaten their relationships with each other.

In short, there is more room for interpersonal difference on Elise's blog, when compared to the often more personally oriented conversations on Maggie's blog.

It should be noted that to ensure a proper and tolerant atmosphere of debate, Elise indicates in the interview that she actively seeks to promote a positive tone on the blog. She opposes verbal fights and if people come to her blog to provoke and stir up a fight, she makes them leave. 'One can drive people away. It is felt clearly between the lines, even if I am not decidedly rude, whether or not you are wanted' (Elise). By engaging her readers in collaborative storytelling and debate while keeping a proper tone, Elise's blog not only serves as a space for interpersonal support and phatic markers of social relationships among peers, but as a forum for exchanging insights, and for learning from others' experiences and accounts.

Ben's Blog: Cycling Talk and Male Bonding

Ben has been a central figure in the development of the Danish cycling blog community and is well known by fellow biking enthusiasts because of his blog. The blog may be seen as an extension of the biking community, going beyond training and races, and it promotes a rather strict focus on issues related to gear and cycling. Ben characterizes his blog as follows: 'It is of course a bike blog, but it is a bike blog centered on a person [. . .]. So half of what you get is cycling gear and stuff, and the other half is me' (Ben). The blog is centered on Ben's everyday experience of biking, for example, it describes working on improving his condition or his gear, and provides richly detailed reports of the bike races in which Ben participates, complete with photo documentation. Besides the thematic focus on biking, the topical orientation is reflected in the design of most bike blogs, argues Ben, in that they typically use cycling-related images as part of the graphic element on the blog's front page. Indeed, it may be argued that this common graphic focus is a local genre convention.

Surprisingly, despite the strictly topical orientation on Ben's blog, which clearly marks a difference from the women's blogs, Ben actually considers the blog unsuitable for information exchange. 'It is more like [. . .] a social forum where people may present themselves and comment a little. That is not what is important. What is important is our relationships' (Ben). Likewise, he argues that the blog interaction is not really a conversation, understood as an ongoing exchange of viewpoints among interlocutors, because there is no guarantee that the commenters will return to the thread and follow up on the exchange. Commenters post merely to say 'Hi', he contends and continues: 'What I get from them is rarely very meaningful' (Ben). As is the case with the other two blogs, then, the exchanges on the blog have a primarily phatic function—to show that the reader is present, and to mark a relationship.

Against this background, it may be argued that social support is also important in Ben's blog, although it is given a different stylistic expression. It is perhaps most obvious in the threads following race reports, where the participants complement Ben and one another for riding well:

> Jacob: Hi Ben good to see you again and what a top dollar ride [. . .] ;)??see you soon?old man?(see about getting a set of twins whilst you are warm ;)

> Jones: Ben . . . you look great with mud on your clothes! And by the way, that was well done for a newly father ;-)

> Ben: Jacob:YES YES . . . that's me:-)!??Jones,HA haaaa . . . yeah that is not normal , me and mud, but sometimes that is just what happens when you are born under the wrong star;)!

Jacob and Jones both congratulate Ben on his race in a teasing and joking manner—for instance, complementing him on his muddy outfit. Their recognition and support is thus given with some distance and irony, and a rather rough tone. This is characteristic of the blog. The rough tone also means that politeness is less evident on Ben's blog. This does not necessarily imply that there is less emotion and warmth involved in their relations—the sarcastic tone may simply be a specific (male) way of relating to each other emotionally. This resonates well with Ben's description of the blog as a forum for togetherness with peers from the relatively small cycling community, rather than a forum for exchanging information and giving advice on factual matters related to cycling. Ben appears to be ambivalent about the blog. His conversational ideal, and his initial purpose with the blog, information exchange, collides with the phatic and relational, which he does not readily embrace.

The lesser importance of politeness also suggests that there is more symmetry or equality between author and readers on Ben's blog, when compared to the women's blogs. Two things support this claim: in Ben's blog there is less respect for the author's framing of conversation, and thus more topical digression and off-topic remarks, and disagreeing without paying careful attention to saving other participants' faces seems to be acceptable.

Typically, digressions and off-topic remarks have to do with the recurrent use of the blog to coordinate training, as we have already seen, although there are instances where this is not the case, as when Terry asks Ben a question about how to synchronize his watch with his Mac, in the thread framed by a post about training in Mallorca. On Ben's blog, a commenter's change of subject based on an immediate agenda appears to be more legitimatized.

Apart from digressions, there seems to be more room for disagreement on Ben's blog than on Maggie's, in particular. The tone of disagreements is also a bit more direct, and there is less collaborative facework. The following excerpt illustrates this; it is from an exchange about changing biking gear to make Ben's bike lighter:

Derek: And put an American Classic on the back hub instead. Costs half as much, saves almost 50 grams, and you get a stronger spoke housing [. . .] ??/Derek

Will: Aaah those American Classics, watch out for them—they've got no durability. Tried a couple :(. and let's not even get onto the spokes . . .

Ben: [. . .] AC . . . NOPE, Like Will I don't have much good to say about their hub, have seen too many reps on them:-)! Yes, I'm coming to Randers for a few days, maybe we can work something out?

Derek: I know a few quite heavy riders (85kg) who've done a couple of seasons on them with no problems (think it's the 225 version).??Yes, I'll probably be up for it, let me know on [telephone number] which days you're here, and we'll fix it.??/Derek

Derek's suggestion for improving the bicycle is met with criticism from Ben and Will, who do not like the gear produced by American Classic. In contrast to the disagreement between Maggie and Paul, they make no effort to soften their disagreement and offer a repair slot, a face-saving opening, for Derek. Similarly, they do not put effort into explicitly stating that disagreement is okay, as the participants do on Elise's blog. They simply criticize the brand as lacking in durability. However, Ben does attempt to smooth things over, by asking Derek whether he wants to meet up, thereby underlining that the disagreement does not threaten their relationship. Derek does not react by concurring with the criticism, despite being alone in his preference. Instead, he risks losing face by throwing himself into a defense of American Classic, by arguing against Will and Ben's criticism. In sum, disagreement is expressed quite directly, and with less consideration for mitigating offence.

It is likely that participants on Ben's blog are less inclined to stay on topic and concur with the author and each other, because the discussions concern gear and biking—not their private lives. The topic is more factually oriented, and therefore disagreement is not a threat to, and assault on participants' personalities and private choices. Because the blog is not so much a private space for self-disclosure as Maggie's blog, communicative relations between participants is differently defined—they are more symmetrical. The author is still the focus of the conversation, but there is more room for readers to express criticism than on Maggie and Elise's blogs. It may be instructive to think of Ben's blog as more of a common room or 'clubhouse'—a public place for likeminded people to hang out. Furthermore, participants do not have to invest much energy in supporting and developing relationships on Ben's blog by expressing recognition and agreement, because the relations among participants are expressed and confirmed in other contexts.

It seems plausible that the differences in disagreement and repair styles may further be attributed to gender. Several studies have found that men tend to be more factually oriented in their communication, and that they tend to create more tension and confrontation, whereas the communicative style and behavior among women online are more supportive (Baym, 2000; Herring, 1999b). To some extent, the tendency is similar in the blog data (e.g., the different orientations to politeness in the three blogs, and Paul's role as the sole challenger of the conventions in Maggie's female-dominated blog). Elise's blog complicates this, given the sometimes lively and boldly enacted debate among the blog's mostly female participants. Consequently, firm conclusions about gendered practices cannot be drawn based on my material, and a discussion of gender is beyond the scope of this study.

As I have argued, my data suggest another explanation for differences in the norms and management of agreement and disagreement in the personal blog: namely, that the topics around which the interlocutors interact mark whether disagreement is appropriate, or whether it is offensive and face threatening. The differences in content and style among the three blogs illustrate the breadth of the personal blog as a genre—enacted, negotiated, and reworked as a product of locally anchored conventions and practices that emerge in, and are constituted through, the ongoing conversation between the author and his or her readers. In this section, I have established an axis of personal blogs along thematic lines ranging from the personal to the topical, and stylistic lines of confession and support, on the one hand, and debate and banter, on the other. In general, however, debate and disagreement are enacted in a spirit of mutuality and responsiveness, and do not escalate into regular conflict and fighting. It may be that the specific agreement structure and avoidance of conflict are specific to the personal blog genre. Other subgenres of the blog, such as political blogs, for instance, might involve more flaming and disagreement, without participants attempting to mitigate offence.

THE PERSONAL BLOG—STABILITY AND CHANGE IN WRITTEN COMMUNICATIVE GENRES

Bazerman writes: 'reading and writing are deeply social processes, connecting people's thoughts, perceptions, experiences, and projects into wider collectivities of organized action and belief' (Bazerman, 2006: 215). The production and negotiation of genre are driven by tensions between the individual's subjective perceptions and understandings of the genre, and the socially sanctioned genre knowledge. Accordingly, as Berkenkotter and Huckin (1993: 481) assert, genres 'are always sites of contention between stability and change.'

In this chapter, I focused specifically on uncovering socially sanctioned—and often-implicit—genre knowledge, that is, the conventions and expectations by which participants orient themselves in the social organization of their blogging practices. The analysis documented that collaboratively articulated expectations and conventions of adressivity, frequency, responsiveness, thematic relevance, and so forth, guide the participants' ongoing enactment and negotiation of the personal blog. The collaborative orienting to such expectations and conventions are prerequisites for creating interactional coherence, intersubjective understanding, and ultimately, to making sense of the blog. The result is a highly structured communicative genre with very little overall variation in patterns of exchange, and in the topics discussed. Participants have collaboratively constituted a (tacit) consensus of what the genre is about, and how it is produced and interpreted appropriately. In the terminology of Moscovici (2001), their tacit compliance with these norms rests on an objectification of the genre that constrains their communicative practices on the blog. By enacting and meeting certain expectations of appropriate actions and topics, participants tend to reify these same expectations as genre conventions. Hence, the adherence to established genre knowledge serves to stabilize the blogging experience, and give it coherence and meaning (Berkenkotter & Huckin, 1993: 478).

Bazerman (2006) suggests that reliance on, and staying within the genre is a particularly important organizational tool for written communication. Following his line of argument, the clearly articulated norms and reified structures of interactional coherence that are continuously reproduced on the blog are to some extent attributable to the blog as a written form of interaction, as a condition for making the written communication on the blog run smoothly. In written dialogue, in which the communicating parties are typically separated by time and space, the communicative relationship between the parties is, in a sense, more fixed and asymmetrical. One party, the author, takes the initiative in defining the situation, that is, chooses the appropriate topics, and so on. The other party, the reader, may, until writing back, only react to, and individually try to make sense of the written text. As we have seen, to some extent this communicative relationship is quite similar to that of blogs, in which the first and main turn in a conversation is the (often-lengthy) blog post, which frames the subsequent exchanges between the author and the commenting readers as the thread evolves.

Compared to spoken dialogue, with its constantly alternating roles of speaker and listener, written conversation in blogs tends to involve longer units of expression and a different turn-taking system, to adjust to the specific circumstances of the blog (asynchronous communication, multiple participants, etc.). Furthermore, considering the blog's lack of the real-time contextualizing cues that guide participants in spoken dialogue, the mutual adjustment and orientation to each other seems much more fragile and uncertain in written dialogue than in speech communication. This uncertainty may be enhanced by the fact that interlocutors on the blog often do not know each other in advance. The social accomplishments of written dialogue must rely on the communicating parties finding some common framing of the text, and sticking to this intersubjective understanding. Against this background, Bazerman argues that written communication is more likely to adhere to established generic conventions than spoken communication, simply because written dialogue is much more dependent on the participants explicitly stating the situational and contextual premises, to become meaningful:

> The reader and writer need the genre to create a communicative meeting place legible from the very form and content of the text. Further, once that place is recognizably presented, readers may easily lose their place if the text starts doing something different. Thus, the push to remain within genre and use it for positive effect in writing is much greater than in face-to-face interaction, where footing may be changed rapidly and subtly and the success of the change can be monitored in real time. (Bazerman, 2006: 222)

In other words, written communication is more likely to follow pre-established scripts. Consequently, it is not surprising to find quite stable, recurrent communication patterns in the analysis of the social organization and ongoing negotiation of blogs.

The regularity and stability of the blog might further be attributed to the fact that blogging is a well-established and mature genre. If this holds true, newer genres of social media should be expected to have less developed and clear genre conventions. Moreover, considering the possibly conservative effects of asynchronicity and relatively long textual turns on genre development in blogs, it is relevant to ask whether short-form genres display similar genre stability. The next chapter, examining Twitter, pursues these possible hypotheses to clarify further the theoretical implications of thinking of social media as communicative genres.

CHAPTER SUMMARY

I have described the personal blog as an asynchronous communicative genre that is relatively stable, and governed by a well-established and widely accepted set of conventions. These conventions may be found to varying degrees in face-to-face encounters and written conversations, suggesting that the participants in blog conversations draw on and adjust genre knowledge acquired and accumulated in other social situations, to render their activities familiar and interactionally meaningful. Participants' practical negotiation of their ongoing conversations enables them to transcend their spatial and temporal dispersion, and create a sense of mutual social presence and commitment, pivotal to the genre.

The components comprising the social organization of the personal blog as a communicative genre are reified, because they serve the vital function of keeping blogs vibrant. With the accomplishment of a sense of togetherness through mutual social presence and responsiveness, the expectations and conventions by which participants orient themselves in their blogging practices facilitate the necessary foundation on which participants can build networks and close relationships with each other, and continue their conversations on the blog. Likely, the importance of these pragmatic functions is specific to the personal blog—other sub-genres of blogging, for instance, political blogs, may be defined by quite different communicative conventions and fulfill different social purposes for the participants.

NOTES

1. It is unclear exactly what counts as a contribution, but it presumably includes commenting on other people's blogs; if not, the number of active contributors is surprisingly high. Hence, the figures for active blog use should be read with some caution.
2. The three bloggers have granted me permission to use their data for the present analysis. All names mentioned are pseudonyms, and all data excerpts from the blogs and interviews are translated from Danish.
3. I have arranged the exchange chronologically, in contrast to its original appearance in reverse chronological order on Elise's blog.
4. The fact that the author usually leaves a response comment partly explains her large share of comments.
5. The notion of 'face' is taken from Goffman's ideas about facework (Goffman, 1967: 5–10). A person's face is the positive social value that she claims for herself in social interaction, and this face is upheld through the interacting participants' collaborative efforts—their 'facework.'

5 Twitter
A Genre in the Making?

Twitter occupies a different position in the social media environment than does blogging. According to Statistics Denmark, three percent of adult Danes reported having a Twitter profile in 2010 (Danmarks Statistik, 2010), corresponding to a user base well below 200,000 Danish profiles at the time of data collection. Hence, Twitter constitutes a niche site in the Danish social media landscape, whereas the service is among the most popular social media at an international level, with about 175 million registered users in September 2010, according to the company itself (Twitter.com).

Twitter was almost nonexistent in Denmark before 2009, apart from a few thousand early adopters. With an explosive growth in user base in Denmark since 2009, at the time of the second case study, Twitter appeared to be an unstable genre in the making. When entering and adopting a new genre, participants are likely to have a more careful and probing attitude, as they familiarize themselves with the communicative norms and conventions, and determine what specific purposes and needs the genre may cater to (cf. Chapter 3). Norms may thus not be as firmly constituted, but may be more negotiable on Twitter, when compared to those of well-established genres like blogs. Moreover, owing to its 140-character communication format, Twitter is a short-form genre, and thus better suited than blogs for quick, near-synchronous exchanges. This makes Twitter a highly relevant object of study for probing the general value of the findings from the blog study that asynchronicity and long communicative turns create more stable genres. Finally, unlike blogs, Twitter was (and still is) used both used via web and smartphones (including a number of third party clients for accessing the service), which became increasingly widespread in Denmark during the period in which the case study was carried out. This platform independence probably adds to the instability of the genre, because the Twitter interface differs (e.g., foregrounds different communicative functionalities), depending on whether Twitter is accessed through the twitter.com website, or various third party applications.

In this chapter, I analyze Twitter as a communicative genre possibly in the making, by drawing together the diversity of usage practices and unpacking the norms and meanings by which participants orient themselves, when enacting the genre. Similar to the blog analysis in Chapter 4, this chapter examines Twitter through four interwoven dimensions of the genre analysis framework, namely, the composition, style, content, and pragmatic uses of Twitter.

SAMPLING

Given that the 6-month time span in which I had studied genre negotiation on personal blogs had revealed quite little genre development, I revised the research design a bit for the Twitter study. I shortened the archiving period to 1 month, January 2010, and instead included more participants, to have a rich empirical material on the variations in terms of genre enactment, and thus have better opportunity to trace and examine possible genre instability. Participants were sampled purposively, using the typological framework also used in the blog study to ensure variation in terms of content (personal vs. topical), style (confessional vs. objective and formal) and directionality (one-way vs. dialogical communication; cf. Lomborg, 2009). The participants' Twitter communications (tweets and replies) and relevant meta-data (username, date and time, URL of the tweet etc.) were archived through a software script collecting data from the Twitter API and presenting them in a structured, textual archive. The participants themselves assisted the collection by running the script on their computers and using their own logins and passwords to collect and return the relevant profile data to me.

The six Twitter users participating in the study, three men (John, Nick, and Steven) and three women (Betty, Miriam, and Rina),[1] are all in their mid-twenties to mid-forties, corresponding to the demographic characteristics of the average Danish Twitter user (cf. Lomborg, 2011). The typical Danish Twitter user is younger and better educated than the average population, consistent with international statistics for the service (Lenhart, 2009; Smith & Rainie, 2010), whereas sex differences appear to be minor. The participants differ in their use of Twitter in a number of ways, as will be evident throughout the chapter. For instance, some are heavy posters; others primarily read. Some connect with large and diverse networks of likeminded strangers, whereas others use Twitter for personal communication with close friends or simply for themselves. All the participants use Twitter for personal purposes, although for some, Twitter also functions as a source of inspiration, networking, and information related to their professional careers.

ENTER TWITTER—BUILDING NETWORKS OF AFFILIATION

Regarding its structural organization, Twitter, and the microblog in general, resembles social network sites. Users are required to generate a network of other users with whom they share a connection, which enables them to view the activities and traverse the social networks of self and others within the system (boyd & Ellison, 2007: 211). Thus, Twitter relies on 'a highly connected social space, where most of the information consumption is enabled and driven by articulated online contact networks' (Naaman, Boase & Lai, 2010: 1). In other words, to enter the flow of information, and engage in conversations on Twitter, users must establish *connections* with other users, by following, and being followed by them. Embeddedness in such networks is also typical of the blog, in that the blogroll lists the blogger's connections. As is the case with the blog, the articulation of connections on Twitter localizes the individual user within networks of fellow users—typically likeminded strangers with whom the user has no prior relationship. However, whereas with the blog the blogroll is optional, on Twitter, the articulation of relationships is a structural necessity and prerequisite for communicating with others.

On Twitter, the tie structure is asymmetric. The connections are not necessarily bidirectional, but merely reflect an individual's attention to specific others, who may or may not reciprocate the attention. Twitter profiles thus display a list of people that the user follows, and a list of 'followers' of the Twitter user. Accordingly, there is likely to be a difference between the microblogs an individual user follows, and the followers of that user's microblog. In principle, this asymmetry is also seen with blogs, but as was seen in the previous chapter, bloggers tend to operate with the norm of reciprocal links on each other's blogrolls. In this section, I explore how users begin to enact, and thereby enter the negotiation of Twitter as a communicative genre, by initiating relationships with others.

Connecting with Relevant Others

The common account of how the users in this study started using Twitter is a story of curiosity and disappointment. Having heard about Twitter in the media, or seen interesting people (e.g., YouTube gurus, designers, and celebrities) refer to their Twitter profiles and activities, they created profiles on the site. Initially, the participants conceived of the site as being all about individual status updates, and therefore, something that added nothing new to their existing repertoire of communication channels: 'I simply could not see the point of it, I thought it was strange to take such as small part of Facebook' (Betty).[2] Furthermore, because none of them really knew anyone on Twitter, it was hard to figure out whom to follow, no one followed them, and it all seemed useless. Consequently, the profiles of the study participants remained inactive for a long time. Only when they started to make an effort to find interesting people to follow, composing tweets and gaining followers, did Twitter start 'growing' on them. In contrast to the other participants, Miriam was encouraged to join Twitter by the women with whom she already interacted on her blog and on Facebook on a daily basis. For her,

Twitter was an immediate success because it did not take any effort to build a network on the site, or find people with whom to interact.

Judging by these accounts, it seems that Twitter is only perceived as useful and fun when the users have somebody relevant to talk and listen to—when the network is activated. As will be demonstrated through the analysis, conversation with other Twitter users in one's network is widespread, and seems to strengthen the attraction and motivation for being active on Twitter, as has been widely documented in international research on Twitter (e.g., Honeycutt & Herring, 2009; Java, Song, Finin, & Tseng, 2007; Oulasvirta, Lehtonen, Kurvinen, & Raento, 2010). Thus, conversationality appears to be a general motivator for genre engagement on Twitter.

The first element in building a network around one's profile on Twitter is finding somebody to follow. It is quite difficult and time-consuming to find relevant individuals to follow on Twitter. The site does have a search function that makes it possible to search for specific individuals by name, but this requires users to know exactly who they are seeking, which is often not the case. Instead, the most common way of finding others to follow is to traverse the Twitter networks of others already in the user's Twitter network, to locate interesting people in their Twitter networks, and begin to follow them. Thus, from the outset, the Twitter user is highly dependent on her Twitter network.

A collective practice has emerged over time, to enable an easier and less time-consuming way of finding relevant others to follow, namely, the practice of recommending others on Twitter to one's followers. The practice takes the form of an institutionalized, that is, a regular and formalized, weekly happening called 'Follow Friday,' which manifests itself in tweets marked with '#FF.' Every Friday, Twitter users tweet recommendations of their favorite followees, to make them visible to their own network of followers. Follow Friday is a quite efficient way to expand one's network. When somebody who a given user already approves of FF's somebody else, it seems likely that the recommended user might also be relevant to follow.

The possibly relevant others that a user begins to follow are initially screened. As Betty describes it:

> When you just start following each other, you may have a few exchanges, and then it fades out. There are, of course, some people that you continue to stay in touch with every once in a while. It is like sniffing each other, then it is fine, and you move on. (Betty)

These newly added others are evaluated based on what they contribute to the feed, and they will be unfollowed, if they do not offer anything of interest, value, or amusement to the user. In that case, they are considered to be just noise in the feed—something to get rid of. In this way, an individual's Twitter feed is a customized version of the site—you only get what you choose to get, and you can always change your mind. The act of following others is, in a sense, a way of courting them, and a way for the follower to signal that he or she desires an affiliation with them.

The second element of building a network is to attract followers: The user must write interesting tweets so other Twitter users will notice her, and evaluate her contributions positively. To be sure, attracting many followers may be prestigious in itself. However, *who* is in the audience also plays an important role. The individual user may be particularly interested in attracting specific audiences, to establish dialogue and (professional or personal) connections with a few relevant peers, whereas other parts of the potential audience may be considered barely relevant. This may be quite a challenge, considering that the new user may be very difficult for potential followers to find, because she has not yet established a network that makes her visible to a wider audience. Moreover, the new user goes through the same trial period as described above, in which she is put to the test by her newly gained followers, and is deemed either worth following, or unable to sustain the readership. In other words, the user must demonstrate an understanding and mastery of the genre, to be included in the networks in which she aspires to participate:

> I think some people have the feeling, especially as a new user in there, that they just stand there, and nobody hears what they are saying. And they really have to prove that they offer something. (Betty)

It takes time and effort to be included and deemed interesting enough to other users, but once included, it requires less effort to gain new followers, because one's visibility in the network is increased. Stated differently, the growth in the number of followers is self-perpetuating: the more followers, the easier it is to be found by new ones. Moreover, for potential new followers, a user's having already amassed a decent number of followers may be a quality stamp. As is the case with the blog, gaining followers seems to be important on Twitter, because it motivates the user to continue tweeting. As Rina describes it, it is more fun to have an audience, than to 'write to a wall' (Rina).

An important sign of inclusion in a given network is the response to, or retweeting of the user's tweets by relevant others. Being retweeted and receiving @replies are signs of recognition and validation of membership. In her analysis of Twitter use among the members of the San Francisco 'tech scene,' Marwick (2010) documents similar dynamics concerning following/follower patterns, @replies, and retweets and describes them in terms of status and hierarchy. The value that participants ascribe to receiving recognition from their peers may be framed in terms of striving for status through conversational association with relevant others. As John puts it: 'it is quite fun if a guy like Thompson, who has been in it for many years, retweets some of my tweets' (John). Thus, John regards Thompson's retweet as a seal of approval with respect to the quality of his tweets. Furthermore, this example indicates that some well-established cluster participants may be particularly well positioned for granting other members acknowledgement, and, accordingly, for regulating membership in clusters of relevant others. Indeed, all are not equally important in the network—as John's comment reveals, hierarchy and status differences corresponding to those documented by Marwick among US Twitter users appear to exist in Danes' Twitter use as well.

In sum, the analysis of how users enter Twitter identifies two central dynamics in building networks of affiliation on Twitter: First, to establish oneself as a Twitter user, it is pivotal to make oneself visible by 1) identifying relevant and interesting Twitter users to follow, and 2) offering interesting tweets in return, to gain followers and keep them committed.

The basic dynamics through which an individual user courts specific, relevant others may be described as comprising a process of socialization. Attuning to relevant others is not unique to Twitter and other social media, but pertains to a fundamental social dynamic. A person's choice of affiliations reflects the aspects of the individual's personality that he or she would like to emphasize. In other words, a person uses his or her network of affiliation in a given context to enact and sustain a specific self. We want to be seen with specific others in specific contexts, because their company puts us in a certain light: as one of them, part of a group. In many ways, what happens on Twitter is similar to what we see when people choose to wear a certain type of clothing, and consume specific cultural products that make them fit into specific subcultures, professional communities, and so on (Baym, 2010: 112; Simmel, 1955). However, with Twitter and other social media, the influence of the network of affiliation, the dynamics of socialization, and the process of mutual adjustment manifest themselves in a special way, as successful socialization is likely to be reflected in mutual recognition and acknowledgement within the network of affiliation, which are expressed in and through reciprocal linking, and, in some instances, sustained conversational activity among participants.

Characterizing the Networks of the Participants

When I archived the Twitter activities of the six study participants in January 2010, they were all well-established Twitter users who had been active on Twitter for at least 6 months, had connected to other people, and thereby established themselves as parts of various networks on Twitter.

Some of the participants have quite limited networks, whereas others have very extensive networks of followers and people they follow. Table 5.1 summarizes the principal figures relating to each participant at the end of the archived period, including the number of others the participant is following, the number of his or her followers,[3] the ratio of the two figures, and the total number of tweets each has posted, since creating his or her profile on Twitter.

Table 5.1   Networks and Twitter activity

Participant	Following	Followers	Total Number of Tweets
Betty	233	290	1022
John	286	365	5740
Miriam	33	30	1083
Nick	66	39	645
Rina	177	155	1586
Steven	38	54	242

Table 5.1 shows that there is great variation in both activity level and network size among the participants, with John, Betty, and Rina having quite extensive networks, and Miriam, Nick, and Steven following and being followed by smaller numbers of people. There appears to be a correlation between network size and activity level. According to Java and colleagues (2007), users who receive more attention from other users, and have more extensive networks, are more likely to update frequently. My data confirm this to some extent, as the three users who have the most extensive networks on Twitter (John, Betty, and Rina) are also many times more active than those with limited networks. Nevertheless, the data also show that this is not always the case: For instance, Betty and Miriam have almost equal total numbers of tweets, but Betty's network is many times larger than Miriam's network. Miriam is the outlier here, and her high level of activity may be attributed to a) her contact being primarily with close friends, thus prompting more daily contact; and b) her specific, everyday circumstances as a pensioner. This challenges the idea of a direct, causal relationship between network size and activity level.

Whereas for Miriam the small Twitter network is a result of her primarily engaging with people she already knows, for Steven and Nick it apparently reflects a lack of effort put into establishing connections with relevant peers:

> If I were to evaluate myself and my use of Twitter in connection to my book blog [Twitter profile], I have not been very good or very persistent [. . .] it takes an enormous amount of time to find friends or find people to follow, and so on, and I don't have that. I have done it if somebody addresses me, or if some of those I blog with [on his regular blog about books] have indicated that they are on Twitter. Then I hook up with them. But I don't feel like I'm there yet. I would say, for this profile to become really interesting, I have to spend some time looking for more people to talk to. (Steven)

For Nick, the situation is somewhat similar. Despite Twitter giving him access to a collection of international design and media professionals who provide many relevant links, Twitter has yet to reach a 'critical mass' of peers with whom he can interact. He does not really have anybody to converse with on Twitter, because the people in his current network are not peers, but celebrities from whom he cannot expect reciprocal attention. He simply has not been able to establish a relevant audience for his tweets, and currently, his Twitter activities are centered on reading, rather than contributing actively to the stream.

For all the participants except Nick, there are only minor differences between the numbers of followers and followees in January 2010. This indicates that a balancing principle may be at work, at least for ordinary Twitter users. In this connection, the three participants with the largest networks state that they operate with the norm of balancing the number of followers and followees—within a certain norm of reciprocity. Rina and Betty both claim to practice a direct reciprocity, meaning that if someone starts following them, they will probably reciprocate the attention. As Betty asserts, 'Not long ago, I decided to follow people back if they followed me [. . .] I actually think that is very polite, and then, if I am annoyed by them, I can always shut them off later' (Betty). Similarly, Rina reciprocates the following, 'just to see what they are saying. If it doesn't interest me, I just remove them again' (Rina). Thus, both women initially follow, to be polite, but still maintain a screening period for those followed to judge the quality of their tweets.

John's approach is somewhat different, as he does not speak of reciprocity, but of balance. His approach does not necessarily involve following the specific users who follow him. Instead, he operates with what could be labeled 'generalized reciprocity,' to ensure symmetry, that is, a small ratio between followers and followees. Balance between followers and those he follows is important, 'to show this way that you [. . .] take other people seriously. I think that other people's opinions, their tweets, are important' (John). These ideas of reciprocating following and ensuring balance, indicate that norms of mutual recognition and symmetry are central to the participants' Twitter experience, suggesting that they emphasize and are attracted to Twitter's conversational aspects and many-to-many communicative potential, rather than its potential as a one-way broadcasting channel for the user.

A comparison of the followers and followees of each of the participants reveals that while they have many bidirectional (reciprocal) links, none of the participants has near-total correspondence between followers and followees. This underlines Twitter's asymmetric network structure. The general picture shows that slightly over half of the users that each participant follows also follow the participant. That is, about half of the links are reciprocated, or bidirectional. This challenges the idea of direct reciprocation of following as a general norm on Twitter. Rina and Betty, the two participants who claim to operate with such a norm, do not have more reciprocal links than the others do, suggesting that if they practice a sort of reciprocation, it is not at a general network level.

The interview data confirm the point about reciprocity and mutual recognition not being general norms within the networks established on Twitter. Only Miriam seems to have a complete overview of her followers—probably because unlike the other participants, her Twitter network is primarily made up of personal friends. It may be understandable that Rina, John, and Betty, with their relatively large audiences, have difficulties in this respect, but Steven and Nick, with small audiences, similarly lack overviews of their followers. One reason may be that, in a sense, followers become invisible the moment they begin following somebody. When A begins to follow B, the Twitter system notifies B via email, and A then appears in B's profile, in the 'followers' section. However, unless B reciprocates by beginning to follow A as well, the only way A is made visible to B, is if A posts a reply to B's tweets. Thus, it seems likely that being aware of one's followers depends on active interaction with them, and not the mere establishment of the connection.

In conclusion, Twitter does not simply rest on establishing networks, but on achieving reciprocity within a smaller group of relevant others, by activating connections through interaction (replies, retweets, Follow Friday, etc.). In this sense, the network dynamics on Twitter resemble those of personal blogs. Norms of reciprocity do exist, but they acquire a specific shading on Twitter, compared to on the blog. On Twitter, the reciprocity norm seems linked to a very small part of an individual's total network, namely, the relevant others who are deemed attractive conversation partners, whereas norms of reciprocity within the larger network of followers/followees are, at best, ambiguous. In contrast, as we have seen in Chapter 4, on personal blogs, reciprocity is maintained as a crucial norm, not only in the ongoing conversations, but also in the continuously groomed articulation of one's network activity in the blogroll.

Potential and Actualized Relationships

It might be useful to distinguish between potential and actualized relationships within the Twitter network, denoting the total number of ties (following/followers) that an individual user has, and the connections to which the user directs tweets, or by whom she is addressed in the network, respectively. This active part of the network is even smaller, when considering the relationships that are reciprocally activated more than once or twice, and are thus kept continuously vibrant.

Table 5.2 shows a great overlap between users addressed by the study participants, and those who address them, but there are some differences that are important for a general understanding.

All the participants contact more users than they themselves are contacted by. Nick is an extreme case, because he mainly uses Twitter as a response or fan channel to express his appreciation of and agreement with the international design and media celebrities he follows, but from whom he does

Table 5.2 Number of people addressed by/addressing the author

	Author Addresses	Users Who Address the Author	Reciprocal Relationships
Betty	49	36	33
John	151	82	73
Miriam	17	13	13
Nick	15	2	2
Rina	64	40	33
Steven	4	3	3

not expect a reply. John, too, addresses a large number of users who do not respond, indicating that he is very keen on networking and starting conversation on Twitter.

In January 2010, Nick and Steven did not interact with anyone more than once or twice. Therefore, their networks were largely composed of potential relationships, as indicated by very few reciprocal relationships in Table 5.2. John, Rina, and Betty also experienced many instances of very limited exchanges, where they addressed someone without getting a tweet in response, or where the dialogue was limited to one or two tweets. This may reflect many unsuccessful attempts to start an ongoing conversation with fellow users, but it may also simply be that Twitter is more about exchanging short statements and comments in the here and now, implying that lengthy, continued conversation over the course of the day, for example, might not be the goal of @replies at all. For Betty, John, Miriam, and Rina, only a small part of their networks was activated continuously throughout the archived period. Of John's 73 reciprocal relationships, there were only 24 regular interaction partners, with each of whom he had 15 to 30 exchanges each. Betty had seven partners (out of 33 reciprocal relationships), with 15 to 30 exchanges each in January 2010. Miriam and Rina each had six regular interaction partners, with whom they had a lot of interaction. Together, these trends suggest that participants have stronger affiliations to a few peers who matter in the network.

A glimpse beyond the individual profiles shows a tendency for some of those with whom the study participants have many conversations to also have conversations with each other on a regular basis. Rather than reflecting a strong, isolated, one-on-one relationship between two specific participants in the larger network, such vibrant relationships often indicate subgroups or clusters within an individual's network on Twitter. Clusters are small, but densely connected networks of users with bidirectional, mutual links, through which users reciprocate fellow microbloggers' attention by reading, and perhaps commenting on each other's tweets. This indicates that participants constitute a relatively tight-knit group of people who share a niche interest in something about which they exchange information, and make connections, or just hang out and make small talk. For example, Miriam is part of a close-knit group of friends who talk on Twitter (and on the phone, MSN, blogs, and Facebook) throughout the day, and Rina is part of a densely interconnected nail blogger network, with collective happenings and so forth. Betty and John are affiliated with the same cluster of Danish Twitter users, and their networks overlap considerably. However, compared to the blog networks, the conversational clusters on Twitter are much more loosely tied, and even the closest relations (Miriam's network excluded) are only activated sporadically.

The reciprocal relationships rendered visible by Table 5.2, and the discovery of how they often indicate vibrant clusters on Twitter, enable a more precise analysis of the meaning and importance of reciprocity on Twitter. Specifically, it identifies norms of mutuality and reciprocation of interest as being pivotal to the interactional patterns and practices characteristic of the genre. By reciprocating attention, participants in the cluster recognize each other's membership, and reinforce symmetrical relations as normative within the cluster. Concerning ties to people outside the cluster, reciprocity, in the sense of continuous mutual addressivity, may not be as important. This might explain why users are not necessarily interested in the total mass of followers, but mainly in the relevant others. These findings are consistent with a large-scale quantitative study on Twitter networks and conversationality by Huberman, Romero, and Wu (2009). They found that despite following and being followed by many others, people's interactive engagement is limited to a few who matter and build on reciprocation of attention. This seems to be a prevalent tendency in Twitter use in general, and not something specific to my sample.

As is the case with the personal blog, Twitter users create clusters within the larger network of followers and followees, to manage their relationships within a clearly defined group of peers, the relevant others with whom the user shares interests, and experiences a 'good chemistry.' This orientation to relevant others is crucial for the situated enactments and ongoing constitution and reworking of Twitter as a communicative genre, because it designates and delimits the social situation in terms of relevant content, purposes, appropriate behavior, and so forth, as locally sanctioned in specific clusters of activity on Twitter.

SITUATING TWITTER USE IN EVERYDAY LIFE

For most of the users in the sample, tweeting is a daily or almost daily activity, and they speak of Twitter as an integral part of their everyday lives, seamlessly interwoven with other activities. They all access Twitter and read other people's tweets every day. Regarding posting activity, the pattern is a little more diverse. During the sampling period, John, Rina, and Miriam posted every day, and Betty posted on all but 2 days. Nick posted 2 out of

3 days, whereas Steven posted more sporadically, a little less often than once every 3 days. However, Steven also has another, very active Twitter profile that is not part of the dataset, but on which the author exhibits the same daily activity as the other users in the sample. Thus, using Twitter seems to involve ongoing and frequent engagement.

As Table 5.3 suggests, the total activity level varies considerably among profiles—from one or a couple of tweets on active days on Steven and Nick's profiles, to an average of over 40 tweets per day on John's profile.

Whereas the number of updates per day is quite stable among the users, there are days with extremely high activity and surprisingly low activity for the four frequent posters in the material—for instance, John posts only four tweets on his least active day and 130 on the most active day during the archiving period. I suggest that instances of particularly high activity at a given point in time indicate that being active on Twitter has a lot to do with timing, that is, being on Twitter simultaneously with relevant others, so that conversational flow can be maintained.

The participants tend to have Twitter open most of the time. For Rina and Miriam, who never shut down their computers, Twitter always runs in the background. For Betty, Nick, and Steven, accessing Twitter is the first thing they do when beginning work in the morning. Their preferred Twitter applications start automatically when they turn on their computers, and it runs in a separate window on the screen. Being logged on to Twitter the entire day is natural and convenient for them all, because their jobs involve spending a lot of time in front of the computer screen. For Rina, who often works night shifts at a help desk, and whose job involves a lot of quiet time monitoring the system, surfing the internet and chatting with others on Twitter and other services is a way of passing time. Accordingly, Twitter serves more or less as a background activity during the waking hours—something users may opt to use during short breaks at work, and so forth.

John, the most active user in the sample, does not primarily work in front of a computer, but spends a lot of time on the road, consulting customers as part of his job. Although he, too, uses Twitter for breaks at work, he is not constantly on Twitter, but logs on and off throughout the day, when it is convenient. Owing to its portability, his iPhone plays a pivotal role, because it allows him to access Twitter, even when he is not at his office; his iPhone is also his access device at the office. In fact, he does not access Twitter from

Table 5.3 Total activity (tweets + replies) for the six profiles in January 2010

	Betty	John	Miriam	Nick	Rina	Steven
Total number of tweets	392	1311	458	42	633	17
Average number of tweets per day	12.7	42.3	14.8	1.4	20.4	0.6

his office computer at all. Despite his specific emphasis on mobile tweeting, John's Twitter activity aligns with the other participants' use of Twitter as an integral part of everyday activities. It may be argued that the 'portability' of Twitter epitomizes its embedding in daily life (also, cf. Chapter 6).

Miriam's normal use situation is a bit different from that of the other participants. She is a disabled pensioner, and housebound most of the time, owing to health issues. For her, being online is not a pastime that runs in the background, but a main activity during the day. She may even tweet from the couch or the bed, if she is not feeling well, and Twitter is crucial for her maintaining contact with the world. This probably explains her high level of activity, despite having a small Twitter network.

The frequent visits to, and constant running of Twitter in the background is reflected in the daily rhythm of Twitter activity, which shows that activity rises during late morning, is steady throughout the day, and drops off during the late night hours for all the participants—with Rina sometimes being active in the middle of the night. This rhythm is consistent with the findings of Krishnamurthy, Gill, and Arlitt (2008) who draw on global data from the public time-line of Twitter in a quantitative, descriptive study of Twitter. Similarly, and consistent with the study by Krishnamurthy and colleagues (2008), is the fact that there are no systematic activity differences among weekdays, except for Betty's activity level, which drops noticeably during the weekend. She explains that she is less active during the weekend, because she is busy doing stuff with her small kids. It is less convenient for her to use Twitter, when the computer is not turned on for other purposes.

The generally stable daily and weekly rhythms of Twitter use indicate that Twitter is not just a background activity during working hours, as activity does not wane when people go home from work. Instead, Twitter use is intertwined with the daily life and leisure activities of its users.

Several of the participants describe Twitter as a very casual activity. For instance, Betty considers Twitter to be a procrastination activity that she is constantly drawn into at work, and must shut Twitter off when she is busy, so it does not distract her. Users are not obliged to be available, or even to notify their Twitter networks that they will be unavailable. According to Steven, there is a common understanding that Twitter is something that users jump into and out of, that is, other things are more important than being constantly available for conversation on Twitter. Participation in Twitter is something he does

> [. . .] out of a surplus [of time], but it is also something that is quickly put aside if I have a meeting or something to do. Then I can leave in the middle of a conversation, actually, and return to it later. And that. . . I think that is acceptable [. . .]. Now the two of us are sitting here having a conversation, and if I left now, it would be really impolite, but if we talk on Twitter, it might very well be an hour before you had a response,

because then you'd know that some emergency came up, or something. (Steven)

In contrast to the personal blog, in which we have seen how people orient themselves according to the convention of confirming their continued engagement through posts and comments, and thereby creating a sense of mutual social presence, Twitter appears to operate under a different logic. Twitter appears to be highly intertwined with the trajectories and activities of everyday life, and may be described as an ongoing communicative flow. The notion of 'flow' is important for understanding the communicative patterns and norms characteristic of Twitter as a genre. I understand 'flow' both as a characteristic structure of the genre, inscribed at the software level (the organization of tweets in an ongoing stream), and in an experiential sense, as the interweaving of tweeting with other activities in the rhythm of daily life.[4]

Like the blog, Twitter use appears to be based on convenience and available slots in the daily schedule, but at the same time, Twitter disrupts and distracts users from other activities, and creates a certain pressure for constant awareness (Crawford, 2009: 259). The stream evolves continuously, and sometimes at a rapid pace, and because tweets occur in a continuous flow in real time, they cannot be 'frozen' or turned off (John). Whereas in blogs, threading, asynchronicity, and persistence of contributions make participation possible at any time, without missing out on something, Twitter demands the user's attention here and now and thus prompts a constant checking-in and skimming of the stream for new and interesting links and conversations.

A NOTE ON PLATFORMS AND APPLICATIONS FOR USING TWITTER

One of the core characteristics of Twitter use is the easy mobile access, and the multiplicity of channels and applications for web and mobile phones, used for communicating. According to Krishnamurthy and colleagues (2008), 20 percent of all tweets are posted from an external application, that is, not from the Twitter web page. Their data are from 2008, and considering the proliferation of smartphones, mobile applications, and mobile internet use since then, it is probable that the percentage is now larger. To some extent, this tendency is reflected in my data.

All the users except Steven access Twitter from both their laptops and their mobile phones, yet only Nick and John regularly use Twitter from a mobile device. The other participants only access Twitter from their mobile phones when they do not have a laptop at hand, for instance, while travelling. All the users in my case study have a preferred application that they use to access Twitter, and a wide range of applications are used, depending on the user's needs and preferences. For instance, Steven prefers to use

Tweetdeck, an application that allows him to have both of his Twitter profiles open simultaneously and side by side and thereby gives him an overview of his activities and feeds. For Betty, Tweetdeck is distracting, because it has a pop-up feature that is activated every time something new is posted in her feed, and draws her attention to Twitter. She prefers to decide for herself when to dive into the Twitter stream, and she finds that using Twitter's own website as an access point is better suited for this. Tweetie for iPhone is ideal for John, who uses Twitter while on the move, and therefore prefers a simple mobile application. Whereas all the users occasionally access Twitter through the Twitter website, only Miriam and Betty use it as their primary access point.

Evidently, the choice of media platforms and applications is related to users' needs and daily tasks, suggesting that Twitter as a communicative genre is constituted and negotiated through the complex interplay of different media platforms, applications, and interfaces at the software level, and the concrete usage practices. The interplay between a specific application and communicative practice is captured in the data sets to a very limited extent. Therefore, I will not pursue this dimension directly in the subsequent analyses.

MANAGING A CHAOTIC FLOW OF COMMUNICATION

I have mentioned participants' orientation to relevant others in the Twitter network, and the notion of Twitter as a flow in the course of everyday life, as key constituents of Twitter as a communicative genre. In this section, I analyze how these factors are negotiated and managed in the social organization of Twitter, focusing on the structural composition of Twitter communication, the emergent communication patterns, and the conversational norms that participants invoke to organize and make sense of the sometimes quite chaotic stream of utterances that comprise Twitter. This is a prerequisite to beginning to dissect local uses of Twitter for various purposes, as well as the personal and social significance that users ascribe to Twitter in everyday life.

Here, conversation is understood as Twitter activity in which two or more parties explicitly orient to each other in a set consisting of a minimum two tweets, of which at least the second tweet of the pair is marked as a reply to the first, by explicitly addressing the initial tweet to its author.

Twitter has an embedded functionality, the hashtag (#), which enables users to organize topically related tweets in threads. This creates the possibility of large-scale aggregations of tweets that are thematically linked, and is typically used for major events, for example, the #superbowl, and the #IranElection. Although enabling an easy overview of what is said in connection with a given topic, as conversations, these hashtag aggregations are of a different nature, because individual tweets are not sequentially linked in a turn-taking process, and the contributing parties are often not even aware of each other as parts of the same hashtag aggregate. Because these large-scale aggregators are of very limited importance in my data, I will not scrutinize their social organization (but see, e.g., Bruns & Burgess, 2011; Highfield, Harrington, & Bruns, forthcoming).

The Baseline: Distributed Conversation, Flow, and Filters

When compared to blog conversation, it may be argued that creating conversational coherence is both easier and more difficult on Twitter. It is easier, because tweets that are part of a conversation are typically marked with an @ (e.g., @Nick) identifying the addressee (Honeycutt & Herring, 2009), and a link at the end of the tweet connecting it to the previous turn.[5] The use of @ further ensures that the tweet is sent to the addressee, that is, it is archived on his or her profile, and thus directly accessible to the addressee in the @mentions section. In this sense, for the participants in a given conversation it appears quite coherent, because of the underlying structures of Twitter's design. However, establishing coherence requires substantial effort for someone merely following the conversation from the outside. In contrast to blogs, where conversations are embedded in threads with multiple participants in a single blog, every tweet in a conversation is posted on its author's profile, so the conversation is distributed across profiles. To keep track of other people's conversation, the user must either follow all the participants in the conversation, so their tweets appear in her feed, or track the conversation back in time, by clicking on the link to the previous tweet in each tweet in the conversation.[6]

There are other factors that make Twitter a quite noisy conversational environment. Several of the participants note that there is a limit to how many profiles they can manage to follow without their Twitter feeds becoming overloaded. If there are too many tweets in the feed (e.g., if they follow too many, or if someone tweets incessantly), they cannot keep up with it, and the interesting links and discussions drown in the noise created by the rest. Twitter offers a feature for managing this, namely, the 'lists' feature, which enables users to filter their Twitter feeds by grouping those they follow in a separate feed, and thereby creating a 'much calmer stream' (John). Thus, the entire feed may be divided into personalized sub-feeds that are much more manageable. The use of the list functionality for filtering the Twitter stream, does not, however, appear to be widespread among the participants. Instead, the general practice among the study participants is to just jump in, and look at the full Twitter stream at a given point in time.

The common strategy for managing the possible overload caused by the rapid stream of tweets is to simply skim—rather than closely read—the feed, possibly going back a little, to identify relevant tweets and conversations to read more systematically. 'I read the ten first tweets that are visible, but I don't care about the rest,' Rina asserts. Because of skimming, Betty finds herself more likely to notice tweets from those Twitter users she knows best, and from whom she would expect interesting posts. The effect of this is probably self-perpetuating: her relation to, and recognition of those whom she already considers relevant others are confirmed and reified over time.

Moreover, regarding noise and strategies for handling overload: as with blogs, tweets appear in the timeline in the order that they are posted, and not necessarily in sequential order. A fast-paced feed with a high activity level makes it difficult for the user to monitor the feed of tweets addressed to her. Consequently, the study participants who engage in conversation check their personal replies more often than their full feed, and thereby filter the stream of tweets so that only the tweets directly addressed to them are read and responded to.

Creating Interactional Coherence

Despite the noisy environment and the unsupportive interface, short dyadic conversations are prevalent in the dataset, as well as some longer, multiparty conversations that appear quite coherent. Hence, participants seem to be able to coordinate turn-taking among themselves, and thus ensure sequencing and meaningful progression of the conversation. This is largely consistent with the findings of Honeycutt and Herring's (2009) study of addressivity in a sample of almost 40,000 tweets from the public timeline on Twitter. Whereas less than one third of the tweets in Honeycutt and Herring's sample were conversational, more than two thirds of my archived tweets are parts of conversations. Whereas this may indicate that Twitter has grown more conversational, my data do not validly represent a general trend of conversation becoming a more widespread practice on Twitter, as I have explicitly sampled cases with some interaction. However, my study does confirm that conversation is an important part of Twitter. Consider the following excerpt comprising one evening from 8 pm to midnight from John's profile, which is quite typical of his use of Twitter:[7]

John: What's up their sleeve now?—Exciting . . . [link]

John: I checked my bill; 827 kr . . . [link]

John: RT @HowardBeck: With wine, "as with women and horses, the real best is second best." [Link]

John: @HowardBeck "A Good Social Democrat" by Roald Als and Poul Einer Hansen, read/reread Morten Ramsland "Hundehoved", Jo Nesbø's thrillers . . .

John: Go Nelly! RT @nelly: Newspaper article about me is online now: [Link]

Robdk: @John iTablet!

HowardBeck: @John Noted!

John: Løkke warming up for X-Factor now. Prime minister's New Year speech (year's lowest viewing figures) on DR1 versus X-Factor (the year's highest) Knockout!

John: @robdk Hope I get one too!:-)

John: Remember X-factor!! @nelly is with us tonight. Damn!—And the shop assistant, little Carsten Schack from Aalborg is one of the judges :-)

John: @Clayton @HowardBeck the world's most boring book incidentally is War and Peace, according to [Link]

Clayton: @John @HowardBeck Marshall Grover's Bill and Ben series isn't too great either.

Xavier: @John hmm, they're saying the tablet's going to be shown at the event.

John: Don't you think this Bond is a bit too physical? (trick question!) RT @ramona: Daniel Craig in HD. Holy mother of God that's sweet. #DRHD

John: X-Factor-conclusion; Pernille's fetish for 15–16 yr old boys, Remee without his hat (unheard of!), and Carsten SoulShock with a coin-slot. I'm HOOKED!

Nelly: @John And @pernille likes nerds :-) #xfactordk

John: @nelly super cool that you dare! Takes guts:-) (and you need to be a bit mad)

John: @nelly Heh heh. Yes, she's a warm person

John: @Billy and congratulations from here! It's DR that should be congratulated, yes?

John: @Clayton no, you're right. My wrong :-)

John: @xavier also heard they're coming up with something interesting

John: @tjensen I'm pretty sure my boss is going to be understanding when I roll up in the morning and say: "Yeah well, it was my Sleep Cycle App, chief."

Tjensen: @John :-D It's Saturday tomorrow, luckily!

Most of the activity in this excerpt is conversational. John participates in several simultaneous interactions on various topics, with nine different peers. In spoken communication, it would be difficult to interact simultaneously with different people around different topics and situations, without disrupting the interactional coherence, but the written nature of conversation on Twitter makes this manageable. The conversations overlap in the feed, and thereby disrupt the sequential coherence of each of the conversations. The fast pace at which new tweets are posted to the feed adds to this disruption of the sequential coherence of the total feed, because the addressee of a tweet often does not have time to respond before some intermediate, pragmatically irrelevant tweet is posted by someone else. However, this does not seem to bother the participants, and they navigate smoothly in the stream of incoming and outgoing tweets.

Most of the conversations in the excerpt above are short dyadic exchanges between John and one other, although there are a few multiparty conversations. This is the prevailing tendency in the collected material. As on a blog, the dyadic nature of most conversations, as well as the @ symbol as an addressivity mark embedded the in design of Twitter, are important means of navigating multiple conversations and ensuring coherence. As the excerpt shows, the conversations are open to third party intervention—others may try to join the conversation, or the already active parties may try to get a third party to join the conversation, by addressing her in their exchange.

The excerpt further illustrates that the conversational structure is quite open, in the sense that conversations are continuously initiated by both John's own tweets, and tweets from others in the network. All tweets are in principle conversational openings, but actual conversations only develop around a tweet if someone replies to it, and they only last as long as at least one of the communicating parties replies to the 'thread.' Usually, the conversations are short exchanges of less than four turns, but in principle, they are rarely closed. Instead, communication on Twitter should be seen as a continuous stream of openings that may be picked up on by anyone who wishes to have a conversation. In the excerpt, John posts four tweets without an addressee (excluding RTs). Two of these receive responses (by xavier and nelly), whereas the other two are not picked up on. It is quite normal that not all tweets succeed in generating response. This indicates that conversational activity on Twitter has a lot to do with timing: finding relevant others who happen to be online simultaneously, and initiating conversations with them, instead of logging on with the expectation of a specific other being available for conversation.

As Miriam notes, compared to MSN Messenger, for which she will sit and wait for responses, on Twitter, responses cannot be anticipated, because most people are not constantly present on Twitter—they just check in occasionally, throughout the day. Accordingly, they will be more likely to respond to tweets that are posted immediately before they check their profiles because these will be at the top of the feed, and therefore appear on the front page.

Whereas participants cannot expect responses to their tweets that lack addressees, they may and do expect responses to their @replies, that is, the tweets in which they address someone. With the exception of Nick's feed, the participants and their interaction partners seem to operate with a reply norm that guides and structures their conversational activities (e.g., the previously mentioned excerpt). As is the case with blogs, by replying when addressed, the user signals that she has noticed and thought about the tweet she has received, thereby demonstrating mutual orientation and interest. The norm of reciprocation is further noted in the interviews, for instance, when Rina attributes other users' failure to respond to their not fully understanding how to use Twitter. Rina and Miriam further note that when somebody does not respond to their replies, they feel rejected, and will probably stop writing to this person.

In comparison with personal blogs, the reply norms on Twitter are ambiguous, and dependent on the situational context of the tweet. There is a clear division between tweets with and without addressees, when invoking norms for replying. Tweets with addressees appear more ordered: the addressee must respond (albeit not necessarily immediately). Conversely, tweets without addressees impose no obligation on the audience to respond, and are dependent not only on sparking audience interest, but on being posted at a time when an audience is *temporally available* for conversation. In this sense, Twitter communication may be described as the continuous striking up of conversations, casual small talk with those fellow users in one's network who are available at a given point in time. Hence, the set of users with whom one ends up interacting on Twitter is, to a large extent, more coincidental than on a blog, where participants may expect continued, daily interaction with a set of close peers. This explains why, when compared to the blog archives, the Twitter data display far less interaction between the closest peers.

From Social Presence to Immediacy

Timing and simultaneous attention on Twitter seem pivotal to starting and maintaining a vibrant conversation. With this, the accomplishment of mutual social presence is centered not on communication frequency, but on *immediacy,* that is, the temporal co-presence (or near-synchronicity) of interlocutors on Twitter.

As is the case with blogs, the conversation on Twitter is, in principle, asynchronous, and, to be carried on, requires waiting for at least one of the participants to be online. Thus, a considerable time lag may sometimes occur between turns in a conversational sequence. But it is remarkable that longer sequences of more than a couple of exchanges often play out in a near-synchronous fashion. Near-synchronous, or even almost-real-time chat-like exchanges are particularly frequent in the samples from both Miriam and Rina's Twitter profiles, which suggests that timeliness and the possibility of near-synchronicity are part of the attraction of Twitter conversation. Consequently, it may be argued that temporal proximity plays a central role in understanding conversational practices on Twitter, vis-à-vis the blog. In blogs, a comment may be left anytime the reader finds it convenient to read and respond to the post, because the comment is posted in the context to which it belongs: namely, the thread. In comparison, conversation in Twitter entails a sense of immediacy. As Miriam explains, you cannot respond to an old tweet in the twitter stream: 'you cannot interfere with something and begin to comment on something that happened a hundred tweets ago, because it is all out of context' (Miriam). Although a reply to someone else's tweet automatically generates a link to that person's tweet, he or she may have moved on to other conversations, meaning that the context of the original tweet is no longer relevant. As further exemplified by Miriam: 'Sometimes, I get a reply that says "Ha ha that sounds funny," and then I have to go back and look for what it could be that sounded funny. Because I've written twenty things since' (Miriam). Hence, at least when used for conversation, Twitter is biased toward synchronicity, the short 'here and now' exchange, and consequently requires the immediate attention of the participant. Because Twitter is organized as a continuous stream, rather than as separate threads, the topic and context of conversation change rapidly, making it critical to enter the stream 'here and now,' where it currently is, if one wishes to make relevant and meaningful comments to fellow users' tweets.

Milne, in her analysis of presence and absence in written genres, writes of letter-writing interlocutors who seek to invoke a sense of 'here and now' immediacy, despite the temporal and spatial dispersion assumed in written communication, by providing the reader with details of their current corporeal context (e.g., 'I'm sitting here . . .') and discursively constructing the communication 'as if' interlocutors were co-present (Milne, 2010: 15). In Milne's analysis, the sense of immediacy is imagined by both the writer and the reader. In contrast, I would argue that a key quality of Twitter as a written communicative genre is that it evokes a sense of immediacy in a very literal fashion—interlocutors can see their interaction unfold in almost-real-time, thus in a sense collapsing contexts, despite users' spatial dispersion. As Donath argues, synchronicity in communication may reduce the spatial distance between interlocutors and create an experience of entering a common space (Donath, 2004; also Baym, 2010: 8). Along these lines, synchronous or near-synchronous Twitter conversation may generate a sense of mutual social presence, but it is achieved differently, and arguably has a different expressive value and function than it does in a blog or a letter. In a blog, *continuous* social presence was described as a vehicle for relationship development and intimacy over time. On Twitter, social presence is *immediate,* between interlocutors in the here and now, without a normative require-ment of continued responsiveness (e.g., to 'meet' on Twitter again the next day). Hence, immediacy on Twitter nurtures a different conversational at-mosphere, which encompasses shifting relationships among simultaneously co-present Twitter users, which are actualized as the Twitter stream unfolds. This has consequences for the themes that may be addressed, and for the stylistic patterns characteristic of Twitter as a communicative genre.

CREATING TOPICAL COHERENCE IN THE TWITTER STREAM

Unlike on blogs, where there is no limit to the number of characters in a turn (a post or a comment), Twitter exchanges are very short—the software imposes a 140-character message limit. This can be a challenge: 'When you have 140 characters, you sometimes accidentally write something that could be misunderstood' (John). There is simply not much room to express oneself clearly. In other words, Twitter conversations entail a potential obstacle to topical coherence and intersubjective alignment between the sender and the recipient of the tweet, and consequentially, for a meaningful, ongoing nego-tiation of Twitter as a communicative genre. Moreover, the quick obsoles-cence of the context of a tweet, and the urge for immediacy in a fast moving stream may disrupt the topical coherence of the conversation.

The 140 characters available for composing tweets pose a structural and linguistic challenge to both the writer, who must boil down her message to a minimum, and the reader, who must make sense of this brief message, in order for a meaningful conversation to take place. Despite this, participants seem to accomplish mutual understanding, and experience their conversa-tions as meaningful. In this section, I examine the strategies used by con-versing participants to maximize the expressive value of their tweets and replies, and thereby create a relevant context for the reader and conversation partner's interpretation of the tweet.

A widespread, emergent practice for establishing a shared conversational context is to organize tweeting around recurring topical 'events' occurring in the world outside Twitter. Such events may be scheduled (e.g., #xfactor, or the 2010 men's soccer #worldcup)[8], or unexpected (e.g., the #haiti earth-quake). Events also evolve around Twitter-based 'memes' (such as the previ-ously mentioned 'Follow Friday'), that is, cultural practices and events that are spread and passed on by members of a network through repeated enact-ment. In addition to #FF and other internationally enacted Twitter memes, participants in the cluster that includes Betty and John, for instance, have developed various local memes, such as '#dirtyfriday' and '#networkfriday'. Common to Twitter memes or events are that they are user-generated: A [group of] core user(s) start a trend, and other users sustain the collective commitment to it. Skilled Twitter users appear to orient themselves towards recurring Twitter memes in the flow of communication.

Recurring memes and events may serve to provide a topical structure and organization to Twitter as a communicative genre. By orienting to, and enacting recurring events on Twitter, the users may assign a sense or order to the otherwise relatively chaotic stream of tweets. When contributing to an event in a tweet, the context of the tweet is already given, and this makes it easy for at least the knowledgeable Twitter users to inscribe the tweet in a meaningful social context, and thus provide direction and focus to the Twitter flow. At the same time, participating in such events is a marker of inclusiveness—a way for the user to demonstrate skillful navigation of Twitter as a communicative genre.

Stylistic-Expressive Means as Interpretive Cues in Conversation

In addition to the repeated event-making on Twitter, participants orient to stylistic norms for creating an intersubjective understanding and interpretive alignment in the Twitter stream, despite the short message length. The short-length format framing tweets seems to encourage spontaneous outbursts and creative linguistic and non-linguistic means of expressing a point in a tweet.

One way to boil down the essence of what the user wishes to express is by constructing the tweet as an embodied action, that is, 'doing' something, instead of providing a more lengthy description of it. This is the case when Rina 'throws confetti' at a fellow user, to celebrate her having reached almost 300 followers, instead of writing to congratulate her, or when Miriam 'burps' to explain to the reader that she is full, after eating dinner. Such playful and creative uses of language to convey physical actions enable users to construct tweets rich in meaning, without exceeding the 140-character limit. In a sense, textualized bodily actions may express actions and states of mind more effectively than written descriptions, because they carry subtle clues to the context of the writing, for example, the physical location and emotional state of the author. Such stylistic-expressive elements are quite effective means for contextualizing the tweet, and guiding the reader toward a certain intended meaning.

Twitter users have developed a distinct linguistic code to compensate for the limited space for interpretive clues in tweets, namely the widespread use of the '#' (e.g., #fail or #FTW [for the win]) at the end of tweets, to provide a relevant context for the reader's interpretation of the tweet, and thereby ensure intersubjective understanding in the communication process. A particularly notable example, consistent with the idea of playfulness and creativity in the formulation of tweets, is a tweet from Betty on a Monday: '#iwantagrownup #whenarewethere? #ivegottopee #mondaymorning.' This tweet is unusual, consisting only of hash-tagged, collapsed sentences that apparently describe Betty's Monday morning frustrations, returning to work after the weekend, and starting with a hectic morning with her children.

'#iwantagrownup' is a regularly invoked hashtag in this particular cluster, typically used to signal that the user cannot handle something. This indicates that hashtags are not only used to organize topics into multi-participant threads, but to make the author's mood, opinion, and so forth, more explicit to the reader. The use of the hashtag as a stylistic marker may not only serve an economizing function, but as a 'code' for exclusivity, marking insiders as opposed to 'outsiders' (i.e. newbies and less skilled Twitter users). The use of the hashtag is particularly characteristic of the conversations among those who have extensive networks and many conversation partners, in this case, Betty, John, and Rina, and their conversation partners. Accordingly, mastering the use of the hashtag signals mastery of Twitter as a genre—it is a stylistic trait of core users, genre insiders, who, through a specific writing style, demonstrate knowledge of the stylistic codes that underpin the creation of an intersubjective understanding, and a smoothly-running conversation on Twitter.

Another, more widespread, way of providing context to guide the reader's interpretation of the tweet is through the use of emoticons and acronyms such as LOL ('Laughing Out Loud'), which is also common practice in the blogs studied, and in CMC in general (Walther & D'Addario, 2001). However, smileys are contested as an appropriate general code on Twitter. Rina (and to some extent Miriam) uses them a lot, because 'a smiley says it all [. . .] if you forget the smiley, it [the tweet] may be misunderstood' (Rina). In contrast, Betty is annoyed if there are too many smileys in the Twitter communication, although she recognizes them as useful nonverbal cues. Still, smileys are prevalent in her feed, indicating that, at least to some extent, they are broadly accepted, extra-verbal, interactional cues to communication on Twitter.

In sum, the stylistic markers used by participants in Twitter conversations to create intersubjective understanding and interpretive alignment seem vital to creating topical coherence in communication, as they have become highly institutionalized as everyday practice in the genre.

THE GOOD TWEET: NEGOTIATING RELEVANCE ON TWITTER

Tweets are written in a textbox framed by the question, 'What is happening?' a question that was, in fact, changed in November 2009 (just before my data collection), from 'What are you doing?' a question that puts the author's personal experiences and whereabouts at the center of the communication, and encourages what Naaman and colleagues (2010) call 'me now' tweets, roughly defined as tweets about the author's thoughts and activities. The change in question indicates a subtle shift of focus in the service. With the new question, Twitter began encouraging a broader range of statements than the purely personal status update for which it was originally intended, but that users had been partly ignoring. 'What is happening?' constitutes a less specific question about the user's world, which may encompass anything from major news events to the author's current moods and activities. Furthermore, the question directs the user toward writing statements about whatever is on his or her mind, here and now, something that is likely supported by the high updating frequency and the brevity of Twitter. This further advances the sense of immediacy, and promotes impulsive and shifting types of statements, rather than a consistent theme on a microblog. My data clearly support this—tweets are much more diverse than the original idea of a personal status update about what the user is doing 'right now'— the data archives reflect a broad range of topics and purposes that users deem appropriate for the microblogging genre.

Roughly one third of the tweets from the six authors are tweets without any specific addressee, that is, they do not include @, which marks and directs a message to a fellow user. Although some of these tweets fit the model of the self-absorbed 'me now' status update, such tweets are far from dominant. The tweets without addressee are about all sorts of topics: here-and-now activities of the author, links to interesting content elsewhere online, opinions, requests for input or help, and retweets of other people's tweets. Accordingly, the centrality of the author's personal experiences and whereabouts, as promoted at the software level by the interface design of Twitter, is not entirely embraced and accepted by the users, because they share things that are not about themselves.

Nearly two thirds of the tweets from the authors are parts of conversations ('tweets with addressee'). These tweets address somebody else, and thus reflect attention to specific topics and relationships with others, rather than just attention to oneself. Therefore, tweeting must be described not only in terms of self-centered status updates, but also as a highly other-oriented activity, in that the user's tweets often seek to engage an audience in conversation. Hence, as already indicated, tweets—and with this, the ongoing negotiation of relevance—are influenced by the dynamics of building networks of affiliation, and of timing the participation to achieve immediacy with other users. The negotiation of relevance mirrors the dynamics of a blog, for instance, in that appropriate and relevant tweets are more likely to initiate conversations, whereas less interesting tweets discourage responses from the readers. In this section, I examine the norms of 'the good tweet,' and how Twitter users orient to their audience when posting tweets. In the background of such an examination of the negotiation of relevance are the network dynamics and consequences (following/unfollowing as reward and rejection) of a given user's performance.

One criterion that is voiced in the negotiation of appropriate tweets is that the posted content should be appealing to, and inclusive of a broad range of users. A common practice for supporting this convention is to take the conversation to other communication channels when it becomes irrelevant in the network, for example, when two people have a long dialogue about something irrelevant or inaccessible to others. In such instances, it is more appropriate to take the conversation to Twitter's backchannel, the direct message system (DM)[9]. This ensures that other people's feeds are not overloaded with irrelevant tweets that do not concern them. This practice is regulated quite explicitly in the network to which Betty and John belong. For instance, John retweets an explicit call for Twitter etiquette by one of his peers to 'keep long conversations on DM!!' Following this call for proper etiquette, John and other members of the cluster start what they call 'a long, irrelevant conversation' about the colors of their living room walls, which runs for 2 days, for a total of ten tweets. The conversation is deeply sarcastic and seems to be sort of a protest against users who fill other users' Twitter streams with irrelevant content. All in all, these more or less explicit calls for etiquette may be considered attempts to correct users who violate the norm, without explicitly addressing them. This further contributes to reifying the convention that tweets should be of general relevance to the network.

The study participants seem to agree that a good and relevant tweet is one that is both informative and funny. None of them cares to read about trivial matters from the everyday lives of others, even less so, when they are not served with a surprising twist, or a touch of self-irony, so that the reader feels that the author is invested in the tweet. Whereas the participants may have varying conceptions of what kind of information is relevant, simply because they have different interests, the idea that good tweets are served with a hint of humor and personality indicates norms at play concerning *the tone and stylistic framing of content* on Twitter. In the participants' descriptions, Twitter is characterized by an informal, spontaneous, and sometimes playful communicative style that reflects and enhances the temporal proximity and immediacy characteristic of Twitter as a communicative genre. Generally relevant and engaging themes, and a casual and informal style may make it easier to get a conversation started with whoever happens to be present on Twitter at a given point in time. As Steven asserts, regarding funny tweets: 'it goes down [is digested] quicker, and you can have a chat about it' (Steven).

Attracting followers and receiving responses is contingent upon offering interesting and well-written tweets, that is, mastering the informal and sometimes self-ironic and humorous writing style. Several of the study participants give examples of how they orient themselves to this stylistic norm. Nick, for example, contends that he is careful to not deploy a too-academic discursive style, and tries to express himself in either a banal manner or by stating things with a bit of edge in his tweets. Betty sometimes rewrites and reformulates her tweets, until she finds them suitable for posting, and Rina thinks twice before posting acerbic tweets. In sum, participants are concerned with how to please their audience:

> To be completely frank, it is a question of making it interesting, making yourself interesting, making yourself sound funny, and not crude, or too

much, or annoying. [. . .] to appear appealing to others, fundamentally. (Betty)

In this quote, Betty orients not so much to a topical norm, but to a stylistic code, when trying to tweet relevantly. It might be argued that because content shifts, the negotiation of relevance relates to stylistic criteria more consistently than to thematic conventions. In other words, users' ideas of 'the good tweet' may be more adequately described according to their style than their content.

Accordingly, in working their way into—and maintaining—Twitter networks, users seek to adjust their modes of expression to fit what they perceive as their peers' preferences. The network dynamics simply nurture and sanction a specific expressive style, characteristic of that network. Users are socialized, and, if successful in creating a network of relevant others around them, become accustomed to the informal and playful style on Twitter. This, in turn, creates and regulates the relevant context for the conversations on Twitter, or a certain ambience framing the communication: informal, funny, and casual.[10]

Despite this informality and casualness, several of the participants describe how spontaneity is both hindered and encouraged by the 140-character limit. Hindered, because it takes effort to say something meaningful in this short form: As Nick describes it: 'In a purely technical and structural sense it is very . . . quite extensive, actually, for such short messages, the amount of work I put into it' (Nick). Steven's experience is somewhat similar: 'You often spend some time writing these messages, because you have to shorten them, really' (Steven). The short-form favors strong communicators, that is, those who are skilled at delivering one-liners, and appreciate the aesthetics of punch lines. This is probably part of the reason that Twitter is very popular in the media and communications industries.

However, spontaneity is also encouraged, because the 140-character limit frees the users from having to express deep thoughts in a careful and reflective manner. Instead, it makes writing quite casual and easy, when compared to other online genres. As Miriam argues, 'If one's attention span is not up to much, then 140 characters, one can handle that' (Miriam), something that is confirmed by Nick: 'It doesn't feel like work the same way, because it is just that sweet little innocent textbox. It is not a big, empty page that has to be filled with deep thoughts' (Nick), like, for instance, a lengthy blog post. The 140 characters and the continuous stream make Twitter well suited for quick, lively exchanges and small talk between users. This implies that the tone of the communication is more direct and to the point. Probably as a consequence of the 140-character limit, there is not as much polite acknowledgement of each other's postings on Twitter, compared to that seen on blogs, in which participants put a lot of effort into expressing the importance of each other's perspectives and input in their talk back and forth.

The direct tone on Twitter could lead to more fighting and flaming, but this is not at all the case in my data. In fact, several of the participants note that is it quite difficult to fight on Twitter, because participants put effort into resolving potential conflicts before they escalate. According to John, the 140-character limit to tweets makes participants very aware of the risk of misunderstandings, and they are thus more careful to avoid it. Smileys and hashtags play an important role in this respect, but more importantly, Twitter's communicative tone itself creates a friendly and relaxed atmosphere that contextualizes and shapes the conversation.

If a user violates the tone, it is likely to have consequences. For instance, Betty mentions that she unfollows other users, if their tweets are rude or offensive to others. John reports something similar, when unfollowing a fellow user whose tweets were too rabid. He simply does not want to be associated with that kind of behavior, and unfollowing is a way to indicate his disapproval. An inappropriate tone may repel one's network, and result in losing one's audience. Apart from severe sanctions, such as exclusion from the network, there are other, less drastic ways to regulate the tone on Twitter, by correcting each other. Consider the following exchange between John and Celia:

John: Fitnessworld the first day after holiday. Should be named fatnessworld.

Celia: @John Well isn't that harsh? At least they are trying ;)

John: @Celia yesyes. Sorry. Was being a little self-ironic :-)

Despite not being intended as an offensive comment about people struggling to lose weight, Celia reads John's tweet as such, and protests, by defending the overweight, and correcting John's perceived harshness. The interaction sequence displays similar facework and repair mechanisms as were seen on blogs, in the previous chapter. For instance, by presenting her criticism as a question, Celia gives John a chance to explain and correct himself. She further puts a smiley at the end, as a means of softening her criticism, and thereby moderating her threat to John's face. He, in turn, replies with an apology, and a face-saving explanation of the intended meaning of the message, to repair the situation—again, with a smiley. By underlining the self-irony in his message, John repositions himself as an insider in the network, knowledgeable with regard to the tone and norms of not being too self-important. With this move, the conflict is avoided, and everything returns to normal.

Such instances of apparent offence and misunderstanding are extremely rare in the collected material, especially so-called other-initiated repair situations in which someone other than the offender initiates a corrective process (Goffman, 1967: 18–23; Schegloff et al., 1977). Usually, possibly offensive remarks are corrected immediately by the person writing them, typically in a humorous and self-ironic manner, as seen in the excerpt above, again underlining the informality and casualness of Twitter as a communicative space.

What is accomplished by the informal and mostly humorous tone to which participants orient themselves, in terms of defining the interactional frame of reference on Twitter? Efforts to uphold a relaxed tone in Twitter, and the rarity of conflict and misunderstanding in the data suggest that users consider Twitter to be a particular type of space, namely, a welcoming, inclusive and sociable space, where users may 'drop in' and 'hang out' at their convenience. Unlike the blog, there is no 'host,' a person owning the space and responsible for moderating and keeping a friendly atmosphere, because the conversation is distributed across profiles, and only united in the individual users' personal Twitter streams. To sustain an appropriate tone, and maintain the smooth stream of conversational flow, participants must collaborate in policing the 'common space,' and upholding the informal ambience.

PURPOSES AND PRAGMATIC FUNCTIONS OF TWITTER

My data confirm the presence of a wide variety of posted content, even within individual profiles. Although there are recurrent themes in all the archived profiles, reflecting the interests of the authors, these recurrent themes are not dominant, apart from in Steven's profile, which has a strict thematic focus on literature, and—to some extent—Rina's profile, which involves much communication about her passion for nail polish. However, generally, the content of the archived profiles is a mixture of diverse topics of interest, personal matters, news and links, and small talk. This leaves the impression of a thematically incoherent and constantly shifting communication. The lack of clear thematic focus is also a natural consequence of many of the tweets being parts of conversations in the form of replies to tweets and themes originated by relevant others in the network. The different topics often overlap and run parallel to one another, and fluctuate over the course of conversations. Consequently, from a genre perspective it may be pointless to analyze and categorize individual Twitter profiles in terms of the local content and stylistic nuances.

To do justice to the empirical data, the analysis of variations in themes and pragmatic functions on Twitter is given a different form than the blog analysis. Instead of exploring the profiles one by one, I will analyze them jointly, examining the purposes and meanings of Twitter revealed in the data. I specifically attempt to connect various types of content to the purposes they serve for the users, including how they facilitate conversations and relationships between author and audience. The aim of this part of the analysis is to explore the range of functions and meanings that users assign to Twitter in everyday life, that is, to examine the breadth of expressions and meanings of Twitter as a communicative genre.

In the resulting analysis, I weave together three perspectives, to illuminate user engagement with Twitter. First, as a point of departure for grouping types of purpose, I draw on Java and colleagues (2007), who, in their taxonomy of Twitter intent, identify four main purposes of microblogs: daily chatter (equivalent to 'me now' tweets about users' daily lives and activities), sharing information, reporting news, and engaging in conversation or small talk with fellow Twitter users. These categories are very broad and qualitatively empty, as they appear in the quantitative analysis of Java and colleagues (2007), yielding no insight into the functions and significance that each type of purpose may have for actual users in specific situations. To begin exploring these qualitative questions concerning Twitter's purposes, I draw together analyses of thematic orientations from the six Twitter archives and interviews in my study. Second, I connect thematic orientations to the notion of directionality of communication on Twitter, informed by the analyses of the six participants' networks, and the division into self- and other-directed tweets. This allows me to further elaborate the categories of purpose classification of Java and colleagues (2007). In particular, I distinguish news reporting and sharing information—two purposes not clearly distinguished in the classification of Java and colleagues—according to differences in the degree of conversationality. Whereas reporting news is considered a practice of disseminating, or broadcasting to one's followers, information sharing is characterized by interactional exchanges among peers in the Twitter network. By using directionality as a descriptive parameter, it becomes possible to link content and purpose to the qualities of the different types of network relationality on Twitter. Finally, I draw a distinction between instrumental, and expressive or intrinsic, purposes of communication, as advanced by Crawford (2009) and Bakardjieva (2005), among others. I do not treat this distinction as a bipolar one, but as a continuum. Instrumental purposes are reflected in goal-oriented uses of Twitter (e.g., coordination, being informed, etc.), whereas entirely intrinsic uses at the other end of the spectrum concern 'personal, "unpressured" exchanges, also known as idle chat' (Crawford, 2009: 255), including more relational and phatic dimensions in the users' enactments of Twitter as a communicative genre. The topical discussion in pursuit of personal interests lies somewhere between these.

Against this background, I identify four main enactments of the genre, namely, Twitter as *news dissemination and aggregation, broadcasting the self, information sharing,* and *hanging out.* These four main pragmatic uses are more or less seamlessly interwoven in the archived profiles, and even in the same tweets, so the categories are not mutually exclusive, and the boundaries are not clear-cut. However, as will be evident from the analysis, the participants may be said to have preferred uses and a primary purpose for using Twitter, reflected in their patterns of communication. Furthermore, each of the functions reveals specific nuances in why participants engage with Twitter as they do, suggesting different ways in which participants make sense of, and ascribe significance to Twitter in their everyday lives.

Twitter as a News Source and Aggregator

In popular discourse on Twitter, a prominent, recurrent theme is the celebration of how Twitter may facilitate the quick dissemination of news. In the scholarly literature, this perspective seems less dominant, but has been explored, for instance, in relation to the Iranian elections of 2009, and the death of singer Michael Jackson, also in 2009 (Murthy, 2011; Sanderson & Cheong, 2010). In my data, the news dimension is present in the sense that some of the participants identify Twitter as an important tool for gathering an overview of personally or professionally relevant information, as well as for disseminating news and links to followers.

Monitoring and Reading

For some of the users in my case study, Twitter functions as a news aggregator for topics that they find relevant, tweeted by others. Nick explicitly describes Twitter as an enhanced RSS feed that collects and serves up news and links about graphic design. Similarly, Steven asserts that

> instead of using it as a social tool for finding people who want to know when I go to the bathroom, or when I grab the bus, or when I am ill [. . .] I use it to find people who share my interest in social media, and in this way, it is an enhanced RSS feed, you might say. That is, they find links, and new information, and new trends, and reference each other [. . .] it is a good accumulator of professional knowledge. (Steven)

Both Steven and Nick express a strong interest in exploring the links that others post, and find this to be a core attraction of Twitter. As Nick asserts, '99 percent of the things only become interesting qua their links' (Nick). By following links, new perspectives and ideas become available to them, as they become aware of news, trends, and interesting content online that they otherwise would not have found. The insights that Nick and Steven gain from using Twitter as an enhanced RSS feed aid their professional lives. In Steven's case, this is because it enables him to track journalistic trends in the use of various social media, which is important, because he is employed as the head of web production in a media outlet. In Nick's case, Twitter is professionally significant because it keeps him updated on new graphic design trends, fonts, and so on—pivotal knowledge for an up-and-coming graphic designer. Thus, Twitter becomes a valuable, even necessary tool and source of information about issues and topics of importance in their work life. Moreover, Steven uses Twitter to monitor his company's brand, and occasionally to spot newsworthy stories. Clearly, these uses of Twitter to serve professional purposes reflect a distinctly goal-oriented, instrumental approach to Twitter: In Nick and Steven's fields, it is a useful tool for professional development and inspiration.

For other users, Twitter also serves as a sort of news aggregator, albeit in a very different way. Rina, for instance, follows various Hollywood celebrities on Twitter, something that allows her to get a peek into their lives.[11] For Rina, Twitter provides free, easy access to information and gossip about the whereabouts of these celebrities, information that she would otherwise get from other sources, such as weekly tabloid newspapers and magazines. Miriam uses Twitter to aggregate a manageable feed of the blogs that she regularly reads, some of which auto-update on Twitter when new blog posts are posted. This way, instead of having to check each blog for new posts, she has only to visit the blogs when her Twitter feed indicates that there is something new that seems interesting. Thus, Twitter becomes a tool for keeping up with the activities of heavy blog posters, in 'headlines.' Rather than being motivated by a professional need, these uses are of a more entertaining nature, thus more adequately described in terms of intrinsic motivation. These more personal, interest-driven orientations to Twitter as a tool for aggregating and monitoring personally relevant content are, however, marginal to the two women's uses of Twitter.

The very goal-oriented use of Twitter as a work tool, characteristic of Nick and Steven in particular, has implications for the reading patterns of these users. Unlike the common practice of diving into the Twitter stream where it currently is, and just skimming the Twitter feed for possibly interesting items, as described previously, Nick and Steven's habit is to read more thoroughly and carefully through the entire stream. This means that when they visit Twitter, they prefer to read back in the stream, from where they last left off, and check out most links, to not miss anything that might be relevant to them. Steven further ascribes these differences to the following/follower-ratio: 'I am the kind of user who is not that good at [. . .] socializing much, who listens more than speaks. And that may be inferred from my following more people than follow me' (Steven). The specific practice of using Twitter to monitor and keep up-to-date on relevant trends in specific professional fields is identifiable by the different reading strategy (close reading, instead of merely skimming), which positions the user primarily as a recipient of other people's broadcasts of news items, rather than someone seeking conversation with peers. In this role, the user becomes a 'lurking spectator' who exploits the network of followees, benefiting from other users' active content production and sharing. Consequently, when used for news aggregation, Twitter does not necessarily encourage interaction, but is reminiscent of broadcast genres, with their clear separation of producers and audiences.

Providing News and Links for Others

A pendant to the use of Twitter as a news source is the widespread practice of posting links to interesting content (news articles, blog posts, etc.) that the user has stumbled upon elsewhere online, and considers potentially relevant to her followers. By posting links, the user filters news and resources, and makes them available to the audience, thereby providing the service of screening the web for interesting content from online news outlets, for example, and possibly introducing followers to things they might otherwise not have found. Followers may then pick up on the recommended content, and follow the posted link, if they consider it relevant. Of the participants in the study, Steven and John share links most often—in fact, Miriam, Nick, and Betty seldom or never post links.

The links posted by Steven and John reflect their interests. Steven solely posts links to book-related news, in keeping with the thematic focus of his Twitter profile, whereas John primarily tweets links to gadget news and political news in established media outlets. To accompany the links, he often posts a commentary, expressing his opinion of the story in the tweet. John considers it a civic duty to create awareness of, and debate political issues, and he tweets about 'covering' stories on Twitter—as if he were a journalist. Confirming this incentive to use Twitter to create political awareness, in the interview John asserts: 'If I discovered a political scandal that I could disclose, it would fulfill a childhood dream' (John).

These examples of how users disseminate information via Twitter bear a resemblance to the broadcast model, albeit in these instances, with the Twitter user in the role of the 'producer' who actively and selectively filters content, and makes it available to an audience, thereby functioning as a substitute for, or extension of the traditional news broadcaster. The underlying purpose is not dialogue with, but the enlightenment of fellow users. In terms of the instrumental-intrinsic continuum, it may be argued that although probably serving an intrinsic purpose and expressive function, as the author-broadcaster may find it personally rewarding to offer something relevant and valuable to an audience, this usage patterns is also highly instrumental in character, because it is part of an ongoing effort to make the author-as-news-broadcaster attractive and relevant to follow.

Twitter as Self-Broadcasting

As Twitter is a communicative genre driven by personal authorship, content necessarily reflects the issues that concern the authors. The point of departure for any user's tweets lies in personal activities, opinions, interests, and experiences, whether or not the intent is to spark conversation. The personal investment in the tweets may take various forms, from the interest-driven, topical, and in a sense more impersonal tweeting (characteristic of Steven), to the sometimes deeply private tweets on family life, moods, and health (especially evident in Miriam's tweets). In this subsection, I explore the functions of the so-called 'me now' tweet (without addressee) to its producers, to provide a complementary analysis to the framing of tweets as news dissemination.

Documenting the Everyday

Even though self-centered tweets without addressees are not dominant in my data, observations from the everyday lives of participants are quite common in the archived material. For instance, participants tweet about their here-and-now activities, their children and so on. Furthermore, several participants post 'twitpics,' that is, links to photos that illustrate their current whereabouts and activities, as when Rina posts a photo of the nail polish that just arrived in her mailbox, or when John posts a twitpic of his dinner. Such posts clearly reflect a personal 'here and now' focus, and may be regarded as thematically trivial, and serving mainly intrinsic purposes of 'daily chatter.'

A related use of the 'me now' tweet is the voicing of an opinion or mood, to get something off one's chest, that is, the content reflects an attitude, a state of mind, or mood. For example, Miriam considers Twitter a 'free space' where she can openly state that she is having a bad day, without having to elaborate on the details, as she would feel obliged to do, if she were to write about it on her blog. Nick reports using Twitter for something similar, although perhaps less personal:

> I try to keep the banalities at a tolerable level, but if I have a thought, or really think that people ought to know that this movie is the best thing since buttered bread, then I can voice my opinion immediately, and I can archive it [. . .] then it is out there in black and white on the internet, and I don't have to think about it anymore, unless I get response. It is a way to externally archive my thoughts. (Nick)

Whereas these tweets without addressees are in a sense detached from the pressures of temporal proximity that we have established as characteristic of Twitter, timing and a sense of immediacy may still be important. However, it is in a different sense, because timely participation is not bound to conversational activity and context already in progress. Timing becomes a matter of establishing a timely connection between the actual activity in which the user is engaged, and the representation of that activity on Twitter. In other words, tweets about the user's here-and-now activities invoke a sense of being live. Marwick (2010), for instance, labels this form of tweeting 'life streaming,' to indicate how Twitter may document everyday life in detail, in real time.

As a result of the 'me now' tweets, and the connection they create between the actual activity and representation of the activity in tweets, Twitter may become a kind of personal archive that documents users' everyday lives. For Nick, the archive function is particularly important, and for this reason, he has integrated his tweets into his Google calendar. The calendar then shows when he tweeted various things in the past: 'It is this timeline of what I do, it is also, in a sense, a diary, when I look back, so I very much want to save this now-integral part of my life' (Nick). Accordingly, tweets without addressees may serve a highly self-directed function, namely, that of keeping track of one's experiences. In this perspective, tweeting is self-directed, rather than other-directed, and constitutes an expressive practice for reflecting on and documenting the user's activities and sense of self in everyday life.

Visibility and Self-Promotion

Whereas tweets that are parts of conversations must adhere to the norms of spontaneity, immediacy, and reciprocity, tweets without addressees allow their authors to compose tweets in a more calculated and thought-through manner, often with the goal of inviting conversation, and creating interest in the author. In this shading, 'me now' tweets serve a strategic and instrumental function for the author.

Practices of strategic editing seem to be more prominent when tweeting without addressees, and most of the participants report editing behavior when writing tweets, not only with regard to the stylistic dimension as already described. As Miriam explains, 'Sometimes it can become sport, what can be said in 140 characters' (Miriam). In a similar vein, Nick compares the tweet to a Haiku poem in which the challenge is to portray oneself in the best possible way. He claims that this strategic self-presentation is particularly important in relation to his ambition to use Twitter to create professional connections with other graphic designers, again underlining the point that tweeting is often about making oneself interesting in the eyes of relevant others.

The strategic use of Twitter to create interest among the audience is also very characteristic of Steven, who uses Twitter to generate traffic to his literature blog. He sometimes uses his tweets as teasers, and explains: 'if I want to advertise my latest blog post [on the book blog], I may go about thinking how to make the sentence exciting, so people will want to visit the blog' (Steven). John engages in similar promotional activity on Twitter, with regard to his Tumblr blog, on which he collects a wide variety of content found elsewhere online. He, too, supplements the link with a teasing comment to entice the reader into following the link.

In contrast to Steven, in particular, who puts a lot of effort into advertising new posts, Rina has simply set up an auto-update, so that when she has written a new blog post, it automatically appears with a link in her Twitter feed. Moreover, Rina and Nick both automatically feed their tweets into Facebook as status updates.

The self-promotion inherent in these practices is subject to a conflict of opinions among the participants. For Miriam it is almost a faux pas: 'They are so self-conscious, all those "I've posted a new post on my blog" and so on. I am not trying to promote myself in any way' (Miriam), whereas Rina and Nick think of auto-updating as something good, because it makes them visible on multiple services without the effort of being constantly logged into them all. For Rina and Nick, auto-updating is an efficient tool for establishing constant visibility and availability on a variety of social media, whereas for Miriam it is a sign of superficiality, shameless self-absorption, and a need for attention. Part of the problem she has with this is that if she follows someone on Twitter, *and* is also a Facebook friend of that person, *and* reads their blog, she will see the same content many times. As she says, 'I drown in having to read the same thing in four places' (Miriam).

The ambiguous attitude toward auto-updates and self-promotional tweets may be linked to discussions of activity level and overload on Twitter, as the quote from Miriam hints. In line with Rina and Nick's arguments for visibility as an important factor in using services such as Twitter and Facebook, John considers it prestigious to be very active. For instance, in one tweet, he shows off his ranking as the most active Dane on Tumblr, something that he also talks about with pride in the interview. But he has also been criticized for being too active on Twitter, for instance, with regard to Follow Friday, leading him to make a list of recommended Twitter users, instead of recommending them every Friday. In conjunction with finding the appropriate activity level, Betty recounts the call by a prominent fellow Twitter user, to establish a maximum number of tweets per person, per day, to regulate the total activity level:

> She has generally argued that people tweet too much, and suggested that there should be a limit of five or ten tweets per day, an unwritten rule that people restrain themselves [. . .] some people in there have gone crazy, written ridiculous numbers of tweets, but some of them lose followers, on that account. (Betty)

Although such a rule has not been affected or become an accepted convention, the mere suggestion of a need for regulation of activity identifies the norm of self-control as important for successful participation and networking on Twitter. In line with Betty's description of sanctions on excessive activity, Rina tends to unfollow those who do not exhibit self-restraint. Even John finds it annoying, although it will not make him unfollow the offender.

Returning to the issue of the strategic use of tweets for self-promotion, and for creating awareness of, and interest in oneself, there is apparently a delicate balance between adhering to the demand for active participation, visibility, and availability, and not overdoing it by overloading other users' feeds, and thereby becoming a source of annoyance.

Connecting and Networking Around Topics of Common Interest

Earlier in this chapter, I argued that every tweet is a potential conversational opening, so it is important to note that tweets without addressees are very likely to be (sometimes unsuccessful) attempts to start conversations. Many of the tweets without addressees do in fact receive responses, and become openings to conversations in which users exchange viewpoints, experiences, and ideas. In this section and the following, I turn to the functions of conversationality. This section focuses on an exploration of the purpose of the widespread conversations about particularly salient topics of common interest in the Twitter practices of Rina, John, and Betty. All of them indicate that information exchange and conversation are what they appreciate most on Twitter. As we have seen, these participants primarily use Twitter for conversation, and thus enact Twitter in ways that confirm their status as relevant interaction partners for their peers.

Honeycutt and Herring (2009) find that information-sharing users are more likely to engage in conversations, whereas broadcasting the self through 'me now' tweets encourages less interaction between author and audience. This is consistent with my findings, which suggest that much of the activity and networking on Twitter is generated around topics of mutual interest to members of clusters in the network. As noted, sharing information differs from news dissemination and aggregation in that it is conversational (i.e. the communication is bidirectional). Instead of regarding the user in terms of a fixed position in the network, as author (broadcasting news) or reader (receiving news), this purpose entails a structure in which participants may be considered interaction partners in ongoing exchanges in a distributed network of peers, sharing information about their interests in one-to-one or many-to-many encounters on Twitter. Each user participates actively in the accumulation of knowledge, by generating and sharing content in the network.

Discussing Cultural Products

Sharing and discussing information about issues of common interest may take its point of departure in a posted link or a user's observation concerning a given event (news stories, concerts, etc.) or product (e.g., movies, books, gadgets) that other users in the network are eager to learn about and discuss. It is remarkable that the information-sharing activity in the collected Twitter feeds often evolves around discussions of new technologies, social media services, and gadgets. Google Streetview, Google Buzz, Kindle, and iPad are just some examples of this sort of topic in the data, especially invoked in the cluster in which Betty and John are embedded. The frequency of technology and media-related topics identifies these as core interests of many participants in the cluster—an interest that unites them. Certainly, a number of other participants in the cluster work in the media and communications industries (including journalists, marketers, developers, researchers, etc.) and may have a professional interest in new services and gadgets. Betty, who works with e-learning, and John, who is a financial advisor, are not professional experts on these topics, but by participating in discussions and being recognized for their contributions, they come to see themselves and are seen as knowledgeable frontrunners when it comes to information technology and gadgets.

Another common, overarching theme encompasses reviews and discussions of various cultural products, such as television shows, sports, movies, and books. Whereas these topics may represent idiosyncratic interests, and the users who discuss these topics presumably have some personal interest in them, I suggest that users orient to these cultural products as topics for information exchange because they lend themselves particularly well to initiating casual conversation among those who would like to enhance their connections, but who do not know each other very well. That is, there is a sociable and phatic dimension to the ongoing exchange concerning these topics: they function to establish contact. Cultural products are common enough for many users to be able to relate to them, as they invite accounts of personal experiences and tastes, and may serve to establish a more personal relationship and sense of togetherness among interlocutors.

Seeking Advice and Assistance
In keeping with information sharing, in the data there are several examples of users explicitly requesting help and advice from their Twitter network. Explicit requests for advice typically generate many responses, and are good conversation starters. For instance, Steven, who characterizes himself as less inclined to engage in conversation on Twitter, considers himself to be more likely to reply to someone in a situation where he can offer practical advice and answers to concrete questions. The following excerpt from Rina's feed, about nail polish remover, further underlines how asking for advice is a good conversation starter:

> Rina: eeeek.! I am on a no buy. . . . but I am running low on polish remover . . . is that allowed when on no buy? I mean it's a necessity!
>
> Glamprincess: @Rina I think that's allowed! You can't not have polish remover. . . .
>
> AllAboutNails: @Rina You said you had a no-buy for polish! I don't count remover as polish ;)
>
> Eve: @Rina No remover is supplies not part of a no buy
>
> Pixellicious: @Rina Totally allowed, it's a need not a want! *nods*
>
> Rina: @pixelliscious @eve @allaboutnails @glamprincess thanks! now I just need to explain that to the boyfriend haha :D

In the excerpt, Rina asks for her network's opinion on whether she is allowed to buy nail polish remover, when she has currently decided that she cannot spend more money on her nail polish hobby. Within less than three minutes, four of her nail-polish-interested friends have posted replies to her tweet, in which they argue for her right to buy the remover. She thanks them almost immediately for their supportive arguments with a joint response, asserting that she will use their input to convince her boyfriend that she can buy the remover. The excerpt illustrates how a lively interaction sequence is sparked by a question and dilemma to which other users may relate. In this case, Rina's question leverages a common passion for nail polish in the Twitter network, around which users may bond. Thus, apart from the instrumental function that the exchange serves for Rina, the interaction sequence adds intrinsic value, a confirmation of common interests, to the nail-polish-interested Twitter cluster.

Goal-Oriented Networking: Making Useful Connections for 'Doing Business'

Connecting and engaging in conversations built around topics of shared interest within the network has added value to the participants, apart from enhancing knowledge and conveying inspiration through information sharing among peers. Several of the participants describe this in terms of both personal and professional networking. In essence, 'goal-oriented networking' involves using Twitter to mobilize a professional network, to facilitate and support the individual user in his or her professional achievements, occasionally resulting in real-world partnerships and business projects being launched. For instance, Betty has used her involvement in a Twitter subcluster about e-book readers and her Twitter talks with other entrepreneurs as a kick-start for starting her own business.

A core element of networking is making one's personal network available to others. This is particularly evident in John's use of Twitter. To John, Twitter is an opportunity to expand and develop networks, by contributing very actively and helping others. Mutuality is pivotal to his networking. For example, by offering assistance to others, he himself may perhaps benefit at a later date, and receive help in return. For John, making his network available to others is a win-win situation. Accordingly, he is very generous when recommending other Twitter users on Follow Friday, retweeting others to make them visible to his own network, advertising the release of a fellow Twitter user's brother's album, and offering input on and discussing business ideas. Additionally, John emphasizes the importance of thanking others, for instance, when they retweet his tweets, and complimenting others for contributing inspiring tweets. This, in turn, may be seen to reflect the broader norms of professional networking.

Networking is particularly intense within the densely knit clusters that characterize the networks of some of the study participants. For Rina, Twitter functions as a facilitator for the nail polish network in which she is active. Apart from discussing and reviewing nail polish, the women in the network help each other get access to various products. Some nail polish brands and swatches are only sold in certain countries, so the US members of the network send nail polish to their peers in Europe, and in return receive European brands of nail polish. Participants also swap already open bottles of polish among themselves, to try out new swatches, and so forth.

Similarly, various forms of networking epitomize Twitter's role for users who are part of the cluster in which John and Betty participate. Besides reading and commenting on each other's tweets, and recommending each other on Follow Friday, the cluster participants connect with each other on LinkedIn and Facebook, typically on the so-called 'network Friday'—a Friday happening initiated from within the cluster. Many of them meet for a drink on the first Friday of every month for 'Twiday bar,' a social event where people mingle and make small talk over drinks, to mark the transition from workweek to weekend. They have a Twitter Christmas party, go to the movies, and organize an annual, international Twitter-based charity event, 'twestival.' All these events serve as opportunities to mingle with people with similar professional and personal interests in IT and media, and possibly make valuable connections for business and pleasure. Some of the participants in these events have even begun to see each other privately in small groups, and romantic relationships have resulted from Twitter-based get-togethers. Accordingly, some of the core participants in the cluster are connected across contexts and socialize on a regular basis. This implies that from a networking perspective, instrumental functions, such as professional networking may be fulfilled alongside simple togetherness with like-minded strangers, possibly over time, resulting in the development of more intimate personal relationships, like those that may emerge on personal blogs.

Hanging Out, Making Small Talk: Tweeting for Togetherness

There is a very subtle line between information sharing and pure sociability, in the archived data. Indeed, as we have just seen, togetherness and socializing often work in tandem with information sharing and networking. The line between gathering to share information and gathering to simply hang out is blurry, in the sense that both purposes are often fulfilled in the same conversation. That said, there are exchanges in the data in which Twitter's primary function is clearly to serve as a sociable space for small talk and fun, because the conversations are almost devoid of informational exchange, and entirely about fun and socializing. Consider the following exchange between Betty and Christine:

Betty: Checking my legs every 5 minutes. Can't feel them. Considering having them off before gangrene sets in.

Christine: @Betty Good to take precautions

Betty: @Christine Precautions like ski pants I'm guessing?

> Christine: @Betty Naw, I was thinking more of amputating … No legs, no gangrene
>
> Christine: @Betty amputATION just to be a #pedant
>
> Betty: @Christine No fingers, no cake. Good thing I've got big mittens on. Just such a hassle without legs and fingers …

The first tweet, by Betty, refers to her freezing at work, owing to the cold winter weather. This remark initiates a five-turn-long exchange about the possible amputation of Betty's legs, with a clear ironic distance. In other words, they have a lengthy, lively exchange on an informationally poor topic. The conversation between Betty and Christine is very illustrative of the small talk characteristic of many of the exchanges in the collected data. The informative output of such exchanges may be minimal, but the relational output is likely to be quite good. That is, these exchanges are all about sociability, social grooming, and enjoying each other's company.

Most often, the sociable encounters on Twitter center on the fast and humorous exchange, and togetherness takes a different form here, when compared to the blogs studied, in which the phatic markers of togetherness are typically explicitly, mutually supportive, at least in the women's network (recall, for example, the prevalence of 'me too' comments). Betty explicitly describes her Twitter activity in terms of fun and 'coziness,' especially in the evenings, and on Fridays:

> At work, I can sit behind the screen and simply hide and giggle half a day over it [Twitter], because, I would say, especially on Fridays the atmosphere in there is unrestrained [. . .] Themes like #dirtyfriday and other ones run, so it is usually quite funny in there, and cozy, and people are happy, clearly a different atmosphere. (Betty)

The idea that Twitter becomes more relaxed and unrestrained in the evening and on Fridays is interesting, because it identifies the context of use as important to Twitter activity. Especially on Fridays, many recurrent themes play out in the network for which John and Betty have an affinity, including '#networkfriday' and '#dirtyfriday,' where users send links to funny and sexually loaded images, videos, and writings online. In the data, another prominent example of using Twitter for simply hanging out is the recurrent Friday activity of live-tweeting *X Factor,* mimicking the act of sitting together in front of the television set, and commenting on and discussing the television show while watching. With these activities, Twitter fulfills highly relational and phatic functions as a communicative genre, whereas the instrumental and goal-oriented uses of the genre appear less important.

Perceptiveness and Intimacy

In general, the participants in the networks studied know each other primarily or exclusively through their online activities. Apart from Miriam, the participants describe their closest contacts as friendly 'acquaintances,' professional colleagues, and like-minded strangers, not personal friends. In contrast to the blog, where, over time, it becomes quite normal for participants to orient to their closest interaction partners in terms of friendship, Twitter seems to typically facilitate relationships that are more superficial. Miriam's use of Twitter is distinct, because she is the only study participant whose interaction partners on Twitter are also her closest friends. The five female users with whom she interacts most on Twitter, and who also interact with each other, are women who she initially met online through blogs (they are all bloggers), and has now come to know so well that they see each other regularly, and are in contact on a daily basis on the phone, Twitter, MSN, and their joint and secret blog, which they refer to as 'the front.' As previously noted, Miriam suffers from severe health issues that make her unable to work. For someone who is often unable to get out of bed because of the physical pain, Twitter provides an ideal communicative tool for staying in touch and in tune with her friends. In addition to her problematic physical health, she describes herself as suffering from a social phobia, meaning that she is not at all comfortable with meeting new people. Some of the women in her network also suffer from social phobias, according to Miriam, and for them, leveraging social media for developing close relationships has been and is a key motivator for their engagement with genres like Twitter. Together, these women constitute a tightly knit group, and share a relational closeness unusual on Twitter, where most users form looser connections. For these women, because they mainly communicate with each other, Twitter is a safe and familiar social space for hanging out with friends.

One way of creating this safe social space is to fence out possibly curious strangers. In Miriam's communication, perceptiveness is expected and extremely well nurtured, not only in the backchannels, but also in the public Twitter feed. First, in Miriam's feed there are conversations of a more personal nature, for instance, those regarding problems at work, health issues, and expressions of affection for one another. Secondly, there are often implicit references to private communication in Miriam's dialogues, meaning that part of the context for interpreting the tweets is omitted. For instance, this is the case in an exchange between Miriam and her close friend Iris, following a tweet in which Iris complains about her ex-boyfriend:

Miriam: @Iris So, what's up?

Iris: @Miriam Not a lot, but it's on the Front . . .

Miriam: @Iris He is such a whiner.

In response to Miriam's requests for an explanation of what is happening, Iris refers to 'the Front,' the group's secret joint blog, on which they share their personal crises, comfort each other, and gossip. Miriam then responds, noting that she has now read through Iris' explanation on the secret blog, and adding a comforting remark referring to a third person ('he'), the ex-boyfriend, who had, until now, not been mentioned in their conversation. To someone without access to 'fronten,' this sequence would make no sense, but for Iris and Miriam, who have access to the contextually relevant information, it makes perfect sense, and accomplishes important goals: social support and the demonstration of an intimate friendship. Such a highly personal communication makes it more difficult for other, less informed users to enter the conversations in Miriam's network, and this seems to be exactly the point. As she asserts, 'I use it, primarily, to communicate with my close friends, so when I write that I'm feeling bad, they will know, and they will know where to catch me, apart from on Twitter, so it is a way to announce it' (Miriam).

Miriam's close-knit group navigates seamlessly among communicative platforms and genres in their daily conversations. The continuous, informed conversations not only strengthen the relationships within this small group of core users, but also function to shut others out of the conversation. In this way, Twitter becomes a vehicle for a very exclusive group of insiders, and in and through the extremely informed conversations, Twitter is established as a kind of intimate sphere that is part of a cross-media communicative circuit, exclusively for the invited few.

> It gives a sense of closeness and intimacy, but it is a false intimacy, because it IS electronic, and it IS in writing, but I still feel that they are there for me, and I feel that it makes a difference to them that I am there for them as well. (Miriam)

For Miriam, who is often homebound, this is extremely valuable. The way her circumstances fundamentally shape her use of Twitter, and the meanings she ascribes to the genre, demonstrate how everyday life and personal needs are inextricably linked to, and color individual usage patterns in the enactment of the genre. Demonstrating perceptiveness is important on Twitter, because it may be a vehicle for, and signal of a stronger relational affiliation among the communicating parties, further marking a boundary between insiders and outsiders. In short, it contributes to creating relational closeness, and making this closeness visible to others in the network.

IMPLICATIONS FOR GENRE ANALYSIS

Twitter use comprises a range of relatively well-established genre conventions. These are invoked across profiles, regardless of the individual purposes for using Twitter, and the various configurations of personal networks on Twitter. Norms of immediacy, responsiveness, orienting to and developing stronger affiliations with what I have called the 'relevant others,' and so forth appear generally adopted in participants' genre enactments, and contribute to creating a more stable—and less uncertain—expression of Twitter as a communicative genre, than I had initially expected. Hence, the hypothesis that short-form genres of social media per se involve greater genre instability has not been confirmed.

Still, as a communicative genre, Twitter displays a strong fluctuation, when compared to blogs. This fluctuation particularly involves the thematic orientation—shifting types of statements are interwoven in the continued stream of tweets, even on individual profiles. Furthermore, as we have seen, ordinary users adopt Twitter as a software genre according to a range of specific personal or professional needs and purposes in everyday life, corresponding to these varied thematic orientations. In this sense, Twitter appears to be a highly dynamic genre.

Given that topics shift rapidly, other defining parameters of genre become central in providing genre stability. For instance, the consistent stylistic conventions—the use of the hashtag, the informal and humorous tone, the sense of spontaneity, and so forth—may counterbalance the topical fluctuation and provide fixity to the genre. Moreover, the analysis suggests that the temporal organization of Twitter, as well as the network dynamics stabilize Twitter as a communicative genre, by constraining in different ways what communications are actually appropriate and meaningful. Extending the theoretical implications from the blog analysis, the analysis of Twitter suggests three major contributions to the genre perspective in social media analysis.

First, the prominence of stylistic conventions in defining competent enactments of genre and thus creating genre stability on Twitter suggests that the relative importance of the dimensions of the genre analysis framework may vary in terms of their explanatory strength, depending on the social media object of study. Hence, on other social media than Twitter, negotiations in terms of thematic orientation, composition or pragmatic uses may play a more prominent role than stylistics in shaping the genre. For instance, as we saw with the blog analysis, stylistic conventions largely followed thematic ones, indicating a lesser importance of style vis-à-vis thematic (and compositional and pragmatic) genre expectations and conventions on blogs.

Second, networking and relationality are central components in the enactment and negotiation of social media as communicative genres. As already suggested by the blog analysis, the Twitter analysis underscores how networks of affiliation create relational pressures to 'fit in' certain clusters of users on social media. Along these lines, I have further expounded on how the communicative purposes facilitate and reflect different types of relationality within the network, depending on whether participants know each other solely through their online exchanges, or are connected across contexts in daily life. Although the role of networks in creating pressures for certain preferred enactments of genre has been documented in this and the previous chapter, it remains to be clarified if and how the difference demonstrated between types of networks on Twitter and blogs travels to other types of social media, for instance, those that build on networks of already-existing relationships among participants.

Third, so far I have studied social media genres that are 'pure' in the sense that they have a simple and streamlined software setup, and that are relatively niche-oriented and have a limited user base. These characteristics combined possibly add to the genre stability found in the empirical analyses of blogging and Twitter. One way to further clarity these points is by asking whether genre dynamics and instability can be seen to a greater extent in social media that cater to a broader and more diverse user base, and that have multi-functional software features, such as Facebook which incorporates and mixes a number of 'pure' genres, including microblogging, chat and email. This will be a task for the final case study in Chapter 6, on Facebook.

CHAPTER SUMMARY

As a communicative genre, Twitter is characterized by networked connections and conversations, a fast-paced, continuous flow of utterances united in a stream, and immediacy, denoting the pressure towards 'here and now' participation among other activities in everyday life. Spontaneity, directness, and rapid, lively exchanges underline the notion of flow and sense of immediacy in Twitter conversations, and suggest an affinity with conventions of oral small talk, as well as synchronous genres of social media such as online chat. Twitter is adopted for a myriad of purposes, often at the junction of professional interest, need, or curiosity, on the one hand, and sociability, on the other. As a communicative genre, Twitter continuously oscillates between instrumental functions and an augmented form of phatic communication.

When compared to blogging, the brevity of postings, the near-synchronicity, and the networked structure of Twitter do indeed nurture a highly dynamic and fluctuating communicative environment, but not necessarily an unstable one. An unstable genre 'in the making' would presumably display more uncertainty in its norms and interaction patterns, and probably more conflict, owing to unclear conventions of participation. In contrast, the participants, and their interaction partners appear to unproblematically navigate the chaotic communicative Twitter environment with a clear sense of the purposes and meanings of the genre in their everyday lives.

NOTES

1. The six participants have all granted me permission to use their data for the present study. All participants are pseudonymized.
2. The 'tweet' function resembles the 'status update' on Facebook. Whereas on Twitter, the tweet is the core element, on Facebook the status update is only one functionality among many, cf. Chapter 6.
3. The number of followers should be taken with a grain of salt because there are many spam-followers (such as porn bots and the like) on Twitter.

4. Along similar lines, Raymond Williams (1974) described television as a cultural form characterized by the organization of *programming* as a sequential 'flow,' with a strategic view to keeping the audience tuned in to a given channel, and, at the same time, by the experiential 'flow' in which television *viewing* as a social activity is organized and rendered meaningful in everyday life.

5. In their study of the uses of the @ sign, Honeycutt and Herring (2009) found that @ is mostly used as a marker of addressivity, to facilitate conversation (almost 91%). Other functions of the @ sign are to refer to someone, as part of an emoticon, as part of an email address, and as an abbreviation of 'at,' to mark the location of the author.

6. Since the study, Twitter has launched a new version of the website, including a threading feature that allows easier conversation tracking. By pressing a button in the individual tweet, the conversation of which it is part unfolds in a sequence of tweets.

7. The Twitter stream represented in the excerpt is simplified and artificially coherent, compared to how it appears for the user on the site, owing to the archiving technique, which organizes the captured tweets in chronological order.

8. Using Twitter for live-chat while watching television is quite common. In Denmark, *X Factor* 2010 was the first major event to be covered by Twitter, to a great extent because the judges and one of the participants were very active on Twitter during the show. This generated a lot of traffic to their profiles, a lot of discussion about *X Factor* among Danish Twitter users, and many new users joined Twitter.

9. The direct message system in Twitter is a backchannel in which users who have a reciprocal relationship may communicate one-on-one, as in email.

10. As on a blog, the tone tends to go in tandem with the topic of conversation. When the subject is more serious, the tone becomes more serious and diplomatic. For instance, this may be seen to be the case the few times that participants discuss politically sensitive and controversial topics, and end their opinionated statement with 'IMHO' (i.e., In My Humble Opinion) (e.g., John, when discussing a case in which a Danish citizen has been turned over to the American authorities, accused of smuggling drugs).

11. For an analysis of how these celebrities relate to their fans on Twitter, see Marwick & boyd (2011).

6 Facebook
Genre Mixing and Portability

Of all social media, Facebook is the most internationally diffused and used service with one billion users worldwide as of 2012. In Denmark, GemiusAudience's log-based measurement registered about 2,800,000 unique Danish users of Facebook in April 2012, a figure that is largely consistent with Statistics Denmark's representative survey of internet use in Denmark (Danmarks Statistik, 2012). That is, more than half of Danish internet users access Facebook on at least a monthly basis. Furthermore, Facebook by far outranks other social media in terms of the time spent on-site per month: on average, each unique user spent almost 8 hours on Facebook in April 2012, according to GemiusAudience. These figures have been stable over the past couple of years.

Since its introduction in Denmark in 2006 and until its mainstream breakthrough from 2008 onward, younger as well as older Danes have appropriated Facebook. Whereas other social media primarily find their audience in the younger parts of the population (the 15- to 40-year-olds), Facebook appears to be quite mainstream across age groups, although Facebook use still declines with age. With other classic demographics such as sex and education, Facebook shows no significant differences regarding who is on and who is not. A similar pattern is evident in, for instance, the US (Hampton, Goulet, Marlow, & Rainie, 2012; Vitak & Ellison, 2013). The mass adoption of Facebook and the greater heterogeneity in the user base, when compared to other social media, could lead to more confusion and less agreement across user groups on basic understandings of Facebook in terms of communicative genre conventions and expectations.

For the present purposes of further refining the genre-based framework for social media analysis, there are other reasons than its sheer size and diffusion for examining if, and if so how, genre norms on Facebook are dynamic or stable. Facebook was chosen as the third, complementary case for three interrelated reasons:

First, unlike blogs and Twitter, Facebook represents a 'mixed genre.' At the software level, Facebook draws together and integrates stand-alone genres such as chat, discussion groups, status updates, photo-sharing, games, and so on. As Vitak and Ellison (2013) note, Facebook's communicative functionalities enable the broadcasting of content to the entire network (e.g., status updates) as well as more directed forms of communication (e.g., private messages and group communication). This poses challenges to the genre-based framework in two ways. Theoretically, the integration of genres in one service calls for a clarification of how Facebook can meaningfully be conceptualized and analyzed in terms of genre. Empirically, it is not evident that all these very different communicative functionalities rely on the same genre conventions. One may expect to find either that the wealth of features confuse users' understandings of what constitutes competent enactments of Facebook, or that the uses of the various functionalities are organized according to a conventionally established division of labor that may stabilize the common understanding of Facebook as a communicative genre. Hence, Facebook as a case may test the elasticity and possible shortcomings of the genre perspective.

Second, unlike blogging and Twitter, Facebook is based on the articulation of networks of affiliation to already known others. That is, the relationships that are constituted and negotiated through Facebook are of a different kind than on Twitter and blogs, where we have seen networks between likeminded strangers to establish around common interests (who may possibly over time develop personal attachment and commitment). On Facebook, the often pre-established relationships with others are typically rooted in personal history: that users went to school with one another, are colleagues or family and thus got to know one another not necessarily because they shared an interest. As suggested by the blog and Twitter analyses, network dynamics play a crucial role in the ongoing negotiation of genre. Examining a genre that relies on different network logics might assist in clarifying how network dynamics affect communicative practices, genre negotiations, on social media.

Third, Facebook represents a social media service that has experienced many changes at the software level, both in terms of expanding the core set of communicative features, frequent adjustments of the interface design, and seamless integration with external applications (such as travel, casual gaming, and self-monitoring applications; e.g., Brügger, 2013). For example, while originally absent from the service, photo-sharing has become a key functionality on Facebook, thus emphasizing visual dimensions of communication on Facebook. With the constant adjustments at the software level, Facebook is arguably in constant flux. This may fuel user insecurity of norms for appropriate communication on the site, and destabilize the user experience of Facebook (McLaughlin and Vitak, 2012: 300). On top, the recent mass diffusion of smartphones allows users to access social media services, including Facebook, via their mobile phones and tablets while on the move. In Denmark, more than half of the adult population regularly accessed the internet from smartphones in 2012, and following this trend, social media too have become increasingly portable (Humphreys, 2013). Examining the subtle shift towards accessing Facebook via the smartphone offers a useful entry point for probing how genres may change over time, and what role platforms and portability might play in this process.

In sum, using Facebook as a final case study, the chapter discusses the wider implications of genre mixing, pre-established relationships, and portability for the pragmatic genre perspective and its analytic power.

EMPIRICAL METHODOLOGY AND DATA

The empirical genre study design for Facebook is different from the two previous case studies, which rely on a combination of in-depth interviews and textual archives. For the Facebook study, no textual archive data were collected, and so it relies more heavily on data gathered through interviews with users. I decided not to archive Facebook data, given the focus of this study on genre mixing and the drawing together of self-contained genres on a single social media service. Hence, one pressing question for archiving would be what to archive, and what to leave out. It would certainly not be satisfactory to archive only data from the public profile elements (i.e. the profile page, newsfeed, and Facebook wall), as this would not help enlighten the analysis of how the different communicative features of Facebook play together and are interwoven in ordinary users' everyday engagement with the service. For that, I would need access to participants' chat logs and private messages, as well as communication from closed groups and games that participants are part of. This, in turn, would raise a number of serious privacy concerns.

Instead, I opted for a strictly interview-based design, extending the interview guides from the blog and Twitter studies with questions regarding the nature of networked relationships on Facebook, the visual dimension, the use of Facebook on PC's vis-à-vis mobile devices, and the experienced change of Facebook over time. As part of the interviews, I further included an introductory session in which participants were asked to give me a guided tour on their Facebook profiles, to get a sense of their content-sharing activities and the communicative practices linked to different functionalities offered by Facebook. The inclusion of a Facebook 'tour' in the methodological setup was inspired by Bakardjieva's qualitative research on the internet in everyday life (Bakardjieva, 2005). These tours serve to clarify and to some extent verify the practices that users claim for themselves in the interviews. Because of the methodological design, the present case study does not allow for detailed analysis of actual communications, their organization, and so forth, as was the case in Chapters 4 and 5. Instead, the interviews prompt a focus on the voiced understandings of genre and genre mixing, as well as participants' changing experiences of Facebook over time.

The study draws on semi-structured interviews with six Facebook users. Participants were sampled purposively, based on the same criteria as for the two other case studies. Thus, participants use Facebook to varying degrees and for different purposes in everyday life. In addition, all participants have a smartphone from which they access Facebook. The sample consists of three women (Anita, Gwen, and Mandy) and three men (Caleb, Luke, and Max), all aged 25 to 40 years, with different educational backgrounds and geographic locations in Denmark.[1]

The empirical analysis is structured around the four dimensions of genre, consistent with the two previous case analyses. The analysis follows a comparative strategy, that is, I focus on eliciting and discussing similarities and differences between Facebook, on the one hand, and Twitter and personal blogs, on the other hand, according to the key constituents of the analytic framework of genre. Before diving into the empirical analysis, I present a brief analysis of Facebook in terms of communicative functionalities at the software level to fuel a theoretical discussion of how Facebook fits with and challenges the framework of social media as communicative genres.

FACEBOOK: A MATTER OF GENRE MIXING?

Facebook is typically considered to be a social network site, a subcategory of social media. Social network sites are roughly defined as web-based services centered on the construction of individual profiles and the articulation of networks of affiliation with other users within a bounded system (boyd & Ellison, 2007). The individual profile contains the personal information that users choose to share: full names, birthday, work or educational affiliation, hometown, political leaning, cultural tastes, whether one is single or in a relationship and so on. Profiles are public by default, that is, visible to anyone on Facebook, but users can adjust their privacy settings to limit the accessibility and visibility of their profiles.

When Facebook was launched in 2004, it was conceived as a simple personal directory only for college students and based solely on personal profiles and the articulation of 'friends lists,' although the Facebook Wall was implemented shortly hereafter as a functionality that allows others in the network to contribute content, for instance in the form of comments, to the individual's profile site. However, over time, Facebook has incorporated a range of other features and thereby dramatically expanded the scope and utility of the service, perhaps most forcefully since its opening to the public in 2006. These include both commercial developments, and additional means for personal communication. For instance, Facebook now allows company profiles of which users can become *fans* but not friends, and the establishment of groups centered on core themes to which users can subscribe or become members. Following the growing success of services such as Twitter in 2006, Facebook added status update and newsfeed features similar to the core features of Twitter—likely as a measure of protection from competition. Similarly, Facebook has incorporated other forms of personal communication including chat, blogging (in the form of 'Facebook Notes,' now shut down again), email, and voice calls (in collaboration with Skype).

Moreover, the boundaries between Facebook and the surrounding web have become more and more porous. In 2007 Facebook Platform opened for external parties to develop software add-ons to Facebook (e.g., games); in 2008, it became possible to import links, videos and so on from the surrounding web to Facebook, and with the introduction of Facebook Connect in 2010, Facebook is now embedded in other websites. For instance, by clicking a Facebook button on a news website users can feed a link to the story onto their Facebook Wall (for a detailed history of Facebook, see Brügger, 2013). With the extensive presence of Facebook on the surrounding web, and the inflow of links from the surrounding web on Facebook, it is perhaps more accurate to consider Facebook a web portal, as suggested by Rainie and Wellman (2012: 185). If we view Facebook as a portal that includes, interweaves and mixes a wealth of communicative genres, the main challenge of applying the pragmatic genre-based framework is to clarify how the interplay of genres can be studied empirically, and possibly delimit relevant points of departure for such a study.

From a personal communications perspective, the two initial ingredients of Facebook, the personal profile and the network articulation, remain central, along with the personalized front page that the individual user enters when logging on to Facebook, which displays the users' newsfeed, along with friend requests, personal messages, groups that the user is a member of, the chat function and so forth. These elements are the core vehicles for interpersonal engagement and socializing on Facebook, and therefore necessary starting points for an empirical analysis of how Facebook is used, negotiated and experienced in the everyday lives of ordinary users.

Even when delimiting the focus to the communicative functionalities associated with personal communication, these functionalities are typically applied for different communicative purposes, with associated genre expectations and conventions. For example, norms may vary depending on whether communication plays out in public features (such as the Wall) or the private channels (such as personal messages and chat), and whether communication is carried out one-to-one, one-to-many or many-to-many (McLaughlin & Vitak, 2012). With the integration of previously existing 'pure' genres such as chat and photo-sharing, their communicative norms enter the genre negotiation on Facebook and possibly destabilize users' shared understandings of the service.

Grasping the at once integrated and differentiated uses of these communicative features requires talking to the users about not only their daily usage patterns but also how they see and make use of the diverse communicative functionalities on Facebook, and how these complement, overlap, and possibly blend into each other in communicative practice. Hence, the assessment of whether and, if so, how Facebook represents a case of genre mixing must rely on users' own practices on and sensemaking of the site.

The focus of the present analysis is on what participants identify as the key functionalities of Facebook: the newsfeed and the status update, and the genre expectations and negotiations voiced in their accounts of using these functions. Hence, it is the public parts of Facebook that seem to matter the most to participants. Private channels are drawn into the analysis as a contrast to the status update and newsfeed, whereas games, quizzes, and so on are not discussed, as these communicative functionalities appear to be almost absent in the participants' use of Facebook.

As a final note, the ongoing changes of Facebook at the software level, and the fact that these often prompt readjustments of users' understandings of Facebook, have implications for the explanatory power of the empirical analysis. Although I strive to emphasize elements of genre adjustment and change over time, the empirical analysis first examines a 2012 snapshot of Facebook, the key communicative practices of a specific group of users, and the meanings they ascribe to Facebook in the course of everyday life.

CREATING PROFILES AND PERSONAL NETWORKS: CONTEXT COLLAPSE ON FACEBOOK

One of the main differences between Facebook and Twitter and blogs is the composition of the network. Facebook principally encourages users to connect to people they already know. As will be evident from the analysis in this section, this often involves bringing together relatively large and diverse friend networks on Facebook. Hence, relationships that used to be articulated and maintained independently of one another in different contexts of daily social life are now brought together on one social platform. This fact has been described in terms of *context collapse* as a general communicative challenge (Lewis & West, 2009; Marwick & boyd, 2011; Vitak & Ellison, 2013). In this section, I examine how the participants manage their Facebook networks and the associated context collapse to elicit a basic understanding of how the relationship between profile holder and audience is negotiated on the service. This, in turn, provides a starting point for identifying key communicative practices and challenges for appropriately enacting Facebook.

The participants' histories in terms of joining and using Facebook differ. Some of them were early adopters and created profiles in 2007 when Facebook began to receive public attention in Denmark, or even earlier. The early adopters among the participants—Luke, Gwen, Caleb, and to some extent Max—are characterized either by a strong interest in and long-term engagement with computers, games and gadgets that prompt a fundamental curiosity towards new forms of computer-mediated communication, or by a fairly large network of friends and acquaintances outside Denmark. For instance, Caleb who lived in Canada for a year during high school, joined Facebook just before returning to Canada for a visit in 2005. He found Facebook a practical tool for re-establishing contact with old school mates, and for coordinating appointments with them while in Canada. Similarly, Gwen signed up for Facebook upon moving to Berlin in 2007 with the intention to use it to find a job and people to socialize with while there. By joining Facebook groups of Danes in the city, she was able to establish a network in Berlin. Only later, when her friends in Denmark started joining the service, did Facebook become a tool for keeping contact with existing relations. The late adopters—Mandy and Anita—describe their general attitude toward new technological fads as skeptic and were reluctant to join Facebook when they first heard of the service. Eventually, when Facebook was more of a mainstream service in Denmark, they did create profiles, apparently after pressure from their friends, colleagues, or family members who were already on Facebook.

Like Twitter, Facebook is structurally built upon the establishment of networks between user profiles, with the important difference that Facebook relationships are bidirectional. To become Facebook friends, one party has to send the other a friend request that the other party must accept. This means that, in contrast to social media such as blogs and Twitter, users typically know the people in their Facebook network in advance:

> There is nobody that I have never met. All of my Facebook friends are people that I have had something to do with in my life [. . .] but there are many of them that I don't see anymore. . . not that it is a conscious choice, but because our life trajectories have taken different directions after high school and so on. (Caleb)

The same holds true for the other participants. Hence, connections on Facebook locate the individual user within multiple, often overlapping networks and relationships: close personal friends and family, colleagues, old school mates, and other acquaintances. This description of Facebook as a communicative genre for maintaining pre-existing relationships is confirmed by several international studies (Ellison, Steinfield, & Lampe, 2007; McLaughlin & Vitak, 2012; Rainie & Wellman, 2012).

Being connected to people one knows from elsewhere has implications for the negotiations of genre on Facebook. Specifically, it means that participants' communication on Facebook often follows pre-existing communicative norms from—and feeds into—other contexts in which the same relationships are articulated and maintained. Communicative conventions are thus colored by not only the software and the participants' understandings of the genre, but also by the pre-established practices and norms guiding the diverse pre-existing relationships that are interwoven on Facebook.

Whereas participants' friend networks vary in size, they all have more than a hundred friends on Facebook. Although this appears to be a general tendency on Facebook,[2] the large networks of the study participants probably also have to do with the relatively broad diffusion of Facebook in Denmark: there are simply many pre-existing connections available on Facebook.

In the context of building networks of affiliation on Facebook, several participants mention that their activities and norms have changed over time. As Mandy explains: 'To begin with, I became friends with everyone I knew and had known, and whom I had once attended kindergarten with and all that' (Mandy). Departing from this practice of collecting as many friends as possible, participants report that they now tend to actively screen and sort their Facebook relationships, so that their personal networks grow at a much slower pace. Furthermore, participants occasionally delete existing Facebook friends that they no longer have relation to and may hardly remember, that is, Facebook friendships that are not meaningful for them to maintain. Anita, for instance, claims that it is not relevant for her to be Facebook friends with someone she has 'played volleyball with for six months seven years ago' (Anita). Thus, building personal networks on Facebook is no longer driven by a need for expanding the number of connections, but about making friends and maintaining relationships with fellow users with whom the participants have more history, more shared experience. This suggests how the common understanding of Facebook as a communicative genre has changed over time, delineating Facebook to first evolve around those people that matter in some way for the participants in their current lives.

One of the study participants, Luke, actively and continuously tries to groom his Facebook network so that he only has 150 friends. Hence, when a new friend joins his Facebook network, someone else has to be eliminated. In contrast to the other participants who will only delete someone if their relationship with the person is very limited, Luke sorts his network without making this kind of personal judgment. Instead, Luke's criterion for deleting is the activity level of the individuals in his Facebook network: he deletes someone if they are not active, or if their activities are invisible to him, for instance, because of them setting up privacy measures to control who can see their profile and status updates. Hence for Luke, engagement with Facebook as a communicative genre not only implies the articulation of an existing relationship through Facebook friendship, but also that the relationship comes alive on Facebook through sharing and the possibility of mutual exchange through communication.

Facebook seems to be particularly well suited for keeping updated on one's personal connections. However, given that participants have several hundred Facebook friends, they do not keep equally in touch with and are not equally interested in everyone else in their personal networks. In the interviews, two types of relationships were described as the most important ones on Facebook: close friends and others who already play an active part in the participants' everyday lives, and 'distant' or old friends and acquaintances with whom the participants seldom communicate directly but with whom they wish to maintain a peripheral or sporadic contact. Some participants particularly emphasize the importance of being able to follow the big events in distant friends' lives: 'it is fun to be able to snoop on people's lives' (Max). Because any user by default receives updates from their Facebook friends,

Facebook offers the opportunity to keep a constant, ambient accessibility and peripheral awareness of the personal network (Ling, 2008: 121; Miller, 2008). Ambient accessibility refers to the fact that the increasing use of digital media facilitates an experience of being 'always on' (Baron, 2008)—always within reach of relevant information as well as communication with our social connections. Peripheral awareness, in turn, may be considered a consequence of our connectivity through digital media—it denotes the possibility to—at our convenience—tap into the flow of communication produced by our networks of affiliation on sites such as Facebook to keep ourselves up to date on matters of importance to individuals in the network and the network as such. The awareness created is peripheral, because it does not per se involve engaging in a communicative exchange with others. We can effortlessly receive updates from them simply by monitoring their communication at a distance. Ambient accessibility to and peripheral awareness of one another may enhance the relationship because 'it amplifies the experience of here and now' (Anita), and by doing this supports a sense of connectedness and mutual orientation in real time.

The participants also use Facebook to follow their close friends' daily lives from the sideline. The close friendships are groomed in a more active and deliberate fashion, namely, through actual conversation on Facebook. Indeed, the interviews reveal that communicative exchanges on Facebook primarily take place between close friends, in the form of coordinating appointments, organizing events, or simply daily chitchat in status updates and comments, as well as the chat function. For Mandy, who is on maternity leave, Facebook is practical for everyday communication with friends:

> It is a fast way of communicating with some of my friends because then I can write an update [. . .] for them and they don't have to answer right away, but maybe they will answer in three hours, and then it becomes a conversation anyway, or communication that does not tie us up as if you're on the phone and then the baby starts to cry. (Mandy)

Here, Mandy suggests that Facebook compensates for her being homebound with a baby and caters to her daily social need for contact with the people she would usually talk to and perhaps see more often. Similarly, Anita sees Facebook, and especially the Facebook wall, as a cozy space for socializing with her colleagues, asserting that they do not discuss work on Facebook but simply 'use it amongst colleagues to have a laugh' (Anita). These accounts suggest that Facebook is appropriated to cater in an easy manner for participants' social need for ongoing contact to specific others in everyday life—others with whom participants may be expected to communicate through other media as well. Hence, along these lines Facebook is part of a media multiplex (Haythornthwaite, 2005) that interweaves frequent communications between close ties in and across media in everyday life.

In comparison with the social presence created by bloggers through frequent commenting activity, and the sense of immediacy created on Twitter by the norm of opting in and out of the communicative flow in the here and -now, the continuous social contact between close friends on Facebook is better unpacked by the concept of *connected presence*, as originally developed as a concept to describe the constant contact family members and close friends keep throughout the day on their mobile phones, which enable them to be within constant reach and available for conversation with one another (Licoppe, 2004). Licoppe (2004) defines connected presence as a form of relationship management 'in which the (physically) absent party renders himself or herself present by multiplying mediated communication gestures up to the point where co-present interactions and mediated communication seem woven in a seamless web' (Licoppe, 2004: 135). Multiple media, including Facebook, may be part of this constant contact, which not only serves to coordinate activities, but also sometimes also simply demonstrates affection, by signaling mutuality and ambient accessibility. As is evident from Mandy's quote above, one of the key strengths of Facebook in this respect is the fact that communication is asynchronous—in contrast to Twitter's near-synchronous temporal structure. That is, Facebook adds to the experience of connected presence without demanding the here-and-now attention of users.

In sum, the users' focus on the maintenance of existing personal relationships points to Facebook as having a fairly agreed communicative purpose for the study participants: In part, facilitating peripheral awareness of and contact to an expanded network of peers through the enabling of mutual monitoring at a distance. In part, supporting a sense of connected presence, by enhancing everyday communication between friends and acquaintances who interact in other contexts as well. Thereby, Facebook seems to be an integral part of the mundane communications and relational maintenance work in the participants' daily activities. Some of them even claim that they would feel left out and fear missing out on something if they did not use Facebook.

Connected presence and the creation of peripheral awareness of one another are framed by the specific network logic of Facebook: The context collapse on Facebook means that participants' communications with friends through, for example, status updates and wall posts can be seen by their families and colleagues as well. Furthermore, these audiences can intervene in specific communicative exchanges between friends and vice versa. That is, Facebook users must attend to multiple audiences when communicating (Donath & boyd, 2004; Livingstone, 2008), without knowing exactly who in the Facebook audience might actually be reading their public messages (Bernstein, Bakshy, Burke, & Karrer, 2013). The overlap or context collapse between previously separate networks entails new opportunities and constraints for communication on Facebook and probably plays a vital role for the development of communicative conventions and genre expectations on Facebook. These are the focus of the next sections.

ORGANIZING FACEBOOK USE IN THE FLOW OF DAILY LIFE

As we have seen, Facebook is profoundly interwoven in the users' webs of affiliation in daily life. In this section, I examine the social organizing principles that underpin participants' understandings of Facebook as a communicative genre to probe how Facebook attains significance for them in the course of everyday life. Specifically, I expound on how the daily routines of checking Facebook reflect compositional genre expectations concerning the actual communicative contributions vis-à-vis merely reading the newsfeed and being accessible, and analyze these expectations in light of the fact that Facebook—in contrast to blogging and Twitter—is centered on the maintenance of pre-existing relationships.

The study participants all report using Facebook several times a day, primarily through the Facebook application on their smartphones. Typically, their visits to Facebook are relatively brief and consist mainly of scrolling through the newsfeed to see what other users in their networks have posted.

> I read . . . login at least a couple of times every day just to . . . let the finger run over the screen to see what funny things people write [. . .] Every once in a while I click on a video, somebody who has posted a video [. . .] just to kill a bit of time. (Caleb)

Participants describe how they run through their newsfeeds for as long as they have time or until they reach the point where they started their previous visit on Facebook. The frequent logins to Facebook to check the newsfeed are considered a routine that serves the main function of passing time. Participants check Facebook while waiting in a line or for the bus, or when needing a short break from other activities, at work or at home. Max, for instance, uses Facebook to 'kill time' at work: 'when I am on telephone duty and no telephones are ringing, and I cannot pull myself up to start doing something else' (Max). Participants also check Facebook at home, 'when I need five minutes of peace and calm in the bathroom' (Caleb), 'when the TV commercials are on' (Anita), or in similar types of pauses from the practical organizing and passing of everyday life. Common to all the participants is that their frequent—for some constant—checking of Facebook must not take too long or dictate other activities. Facebook is considered a secondary activity to other daily business. 'It is not important, or, I don't feel that it is important to keep track of everything that is happening. It is entertainment, primarily' (Max), or as Anita frames it, 'it is not as if it controls my life and that I have to go home [to check Facebook]' (Anita). Max further elaborates on how he sees Facebook as an alternative to reading online news or checking out videos on YouTube, things he would otherwise do in his breaks. Hence, the frequent logins appears to be less motivated by the need to keep up with the fast-paced development of the newsfeed and the associated risk of missing out on something, than it is about creating and filling out small pauses in the everyday.

The participants' self-reported practices concerning the use of the newsfeed suggest a common understanding of Facebook as a genre that first and foremost serves purposes of entertainment and time-passing, rather than a genre that evolves around deep personal communication with friends, where one would expect a greater commitment to keep one another posted at any time. Users can opt in and out of the stream of activities on Facebook at their own convenience in the course of daily life—somewhat like what Twitter users described in Chapter 5. Considering Facebook's specific network configuration centered on maintaining pre-existing relationships, it is perhaps a bit surprising that in comparison with blogs and Twitter, there is no remarkable difference between these genres and Facebook in the experienced obligation to be present and committed to communication on a general level.

The intersubjectively shared understanding of Facebook as a time-passing activity seems to change when considering participants' own communicative exchanges on Facebook. Some of the study participants emphasize the personal notifications as a primary motivator for the frequent logins on Facebook: 'I check whether anybody has posted anything that I am part of' (Gwen). Facebook creates personal notifications to a user when, for instance, there has been new activities in a group in which the user is a member, new comments are posted in a thread to which the user has previously contributed, the user is invited to an event or has received a personal message. By default, notifications are placed behind an icon on the user's Facebook front page, but by adjusting their smartphone settings users can have notifications pushed to their Facebook applications. Luke and Gwen, who consider personal notifications to be a core attraction of Facebook, have set their Facebook applications to notify them this way, so a pop-up message appears on their smartphones whenever they have new notifications. In addition, they assert that they will typically login to Facebook to check it as soon as possible after receiving the notification. The practice of letting oneself be pushed toward logging on to Facebook suggests that a genre expectation of commitment, availability for communicating, and mutual social presence exists on Facebook, after all, at least in connection with the users' own communicative activities and contributions. Once engaged in a conversation, the user is more inclined to feel obliged to follow through and stay available for listening and possibly responding when others contribute to the same conversation, or otherwise try to contact the user. Although this to some extent marks a contrast to Twitter (where users only feel obliged to stay in conversation insofar as they have the time, cf. Chapter 5), it clearly resembles the communicative practices and expectations of presence as embodied in the norms of responsivity among the personal bloggers. In sum, the convention of responding, staying available and attentive when having entered a conversation seems to cut across social media.

Although participants log on to Facebook several times a day, most of them rarely post anything themselves on the site. This corresponds with Hampton and colleagues' recent survey and logfile-based study of Facebook in the US, which found that the typical Facebook user receives more from Facebook than she gives back through content contributions (Hampton et al., 2012). Hence, there appears to be a difference between Facebook, on the one hand, and personal blogs and Twitter, on the other, in terms of practices concerning the frequency of contributing. A lesser pressure to contribute content on Facebook could be attributed not only to the commonly voiced idea of Facebook as a site for entertainment and 'goofing off' (Wagman, 2010), but also to the service being more mainstream and its users signing up not to miss out on anything. In contrast, especially Twitter appears to attract a niche audience of tech-savvy power users, who might for that reason be expected to have stronger motives for active engagement.

The most active study participants, Luke and Mandy, post something a couple of times every week. Mandy estimates that she currently posts more often because: 'I am at home and I don't have to work all day. I go on Facebook more often and write or post a photo more often than I would when the working everyday returns' (Mandy). Her current situation is unusual. Being on parental leave involves having the access points to Facebook—laptop, iPad, and iPhone—readily available all the time, something that she is not used to when at work as an ergotherapist. Hence, her posting more actively is likely a result of her special current everyday circumstances.

The remaining participants report posting once a month or even more seldom. The limited contribution of content leads Caleb, who occasionally contributes content by uploading a photograph, to describe himself as 'a poor Facebook user' (Caleb). The limited activity in terms of status updates, photo uploads and so on may, at least in part, be seen as a confirmation of the baseline understanding of Facebook as no-strings-attached time-passing, in the sense that participants do not want to commit themselves constantly to communicative exchanges. However, it can also be seen to reflect a genre norm of not being too active and thereby overloading other users' feeds with constant updates, as we have also seen is the case with Twitter. As Anita describes it: 'in the beginning people would update about anything, and those who do that now, I have shut them down because I don't want to spend my time on reading that they have been to the supermarket' (Anita). The same norm is expressed by Gwen who writes updates 'more often inside my head than in practice' (Gwen). That is, Gwen often has ideas for a Facebook phrase but refrains from posting it out of a conscious choice of not being a very active contributor. 'I think it is a bit naff, or I think many users become too. . . . eager to stage themselves. I don't like that very much' (Gwen). She continues: 'If I wrote it for me, I would probably write much more, I think, if it were to function as my personal diary or reflection of the things I do' (Gwen). What Gwen expresses here is a genre convention that participants should restrain themselves, and write in a way that is thought through and relevant to their friend networks. 'It has to be worth it [. . .] it is always with a view to what others might find interesting' (Luke). Interestingly, in this respect, Luke finds this to be a key change in his Facebook use over time. He used to post much more often, typically several times a day, and it mattered 'that I could write in the here and now. It made it more intuitive' (Luke). He ascribes his change of behavior over time to having less relevant things to say.

Together, the study participants' own posting behavior and their distaste for massive updating from others convey a norm of limiting communication to relevant matters. The carefully dosed active participation on Facebook in the form of status updates, wall posts and so on may been seen to be about sparing oneself as well as one's audience from the constant commitment to communication. In the practical negotiation of genre, Facebook implies no obligation to post frequent updates, as seen on the personal blog (cf. Chapter 4). This contrasts somewhat to the Facebook software and interface, which actually encourages frequent updates. The status update feature invites sharing content in the here and now by asking the user 'what's on your mind?' a phrase that is quite similar to the one that frames tweets. The fact that users seem to restrain themselves from constantly updating demonstrates the power of communicative practice in shaping social media as communicative genres, and challenging the genre expectations inscribed by the service provider in the software.

Although the convention of communicating only relevant matters appears to be strong among the study participants, it may be challenged by the practices of other user groups on Facebook. At the same time, it is remarkable that such a genre convention is voiced in all three case studies, thus suggesting that adherence to criteria of relevance is a more general convention for social media use.

Summing up the compositional genre expectations expressed by the study participants, it may be argued that, on the one hand, given the users' frequent logins to their Facebook accounts there is an implicit convention of daily use, and thereby, indirectly an expectation that users are accessible and present on Facebook. On the other hand, this convention is not regulated very actively, for instance, through the constant maintenance of daily contact between participants in updates, comments, and so on.

The absence of demands for frequent communicative exchanges could be based in relationships to the relevant others to which the individual user orients on Facebook: old, distant friends and close friends. Concerning the relationship to distant friends (e.g., old school mates), with whom participants just wish to keep a peripheral contact, it is not obvious that constant contact would be preferable. Outside Facebook, it is not the norm to keep in touch on a regular and relatively frequent basis. Rather, the relationship is revived at rare, special occasions such as high school reunions. Hence, the limited contact on Facebook mirrors broader norms for the kind and degree of contact of such relationships to the distant network.

Concerning the close relationships, these are typically not primarily maintained through Facebook, and thus are not dependent on Facebook. Close friends, family, and colleagues keep contact in other ways in everyday life—through phone calls, text messages, and face-to-face communication.

Hence, for these relationships, Facebook is just one more contact point, a further enhancement of an already vibrant friendship—and therefore not something that requires constant commitment to keep the relationship stable and close.

THE DIVISION OF LABOR: MANAGING MULTIPLE FUNCTIONALITIES FOR COMMUNICATION

The commonly voiced understanding of Facebook as first and foremost about reading, entertainment and keeping updated on one another at a distance through the newsfeed, and secondly as a communication channel for close relationships through small talk in status updates and so on, seems to be widely consolidated among participants. However, considering the multiple communicative functionalities of Facebook, it is not evident how goofing off, small talk, and peripheral awareness map onto other aspects of Facebook. This section seeks to clarify if there are different expectations and uses tied to other communicative functionalities—one-to-one, one-to-many, and many-to-many—offered by Facebook. That is, I ask whether participants treat Facebook as a collection of genres on one platform, or as one unified genre.

Participants consider the core features of Facebook—wall posts, status updates, and their display in the audiences' newsfeeds—forms of broadcast that may or may not initiate conversation—an understanding that frames Facebook as quite similar to Twitter (cf. the general description as a chaotic stream of communicative openings, Chapter 5). Along these lines, Caleb argues that most of the communication on Facebook is unidirectional: 'everybody is writing all at once and when you look at your wall there is no connection from top to bottom' (Caleb). For the same reason, he does not consider Facebook to be defined by conversationality.

When I probed the participants in more detail for the experienced difference between public communication on Facebook and the various features for more private one-to-one or many-to-many communication, it became clear that they also use Facebook for interpersonal communication. However, although participants see the utility of the interpersonal conversation functionalities, they express using these with somewhat skeptic attitudes, and do not seem to find Facebook very appropriate for personal conversation.

Most critical is Anita, who almost refrains from using the private one-to-one channels on Facebook (i.e. chat, personal messages). On the one hand, she finds them unsuitable—not personal enough—for communicating with close friends. She prefers meeting or calling her close friends, rather than chitchatting with them on Facebook. 'It means a lot to me that not everything is communicated electronically. Soon you don't have any friends anymore, if it is all about pushing a button' (Anita). Hence, Anita considers

Facebook an inferior platform for personal communication—something that might dilute her relationship with others. If she were to write to her close friends, she would rather use a traditional email or SMS than Facebook. On the other hand, Facebook is also not suitable for formal or professional communication. For instance, Anita recounts she found it inappropriate when a fellow schoolteacher in need of professional advice once approached her through Facebook's personal message feature, which is simply an embedded email functionality. Anita considers an email sent on Facebook different from regular email in terms of communication norms. Whereas regular email for her has long been an established way of communicating about professional issues, Facebook is not the proper venue for professional exchange. Thus, because the email functionality is embedded in a social media service that Anita uses for informal and casual hangout, she finds it unsuitable for anything (personal as well as professional communication) beyond this. Caleb positions himself in a similarly critical fashion, arguing that since at the outset Facebook does not require the commitment and constant attentiveness of its users, it is not an obvious choice for personal communication. 'It is too easy to write on Facebook . . . Oh what a lovely wife I have, if you never say it to her at home' (Caleb). To him—and to Anita, Facebook communication is a bit superficial.

Gwen never uses the chat and other interpersonal communication functions and is always marked as 'offline'—but for different reasons than Caleb and Anita. 'I prefer to choose myself when I have time for a conversation' (Gwen). Her choice not to use these functionalities is thus a matter of regulating her accessibility. Although not necessarily considering one-to-one venues of communication of Facebook faux pas, Gwen considers chat 'bad communication, an all too amputated form of conversation' (Gwen), further asserting that she prefers to be able to answer properly when somebody addresses her. Hence, Gwen claims to limit her accessibility through the one-to-one channels of Facebook out of respect for her conversation partners.

The least critical user of interpersonal communication facilities on Facebook, Luke, is a vivid user of the Facebook chat. The chat function has taken over much of his personal chitchat with friends on Facebook simply because it is practical. At the same time, he remarks that he might just as well send a text message, which—in contrast to the chat—would not imply an expectation of immediate response. Thus, similarly to Gwen's choice of regulating her accessibility, Luke has reservations when it comes to the obligations to respond that one-to-one communicative functionalities impose on him. Again, this confirms the overall understanding of Facebook as first and foremost a casual communicative space to drop in and out of as one pleases. In sum, there are divergent uses and conceptions of the appropriateness and utility of Facebook as a genre for one-to-one communication.

In contrast, regarding many-to-many communication in private channels such as closed groups, the picture converges. Most of the participants are members of one or a few closed groups and find these practical for coordinating events and meet-ups. For instance, Caleb is part of a group of fellow soldiers and a group for his former high school cohort. Both groups are used to coordinate annual parties and events. 'It is not really that much better than if everyone joined an email thread [. . .]. It is just easy to see who signed up for the event and not, and you can write comments concerning the party' (Caleb). Similarly, Luke is a member of a soccer group that is used for coordinating training sessions, and Gwen keeps a closed group with her mother-and-baby group. Even Anita is member of a closed group for communicating with her old study mates. Whereas they would previously have used text messages to coordinate appointments among group members, Gwen and Anita both consider the many-to-many communication in their closed groups much more advantageous and easy: 'you simply ask everybody at once' (Gwen). Gwen further emphasizes as a core strength of the closed group communication that it offers an informal means of suggesting meet-ups. If the other members of the group do not have the time, they can simply refrain from answering. 'It is up to oneself to choose if one wants to be active, and one is not excluded for not being active. One is still part of the group and gets all the messages' (Gwen). Hence, in contrast to one-to-one forms of communication on Facebook, the many-to-many communication in groups—just like the public communication channels on Facebook—does not demand the constant attention of participants and the commitment to responding. This makes closed groups attractive and useful in everyday life.

The participants' attitudes toward personal conversation in the configurations of one-to-one and many-to-many on Facebook are strongly aligned with their overall understandings of Facebook as a casual communicative genre, as analyzed in the previous section. Whereas there appears to be some division of labor between the different communicative functionalities offered by Facebook, these do not result in firm, differentiated communicative norms. Instead, the overall understanding of Facebook and its use for casual time passing and chitchat appear to blend into the use of and expectations to the unique communicative functionalities, regardless of their software-inscribed communicative configuration. This suggests that participants treat Facebook not as a portal for a wealth of different genres, but as a coherent, albeit mixed communicative genre.

THEMATIC ORIENTATIONS AND BOUNDARIES OF FACEBOOK COMMUNICATION

As we have seen, the Facebook users under study generally restrain themselves in terms of posting content to Facebook, out of a normative inclination only to post content that is relevant for their audience. Against this background, this section examines thematic negotiations of relevance, asking what types of content is deemed relevant and appropriate for communicating on Facebook, and how the fact that the audience is already known affects thematic negotiations.

Similar to the Twitter users, participants in the Facebook study express a preference for funny and cleaver posts. 'I have three or four friends on Facebook who are really good at being funny and creative [. . .] that is usually quite interesting to follow,' as Max explains it, and continues by underlining that if he shares anything himself, it would be of a similar kind: 'it is typically funny photos or links to articles or errors in articles or that kind of things' (Max). This tendency of a positive attitude and orientation to content that one finds cleaver, funny and that others could be expected to have a laugh about too is common across study participants.

Furthermore, the quote from Max above subtly indicates that content should also be informative. For example, this includes sharing links to interesting articles, upcoming events in the local area, or a recommendation of a good concert. Along these lines, several of the participants note that over the years they find that the thematic focus of Facebook updates has shifted away from trivial everyday activities to more professional and informative issues. This type of content is deemed more generally relevant and useful for the Facebook audience, especially when compared to mundane updates about the everyday. Several participants express ambivalence towards posts about everyday activities:

> It is like reading a gossip magazine, it is somewhat exciting to read, but it also annoys me a bit. I follow many users who post professional stuff, and I think that is cooler that it can be used as a news channel [. . .] I would rather read about a new coffee shop than about someone's baby having his first tooth. (Gwen)

The preference for informative and funny posts arguably has to do with Facebook's multiple audiences. When communicating to several audience groups at the same time it is presumably a unique quality—but also a difficult challenge—to find a theme that can appeal broadly to the personal network. Funny and informative posts present themselves as convenient and likely candidates for being considered generally relevant, whereas more mundane, personal posts are likely more interesting to those in the audience who have an everyday relationship with the author.

The preference for informative posts appears to hold for adult Facebook users on a broader scale. For instance, Vitak and Ellison (2013) in their qualitative study of US adult users found information sharing and mining, recommendations, and requests for practical help to be among the most valued types of content on Facebook. They further suggest that the presence of multiple, heterogeneous audiences in the personal networks is an asset for furthering information sharing. If the network were too homogenous, less new information would be passed along on Facebook. Hence, the network configuration and context collapse on Facebook seem to promote the sharing of informative content.

Regarding more person-centered updates, some participants point out a difference between mundane status updates from the everyday lives of people in their network and updates about big and extraordinary events and news in the personal lives of these people. As Anita asserts, 'I think it is nice to know when people expect a child or are getting married or are moving abroad for two years [. . .] I think it is that kind of things that need to go out there' (Anita). Along these lines, several of the participants themselves claim to share such events, for instance, in the form of photos and videos of milestones in their children's lives (e.g., sharing a photo of a newborn child with one's personal Facebook network to notify everyone that they have become a parent). Anita reflects upon how such extraordinary updates can make it easier to meet especially the more peripheral Facebook friends face to face, because 'you don't have to start from scratch every time' (Anita). Hence, the sharing of personal news on Facebook can act as a conversation starter in physical encounters.

Gwen generally has a more ambivalent attitude towards personal updates. For her, such updates are not entirely appropriate as they conflict with norms concerning responsivity and active engagement with Facebook. She contends that posts about happy or negative events implicitly involve the expectation of a response as a confirmatory act from the network. 'I think it calls for too much, whereas I think that my own posts are humorous statements that do not HAVE to invite contact, but if somebody thinks it is funny, we can have a laugh about it' (Gwen). Thus, for Gwen, when the content is of a personal nature, it demands a response from the audience, and this challenges the convention that it is up to the individual user to regulate and dose his engagement in communication on Facebook.

As was the case with the participants in the blog and Twitter studies, the Facebook users appear to operate with a genre norm that mundane updates from everyday life are inappropriate and annoying, again confirmed by the US study by McLaughlin and Vitak (2012). 'It is typically updates that are [. . .] very trivial or people who update all the time' (Max). For Max, the most annoying Facebook use is the combination of too frequent updating and uninteresting content. As an example of trivial status updates, he describes 'a photo of a coffee cup on a table with a little spot next to it where it says "Oops, I spilled some". . .' (Max). Posts about the banalities of everyday life also include updates on exercise (e.g., when someone posts that they just went for a run) or location-based communication (e.g., check-ins via Facebook Places). Luke notes 'I generally think that is stupid and self-promoting' (Luke), whereas Caleb wonders about 'what it is that makes people want to express all these things? [. . .] Why can't they just be happy for themselves . . .' (Caleb). Implied in these statements is a sense that what is particularly annoying about such posts is that they are useless for the audience—they are navel-gazing and have no function for others than the person who wrote and shared them and do not contribute relevant information or funny stuff to socialize with the network.

The participants mention other types of inappropriate and irrelevant content on Facebook: political discussions—especially those that contain extreme viewpoints, advertisements, 'the never-ending serial with children' (Luke), and invitations to 'games and various applications that spam' (Max). These topics are deemed unsuitable for two reasons: that either they represent a misfit with the generally casual and funny atmosphere created on Facebook (e.g., extreme viewpoints and political discussions), or that they cater more to the author than his or her audience (e.g., mundane posts about one's child, game invitations).

In addition to content that participants deem irrelevant and inappropriate, there is content that they experience as outright offensive—typically because it is considered too private or because it involves others than the person posting it. However, examples of this kind of content seldom find their way to the participants' Facebook feeds. This indicates that communication on Facebook operates according to a general norm of sobriety and of not involving private topics such as death, sex, love relationships, and outbursts of emotionality. To be sure, such topics do find their way onto Facebook, if only occasionally, but they are not considered an appropriate part of the everyday uses of the service. In the participants' view, posts about such private topics are particularly offensive, because they intrude themselves on the audience and include the audience (often) against its will. As Anita expresses it, 'I am forced to get too close [to that person] and I don't need that' (Anita).

The experienced offensiveness of too personal matters underlines the fact that Facebook is deemed inappropriate for communication that does not fit the casual scheme. It further suggests an ongoing reflection and negotiation concerning the boundaries between appropriately personal and the all-too-private communication—a negotiation that also characterizes Twitter and blogging, and thus appears to be a general concern for social media users (cf. Chapter 7).

The Role of Visual Communication

In comparison with blogging and Twitter, visual communication in the form of videos and photo albums is more prevalent on Facebook. Especially, photos have gradually attained a more prominent role on Facebook over time, as latest illustrated by the March 2013 redesign of the Facebook interface to optimize and streamline photo browsing and sharing on the site. This software evolution feeds into communicative practice and genre negotiations on Facebook, as participants commonly mention photo-sharing and browsing as an increasingly important part of their Facebook activities. For instance,

Caleb argues that photos make Facebook well arranged and more manageable, and thus add value to his engagement with the service.

The participants seem to post photographs more often than written posts. 'I like the idea of posting photos of things I see [. . .] I think it is more fun to post photos because it means . . . it is more real' (Luke). What Luke seems to suggest here is that photos are more valid documentation of his activities than his mere describing them in writing: they show rather than tell. Other participants appear to align with Luke's perspective, and assert that when they contribute content, it will typically be by posting snapshot photos, for instance, of their holiday destinations and activities to say 'look, this was a great trip' (Anita). Similarly, they report browsing holiday photos and other albums uploaded by their friends.

As previously mentioned, participants also to some extent upload photos and videos of their children—and specifically of the extraordinary events in their children's' lives. At the same time, posting these photos and videos is associated with a certain doubt and ambivalence concerning the appropriateness of this practice. The ambivalence is primarily fueled by a negotiation of what is legitimately personal and what is too mundane or inappropriately private for those represented in the photos and videos. Max and his spouse, for instance, have discussed and settled on ground rules concerning sharing photos of their son:

> I was very much in doubt of what to do [. . .] I thought that the amount of information that I give by sharing photos of my kid is actually quite small [. . .] photos of kids with meat sauce all over the face literally don't contain much information, they are simply funny. (Max)

Concerns about photo-sharing are linked to the point that everyone should be able to choose and control what is shared about themselves. This sense of control is considered particularly important because, in principle, once uploaded, Facebook owns participants' photos and videos. For one, Caleb asserts that, given Facebook's ownership of the photos he shares, he does not want to share photos of his daughter 'for her sake. I don't want her to turn 25 and then there are these photos of her on the internet' (Caleb). Similarly, Gwen refrains from posting photos of her son, arguing that 'I don't like being posted myself, when others post photos they have taken, if I'm on them' (Gwen). In addition, she relates the extensive sharing of photos of self and others as a 'teenage' fad, something that characterizes younger users—and that they find perfectly appropriate.

The norms of photo-sharing voiced in this study might not be a general genre convention. Instead, the shared understanding among the study participants that it is inappropriate Facebook use to post photos of others that they could find embarrassing, could be an age-specific understanding of the genre. Like written communication on Facebook, the norms of visual communication arguably reflect a concern of striking a balance between appropriately personal and too private content—similar to what is seen on personal blogs and Twitter. This balance thus appears to be of general concern in social media use and will be explored in more detail in the concluding analysis of social media as communicative genres in Chapter 7.

Regulatory Mechanisms: Responding, Liking, Ignoring, Hiding, Unfriending

As was the case with blogging and Twitter use, the various forms of response and mutual recognition between the author and the networked audience are key elements in the negotiation of genre: through responding, one implicitly sanctions and possibly strengthens specific thematic enactments of genre as appropriate and welcome. The absence of response similarly functions as a suggestion to tone down specific types of content. On Facebook, response is given not only through comments, but also—and perhaps primarily—through *likes,* that is, acts in which the audience clicks a specific button under the post to mark that they endorse it.

The participants describe themselves as reluctant in terms of commenting on other people's posts on Facebook—in line with the overall understanding of Facebook as informal and noncommittal communication and time-passing. Responses are given when relevant and deserved, and when participants have time. Specifically, most of the study participants claim to be most inclined to respond to concrete requests for assistance, for instance, when someone needs help from the network to find a place to stay, or to fix a computer problem. Furthermore, some report being more likely to respond to posts from particular others in their networks: close friends are more often rewarded with comments. For instance, Luke feels obliged to comment when a close friend posts something, in part because they 'work as catalysts for one another' (Luke) and provide mutual inspiration and encouragement, in part because Luke considers commenting a way to confirm a close relationship with them and to provide support. He specifically asserts that he 'wishes to give the other person the attention he deserves' (Luke). This way, exchanges of comments may encourage and inspire new status updates, as a continuous maintenance of everyday relationships between friends.

Apart from commenting, a convenient, easy, and less time-consuming way to respond to others on Facebook is using the like-button, and participants claim to use liking more frequently than commenting. Liking a post may be considered a way for the individual user to show that he has seen the post—a phatic marker similar to much of the commenting activity seen on Twitter and blogs. However, participants find likes to be a less committed and genuine type of response. As Gwen describes it, 'I might press like to an update that I actually find pretty annoying because I want to give the person the experience that "I see you"' (Gwen). Accordingly, although it marks an awareness of the other, liking a post does not necessarily indicate an interest in and acknowledgement of the post. In their study, Vitak and Ellison (2013) similarly found Facebook to be considered a convenient channel for giving and receiving support and recognition, although it was perceived as less genuine than support given face to face.

As analyzed, participants discard some forms of content as irrelevant and inappropriate enactments of Facebook as a communicative genre. However, participants can accept a few inappropriate posts if they are embedded in a thematically varied communicative flow from the sender. In these cases, individual annoying posts are simply ignored. Hence, posting specific types of content is only seen as problematic, as normative breaches of the genre, to the extent that a user solely writes about his kids, checks in, or sends gaming invitations. That is, when a user demonstrates a completely different understanding of the genre than the study participants. In such instances, the participants reaffirm their own understanding of genre by unsubscribing to that person's posts. Whereas on Twitter unsubscribing would imply to stop following someone, on Facebook users can avoid unfriending the other person and simply mute him or her. Facebook has a built-in function that allows users to filter and hide updates from specific persons so that they do not appear in the personalized newsfeed. Only in rare cases, for instance, if someone posts a racist comment or constantly spams with requests from games such as Farmville, will the study participants unfriend that person and cut off the Facebook relationship.

In their study of young Facebook users in the US, McLaughlin and Vitak (2012) analyzed how the use of different acts of sanctioning others' Facebook activities to regulate norms of appropriate content—to delete, hide or ignore a person, depend on the relationships between the norm violator and the offended user. The same holds true among participants in my study. Participants report that they are inclined to 'punish' peripheral acquaintances harder, for example, by ending the Facebook friendship, because it has less, if any, social consequences: 'It is like at a party, right, I sneak out at half past two in the morning and feel tired and go home. Nobody will notice that I have left, right?' (Max). Although several of the participants claim to feel bad and guilty when deleting others, they do it anyway. This is because Facebook allows them to be discrete about it. Facebook does not send the other person a notification that the friendship has ended. Hence, the risk of being exposed is relatively small. Correspondingly, with close acquaintances, family, or colleagues with whom the participants have a relationship outside Facebook, the punishment is milder: it involves ignoring or hiding them. These people are not deleted from participants' personal networks (except for Luke's network, as we have already seen) as deletion could possibly have social consequences for the relationship as such. With these Facebook friends, the flow and content of communication are regulated differently.

The thematic negotiation of genre largely follows the understanding of Facebook as expressed in the participants' social organizing of Facebook use in everyday life. The identified norms of appropriate and relevant themes indicate that, on the one hand, the posted content must offer something useful—an informative or entertaining experience—to the audience; on the other hand, the theme must not evoke a sense of obligation for the audience to accept the offer of starting a communicative exchange—it must not force a response. Hence, again, the underlying logic seems to be that Facebook is first and foremost an *offer*—a noncommittal, casual invitation to produce and share content and thus engage in comunication.

STYLISTIC CONVENTIONS

When participants do produce content on Facebook, they must adhere to certain stylistic conventions to demonstrate genre competence. Concerning status updates that are broadcast to the entire personal network but not targeted at anyone specific, mastery of the style appears to be a matter of hitting a spontaneous tone. It must not seem forced or calculated, and generally 'there isn't so much filter on,' as Mandy describes it. In this sense, the stylistic norm of status updates on Facebook resembles that of tweets, as described in Chapter 5.

Given Facebook's status as an informal and casual communicative genre, the participants generally assert that Facebook communication is often about nailing a funny and ironic tone. Luke, for instance, recounts how he sometimes spends days working on a Facebook update before posting it to find a proper formulation that he himself finds funny. In contrast, participants say they stay out of discussions on Facebook (e.g., about political matters), primarily because the tone often gets harsh and ugly—it loses the informal and funny dimension. The participants' descriptions of what they consider to be the appropriate tone underline, from a stylistic perspective, the convention of Facebook being a genre for informal encounters and casual time-passing in the small breaks during the everyday.

Some of the participants point out that they find it challenging to keep an appropriate tone, to find a balance between being breezy and serious when dealing with multiple audiences simultaneously. This marks a difference between Facebook and the two other genres studied, for which the audience is typically more homogenous. It appears that communicating in the public channels on Facebook is quite demanding, because participants cannot expect everyone in the audience to be completely aligned in their genre expectations, and thus to be equally tolerant to everything that is posted and able to read between the lines. In this connection, Max finds it particularly challenging to convey irony through writing, and he reports that his caution against engaging in communicative exchanges on Facebook partly has to do with his experience that others often misunderstand his humorous-ironic tone. This also explains why smileys are prevalent in Facebook conversation. Similarly to blogging and Twitter, smileys are emphasized as a form of meta-communication that may assist the audience in interpreting the post—supporting posts and comments with facial expressions as conveyed through smileys makes it easier to make the communicative style work in way that is inclusive and meaningful for the broad and diverse audience. Acknowledging that smileys serve a function especially when communicating with people one does not know all that well, Luke still considers them 'stupid, because I think it is a trivialization of language. If you cannot express yourself without it, then don't write' (Luke). Hence, at least for Luke, the use of smileys to some extent represents a lack of genre competence.

The funny and informal tone is also found in communicative exchanges between close friends on Facebook, although in these instances, it serves a different function—namely, as a vehicle for perceptive talk that effectively excludes others from the communication. Again, the context collapse on Facebook is an important challenge. Luke recalls the recurrent instances when colleagues that are in his Facebook network try to join the ping-pong that he maintains on the site with his close friends: 'They don't know the jargon between us friends, and it can be a bit annoying as it can kill things [. . .] but sometimes it actually makes the exchange more fun because it is so untimely' (Luke). Similarly, Anita experiences an exclusive and perceptive community—marked by a sort of a 'code language'—with her colleagues in their exchanges on the Facebook wall, and notes that often, one would have to know the context to take part in their exchanges. Accordingly, stylistic elements in communication may serve to engage specific parts of the audience in conversation, and demonstrate genre alignment among those in the know, whereas others are to some extent excluded from communication. This, in turn, can be viewed as a way to handle the possible confusion regarding communicative norms that follows from Facebook's collapse of multiple audiences. Through small stylistic maneuvers in communication, participants address their audiences in different ways so that they may relate not only to the expansive and diverse network of close and peripheral contacts, but also at the same time signal a closer relationship with specific, relevant peers in their network. Again, we see a similarity between Facebook and the two other genres (cf. the biking discourse on Ben's blog; the perceptive talk in Miriam's Twitter network, etc.): Stylistic communicative practices are commonly used as strategies for marking genre competence and closer affiliation among specific network members.

In the previous chapter, on Twitter, the short-form, near-synchronous communication was found to make style a more defining parameter than content for competent genre enactment. The Facebook study does not seem to involve a similar bias towards style over other genre dimensions, as the analysis suggests that participants must master a tone that supports the organizing conventions of composition and content: namely the creation and maintenance of a casual space for keeping in touch and letting oneself be entertained, without entailing a commitment to contribute to the ongoing flow of communication. Thus, there is no clear correspondence between short-form, status update-centered software, and a specific, prominent role of style when practicing genre in social media. However, the similarity in stylistic conventions between Facebook and Twitter suggests a general link between the humorous, spontaneous stylistic ideal and the short-form of both tweets and status updates.

WHEN FACEBOOK GOES PORTABLE

In 2006, it became possible to go on Facebook with a mobile phone (Yuan & Buckman, 2006), and in 2008, the Facebook for iPhone application was launched (Brügger, 2013). There are no reliable statistics on how many Danes actually use Facebook from their mobile phones, but given the wide diffusion of smartphones in Denmark, it is likely that Facebook use on the smartphone is on the rise. Furthermore, a recent survey by the Pew Internet and American Life project suggests that more than one third of American Facebook users occasionally access their accounts via a smartphone (Rainie & Wellman, 2012: 140).

The participants in the present study all point to their smartphones forming the main access point for daily Facebook engagement. At the same time, they all started using Facebook through the Facebook.com website, and still access the website on their PCs on a regular basis. The subtle shift towards more mobile application-based use of Facebook over the course of the study participants' Facebook histories provides crucial insights into changing enactments of Facebook as a communicative genre over time. Furthermore, the participants' reflections regarding web versus mobile use offer a valuable glimpse into how different media platforms enable and constrain communicative actions associated with participants' Facebook use and thereby come to shape communicative norms. Hence, in this final analysis section I open the door to studying the promises and perils of portability and its possible implications for social media use. The analysis is suggestive rather than conclusive in considering the interplay between portability and communicative genres.

The mobile application is the participants' preferred access point for the daily or hourly logins to Facebook to browse and be updated on what has happened since the last login. However, the mobile application is functionally more restricted than the Facebook.com website. This leads users to turn to web access when wanting to perform specific types of actions on Facebook. For instance, Luke uses web access when he wants to share a post, because the application does not allow this action. Max finds the web platform more attractive and usable for extensive photo browsing. Unlike the mobile application, the website offers better zoom and click-through functionalities when glancing through photo albums. Furthermore, because the website allows him to use tabs to navigate, he is more easily led to other websites without losing track of where he started on Facebook.

> It annoys me that it [the mobile application] does not have tabs, that I
> cannot open a page [. . .] I am distracted from what I was actually doing,
> because I wanted to just take a look at something. You cannot open it
> in a new tab and then look at it later. (Max)

Hence, the website still has its utility for Facebook use, because it allows
for a broader spectrum of actions and better navigation. In addition, screen
size and tactility matter for the participants' choice of access point for
communicating on Facebook. For the reading and production of longer
content bits, participants commonly prefer the website over the mobile
application. Both Mandy and Max assert that writing and reading is
more time consuming on the mobile screen: 'I am more inclined to enter a
discussion and comment on something others have uploaded if I'm on the
PC' (Max).

The choice of media platforms according to the affordances they offer for
communicative action has been conceptualized in terms of *intermediality*
(Helles, 2013), a framework that is further equipped to analyze the interplay
between media preferences and communicative norms in the conduct of
everyday life. Against this background, the interviews suggest two major
lines of development in the enactment of Facebook as a communicative
genre enabled by the platform shift towards more use from the smartphone:
a) participants post more photos than before, something that may be
said to have fueled a genre change towards more visual and multimodal
communication, as confirmed by the participants' preference for posting and
browsing photos rather than written statements; and b) participants check
their Facebook accounts more often than they did before they acquired
smartphones.

> I go on Facebook more often because I always have it on me wher-
> ever I go. Sometimes it may have made the spontaneous happenings or
> thoughts I experience during the day. . . it has made it easier and faster
> to post on Facebook because I can take a photo of it in an instance or
> quickly write what I have just experienced instead of having to wait
> until I get home. (Mandy)

The increasing engagement in visual communication has to do with two
qualities of the smartphone: it is always at the participants' hands, and it has
a quite good camera. Like Mandy, Luke connects his posting more photos
to his increased use of Facebook from the smartphone. Typically, his photos
are combined with a bit of text to comment on the visual display, suggesting
that Luke actually prefers this multimodal communication to pure text or
photos. Scholars have argued that the images taken with camera phones are
at once more intimate and more mundane than earlier forms of personal
photography (Gye, 2007; Murray, 2008). Analyzing the iPhone in particular,
Palmer (2012: 86) suggests a shift toward more spontaneous photographic

practices. Along the lines of such findings, Gwen contends that although she does not embrace this behavior herself, people in her network more often post everyday photos and videos on Facebook. So, in a sense, the smartphone has changed the Facebook experience for her as an audience member.

Whereas D. Palmer (2012) emphasizes instantaneity and spontaneity as key motivators for the use of mobile photography as such, the study participants do not agree on being driven by these factors in the practice of uploading photos to Facebook. As we have seen, they do consider photos a more accurate form of documentation of their activities in the here and now, but several of them also state that it is not necessary for photos to be posted as soon as they are taken. Instead, participants upload their photos when they have the time—in perfect alignment with the generally accepted idea that Facebook use grows out of the convenient moments of the everyday.

The other genre change experienced by participants, and expressed in the above quote from Mandy, is that using Facebook on the smartphone involves an increased impetus to be 'always on,' as Baron (2008) has termed the constant availability of individuals through digital media. Mandy describes how the smartphone prompts her to check Facebook more frequently, not because it nurtures a need for ambient accessibility, but simply because 'I have the opportunity to check, and then I get a little curious to see if anything new has happened since three hours ago' (Mandy). Gwen, whose Facebook application sends her notifications of relevant Facebook activities, offers a similar account for her more frequent logins and further adds that 'since the phone notifies me of new activity, my logins are not limited to when I feel I have the time to have a look at it, it also comes without my active seeking it out' (Gwen). For Gwen the smartphone (and specifically her choice of receiving notifications) has changed her availability—for instance, she will typically respond faster when addressed on Facebook. Lastly, and in contrast to Gwen's changing sense of accessibility, Caleb describes his more frequent logins through the smartphone as followed by a lessened sense of serious commitment to Facebook, simply because it demands less effort.

> If I were to go to the computer and sit down and open it and go on Face-book, I would have a deeper intention with logging on to write a message to someone or posting something or another clear goal. Now that it is frequent log-ons, running through the feed and logging off again then it is actually more seldom that I take the time to write something than before, because it is too easy [. . .] it is not really an active, conscious choice anymore. (Caleb)

Accordingly, the smartphone increases the possibility of being always on. On the one hand, this may make it more difficult to control one's accessibility on Facebook, as experienced by Gwen. On the other hand, as suggested by

Caleb, it may further strengthen the sense that what is going on on Facebook is not that important after all—it is simply becoming more mundane.

GENRE MIXING, STABILITY, AND CHANGE IN SOCIAL MEDIA

Despite the fact that Facebook combines multiple pre-existing stand-alone genres of online communication, this small study suggests that participants largely conceive of Facebook as a unified phenomenon—guided by a set of intersubjectively established practices concerning its pragmatic value and purpose in everyday life. Compositional, thematic, and stylistic conventions converge to anchor Facebook as a casual space for hanging out, making small talk and goofing off whenever participants have the time or need a break during the everyday. Thus, although Facebook involves genre mixing—and perhaps confusion—at the software level, it has a surprisingly stable and unambiguous expression in the practical enactment—at least among the study participants. One possible explanation for this is that by treating Facebook as one genre with a relatively coherent set of conventions, users enable themselves to navigate Facebook skillfully. As a result, Facebook appears relatively unproblematic and inherently meaningful in their daily engagement on the site.

At a theoretical level, I have argued that one of the merits of a genre-based understanding of social media is its ability to grasp the dynamics of stabilization and change. Methodologically, I sought to include a relatively mature genre (the personal blog); a genre in the making (Twitter), and a mixed genre (Facebook) to study in greater detail communicative patterns that reify, or destabilize and transform genres. However, apart from the suggested development towards more visually oriented communication associated with using Facebook from the smartphone, the empirical analyses are much more illustrative of genre stability than change. Arguably, this pitfall has methodological roots, and does not per se challenge the theoretical concepts and analytic framework.

For one thing, the lack of genre controversy possibly has to do with the criteria used for case selection. In striving for data richness, to capture the ongoing 'negotiation of genre' through interactional dynamics, I opted primarily for experienced and relatively active users (in terms of posting content and having conversations with fellow users)—in particular in the blog study, but also to some extent the studies of Twitter and Facebook. This might have led to the selection of more orderly and, from a genre perspective, therefore unproblematic cases. Given their experience and engagement in communication, the participants may already have reached a common understanding with their networks of relevant others of the situated expressions and meanings of the genre. Especially, highly conversational instances of genre might demonstrate greater inertia in the genre—at least, this seems to be the case with the instances of genre I have studied, which evolve around the everyday lives of ordinary users. Other types of cases might have better illuminated the perspective on change in social media as genres. For instance, cases that mix and push the boundaries between the personal, and the political or commercial might have been useful for eliciting more data regarding participants' uncertainty about genre norms and disagreements about what constitutes an appropriate enactment of the genre.

For another thing, the picture of overall stability in the expression of the three genres may be related to the time frame of the empirical studies. Both Twitter and Facebook were studied in short time frames, although the interviews also probed participants' changing experience of the services over time. Only the blog study was longitudinal, but it did not yield insights on genre change over time in the 6-month period studied. This does not necessarily mean that social media as genres are not very dynamic. However, modifying my initial assumption that genres are highly dynamic in a fluctuating media environment, genre transformations may take time, and must be studied in a much broader time frame.

The analysis of the move from stationary to portable platforms for accessing Facebook to some extent addresses genre development in a broader time frame, as elicited by interview data. Portability appears to be an important element in facilitating and promoting new practices that over time become defining for the genres (e.g., immediacy as a governing temporal norm on Twitter; and the development of Facebook as a more visually oriented genre). A focus on genre change may thus benefit from incorporating a stronger focus on the media platform and its relationship to the concrete expression of genre, and the specific software used in the analysis.

CHAPTER SUMMARY

The analysis presented in this chapter confirms the picture from the two other case studies that social media are an integrated part—even a communicative condition—of everyday life: Facebook is interwoven with other communications in a range of work and leisure activities, and not least in the maintenance of personal relationships. The touch of the mundane is particularly evident in the underlying, and commonly accepted understanding of the purpose of Facebook, as enacted in the participants' practical use of Facebook in the small breaks during the daily grind. Through the frequent logins to check the newsfeed and other communicative features, Facebook offers small oases of relaxation from other doings, informal updates, casual chitchat, and entertainment centered in the relationships of the everyday. In this sense, Facebook extends and enhances the everyday, with colleagues, friends, and family.

The extension of everyday communication is tied not only to the concrete communicative exchanges in posts and comments, but also in large part to the peripheral awareness and the presence of the possibility for contact among Facebook friends. This further suggests that phatic communication, similarly to blogs and Twitter, plays an important role on Facebook as a vehicle for the grooming of relationships. Through their routine, daily Facebook use, participants continuously establish and maintain the possibility for contact with one another: they keep the line open, so to speak, for communication.

Even though each user has partly unique understandings of and expectations to Facebook as a communicative genre, given individual expressive abilities, interests and general life circumstances, the four analytic dimensions of genre and the communicative conventions they reveal confirm that competent genre enactment and legitimate participation in the ongoing negotiation of genre is subject to the particular network logics of social media. The embeddedness of communication in networks creates social pressure for establishing and nurturing relationships in one's network of affiliation—a pressure that deeply affects genre negotiation. As demonstrated in this chapter, the multiple audiences and the context collapse on Facebook raise the stakes of appropriate and competent genre enactment. It gives rise to norm confusion and insecurity, because we typically adjust our communication to one concrete social group and context at a time. The overlapping networks and contexts of affiliation shape Facebook as a communicative genre by pushing for communication that is inclusive and broadly relevant across social groups, so that every personal connection can, in principle, take part in communication and for informality and casualness so that nobody feels obliged and forced to engage actively in communicative exchange.

NOTES

1. As with the two other case studies, participants have been pseudonymized.
2. Ugander, Backstrom, Marlow, and Kleinberg (2012) analyzed the total user population on Facebook and found the average number of friends to be around 300.

7 'Personal, Not Private'
The Sociability of Social Media

In the introduction to this book, I described the internet as involving the public enactment of personal, everyday communication. Software functionalities such as the accumulation of contributions into persistent archives make participants' interpersonal communication available to a wider audience across space and time. This raises important questions regarding the negotiated norms for appropriate self-disclosure and privacy in ordinary users' everyday communication in social media.

In the preceding three chapters, I documented ordinary users' enactments of personal blogs, Twitter, and Facebook as personal niches for self-expression and interpersonal relationship management in everyday life. In the ongoing personal conversations with relevant peers over time, participants in online communication are likely to disclose different facets of themselves in public or semi-public fashion. Once produced and posted, the tweet, status update, blog post, and comment have lives of their own; they may spin out of the author's control. For instance, boyd (2008) talks about digital content being *persistent*, *searchable*, and *replicable*, as well as being accessible to *unintended audiences* (also Viégas, 2005). Although the author has control over the production process and may write to a specific addressee or group of addressees, the author cannot control who actually reads the text. Accordingly, the potential audience of the personal communication is expanded, and this has consequences for the way in which users share their personal experiences and what they are willing to share. That is, what is appropriate for the genres?

From a genre perspective, it is crucial to explore how users negotiate the interface between the public or semi-public nature of the software genres, and the sometimes-private conversations taking place, because this yields important insights into the distinctive attributes and experiential qualities of social media in users' everyday lives.

When I probed for participants' experiences, motivations, privacy, and publicity expectations in relation to their use of blogs, Twitter, and Facebook in the interviews, the participants commonly voiced an orientation to, and understanding of their social media practices and behaviors as 'personal, not private.' In this chapter, I will argue that the phatic elements so prevalent in participants' social media use have a crucial function in demonstrating personal engagement and commitment, while also adhering to norms of general relevance and preserving privacy in communication on social media.

The function of the phatic communication on social media may be fruitfully explored through Simmel's concept of *sociability*, which reflects a togetherness that exists somewhere between the public and the private. Simmel defines and dissects the concept of sociability as driven by people's everyday conversations. Sociability is upheld and maintained through conversational activities and reciprocity (Simmel 1971 [1910]: 130–137), and is neither about achieving some common goal, nor centered around one specific topic. Fundamentally, sociability is about being together by keeping a conversation alive. Sociability is togetherness freed from the seriousness and frictions of life, and 'it is tactless to bring in personal humor, good or ill, excitement and depression, the light and shadow of one's inner life' to the conversation (Simmel, 1971 [1910]: 131). In other words, sociability means highlighting similarities and de-emphasizing individuality in conversation by 'hiding' the intimate and potentially uncomfortable topics, because serious discussion disturbs and threatens the continuity of conversation. Consequently, sociability embraces the phatic functions of communication: It is facilitated by the maintenance of the flow of communication and mutual orientation.

In this final synthesizing analysis, I use the conceptual lens of 'sociability' to explore how togetherness with peers on social media involves a collaborative effort to negotiate and navigate the public/private interface of social media in ways that are 'personal, but not private,' and thereby sustain an ethos of mutual privacy protection. I examine how sociability takes on different nuances in blogs, Twitter and Facebook, partly owing to the network configuration, spatio-temporal and topical organization of the genres, and argue that sociability, along with its primary vehicle, the phatic communication, constitutes a critical experiential quality of social media in everyday life.

BLOGGING: CREATING INTIMACY THROUGH PHATIC COMMUNICATION

None of the three bloggers discussed displays his or her full name on their blogs, and they all use pseudonyms as nicknames. At the same time, as Elise observes, many bloggers reveal and regularly use their first names in blog conversation, and loyal readers of the three blogs are familiar with the authors' real names. This gives the blogs an authentic feel—the sense that real people are writing.

Both Maggie and Ben present themselves in portrait photos in the upper left corner of the sidebar on the front page of their respective blogs—a common practice on blogs. The photo is accompanied by a short description of the author and his or her interests, to give readers an impression of the author and of what may be expected of the blog. Elise has a similar blurb presenting herself and her interests, but until meeting fellow bloggers at blog-rallies, she had never posted a photo of herself on the blog. In fact, Elise's visual self-disclosure occurred during the archiving period, when her blog had existed for about 3 years. Her decision to finally post a photo of herself indicates a change in her sense of and need for privacy. These initial reflections concerning the bloggers' self-presentations suggest a careful effort to appear in a manner that is personal, but not private or compromising, on the personal blog.

Concerning the posted content, the three bloggers clearly identify some things as too private to be brought up in blog conversations. The blog is too public for sharing one's inner thoughts and feelings—these are better dealt with in other types of conversation. As Maggie explains, 'in a blog comment you don't get too personal, because you know it can be read by anybody' (Maggie). She goes on to describe telephone conversations with her closest blog friends as opportunities for talking 'about things that you cannot talk about on the blog' (Maggie). However, this does not mean that highly personal emotions and experiences should be filtered out entirely. In the interview, Elise notes that she senses a certain pressure for self-disclosure, not only in her own blog, but in general, and as previously demonstrated, posts about personal issues generate a lot of comments on the three blogs.

Whereas some bloggers build their blogs around the constant sharing of very private thoughts and experiences, and use the blog somewhat like a diary for self-therapy (e.g., mourning a dead child, being diagnosed with cancer, or dating, to mention only a few such sensitive topics), the bloggers in this study do not feel comfortable sharing such private matters. In a sense, they operate with an ongoing meta-reflection concerning self-censorship to avoid exposing themselves (and those they mention) on the blog. As Ben expresses it: 'my blog is a door to my life and my world from a certain angle [. . .] I have decided what I want to write on this blog. I write personally, but within a boundary that I have established' (Ben). For Ben, this means reporting personal ups and downs related to cycling, and refraining from blogging about his love life, for instance. Hence, the blog may convey personal issues, but with reservations.

The balance of privacy and disclosure is described in terms of 'selling out' vis-à-vis 'maintaining self-respect' and dignity (Elise). The concrete boundary setting may vary from blogger to blogger. For Elise, sharing intimate details does not fascinate, and clearly oversteps her boundaries. She refuses to dig into her own pain: 'dirty laundry should not be aired on-screen' (Elise). Regretting the one post in which she feels that she compromised herself, Maggie voices a similarly protective attitude concerning her own privacy, given that she does not know her blog audience with any certainty. For Ben, the question of disclosure to an unknown audience is further complicated by the possibility of his being confronted with audience members from the cycling community at races. Several times, strangers who happened to know a lot about him, from reading his blog, have approached him. Being a 'celebrity' who receives this kind of unexpected attention from strangers in the cycling community is both annoying and flattering, Ben contends, and for this reason, deciding what to share or withhold on the blog demands careful consideration.

Maggie is surprised by other bloggers' willingness to expose their private lives, and at the same time respects those who disclose intimate details in a 'dignified' and 'sober' manner (Maggie). For her, it adds to the depth of the experience of blogging that other bloggers do not just gloss over the surface, but portray themselves in a nuanced manner, and offer personal glimpses of themselves to their audiences. This confirms previous research that suggested that disclosure of the personal and intimate is a driving force in establishing and developing social relationships with the audience on a blog (Kendall, 2007; Sørensen, 2009; Viégas, 2005). Accordingly, as a fundamental aspect of the genre, personal bloggers continuously negotiate the boundaries between the appropriately personal, and the too-private disclosure (cf. Chapter 4).

A crucial component of this boundary work in personal blogging is conveying *authenticity*. Just as they expect other bloggers to disclose themselves, the three bloggers under discussion aim to have their own blogs to reflect them as nuanced persons. Ben stresses the importance of having something at stake: daring to write about both good and bad things in his life, instead of writing an idealized version of himself into being on the blog. To Maggie, it is important that people find her blogging authentic and consistent: 'you establish good contact with some people, then you meet them one day, and so what, what use is it to [. . .] have created a false image of yourself?' (Maggie). Along similar lines, Rettberg argues that blogs rely on personal authenticity (2008: 92–93). This convention of authenticity, crucial for building close relationships with other bloggers, suggests that the author's sense of self must be constituted in and through relationships with others by means of a fairly consistent and truthful self-presentation on the blog over time, to be deemed trustworthy.

As discussed in Chapter 4, the personal blog is characterized by limited topical development, epitomized not only in a strong emphasis on recognizing and confirming the author's account and viewpoint in the post, but also in the recurrence of certain topics and the suppression of others over time. The iterative content pattern on the blog serves to maintain a coherent, albeit also more one-dimensional and socialized expression of the author's self over time. As Elise notes, the blog represents 'a part of me that I would like to enhance, that I would like to be, and that . . . it is not fake at all. But of course, it is [. . .] just a sample of me. You cannot put it all in there' (Elise). Arguably, the blogging self is a restricted version of the author's self: a self that 'fits in' with a group of peers, addresses common interests, and is not offensive to the other participants. Nuances are typically added over time through continuous commitment to and from other bloggers. It seems that orienting oneself to a group of blogging peers through mutual social presence and topical stability is key to conveying a coherent and authentic sense of self.

The notion of sociability captures quite well the communicative dynamics of personal blogs as a balancing act of communicating in a personal and authentic manner, without being too private. According to Simmel, the individual is of course herself in social situations, 'but not quite completely herself, since she is only an element in a formally constituted gathering' (Simmel, 1971 [1910]: 131). The blog allows some room for 'being oneself,' without disclosing one's entire personality, let alone inner desires, and so forth, in a publicly accessible text. We might think of blogging as both authentic and selective self-writing, because the author decides to share some personal experiences, while leaving others untold (Rettberg, 2008: 11–12, 112–115; Serfaty, 2004).

Phatic communication plays a vital role in the bloggers' negotiations of the personal/private tension, by creating a space for experiencing a sense of intimacy. As I previously argued, participation in a blog conversation seems to be more about small talk and demonstrating social presence, than about exchanging information and viewpoints. At least in the cases I have studied, personal blogging epitomizes the sociable conversation, where the channel is kept open through participants' constant reaffirmation of mutual social presence. Although the phatic communication may seem banal, superficial, and even pointless to an outsider, it might not seem so to the participants. The phatic elements in the participants' mundane conversations on blogs function as vehicles for managing personal relationships in a public space, through a more subtle articulation of intimacy. In short, phatic communication designates the blog as a personal, but not private space. Knowledge of the private struggles and joys of other bloggers' lives is often established through continuous participation on one another's blogs, and through more private backchannels, such as email exchanges, mobile communication, and face-to-face encounters. The phatic aspect so characteristic of the continuous signals of mutual social presence and reciprocity among insiders may be a way of demonstrating awareness, perceptiveness, and understanding of one another beyond what is actually said in a blog post. Moreover, in keeping with Miller (2008), phatic communication on a blog may be considered a means of achieving and managing at least a limited form of intimacy within a larger group of people. It is a way of dedicating oneself to the personal relationships maintained through the blog, without exposing oneself or one's peers in the interaction.

TWITTER: MUNDANE EXCHANGES AND THE AUGMENTATION OF EVERYDAY LIFE

Of the Twitter participants, Betty and John use their full names as nicknames on Twitter, whereas Rina, Nick, and Miriam's nicknames refer to their online presence in general, as they have been used across sites and services for many years. Both Miriam and Rina provide real names in the right-hand menu bar on the front page, to complement their nicknames. All the participants except Steven have photos of themselves on their front-page profiles; all except Nick provide a link to their personal homepage or blog; all provide a biography in the right-hand menu bar, stating their core interests, and, in some instances, information about occupation and family. The interconnecting of activities across sites and services through links and the use of recurrent nicknames, as well as the display of personal information, allows others to obtain a detailed picture of the individual participant. This suggests a strong norm of authenticity among Twitter users. Demonstrating a consistent self across contexts is crucial. As Miriam observes: 'I have really put an effort into not seeming different than I am [on Twitter]. And that enables it to persist in real life, when I meet these people' (Miriam). Like the bloggers, Twitter participants demand personal effort and personal investment, giving readers a sense of who the author is. This provides them with useful information for shaping expectations of one another, and assessing mutual relevance. The display and linking of personal information does not seem to worry the participants. For instance, Betty asserts that if someone wants to know these details, the internet would make it easy, regardless of how much or little she shares on Twitter.

Steven presents an interesting contrast to this elaborate revelation of personal information. He has chosen to post under a pseudonym, and thus remain anonymous. However, he has another Twitter profile in his real name. Steven gives several reasons why anonymity is important to him, despite the fact that the topic of his writings (books) is presumably uncontroversial. Most importantly, being anonymous on his Twitter profile is a way for him to protect his private life by distinguishing it from his online presence. As Steven notes, 'everybody can read what I write [. . .] so in that way it is completely open, you are completely naked' (Steven). He further contends that anonymity in his book blogging and tweeting is valuable, because his political inclinations are evident in his writings, something he finds incompatible with his professional occupation in the media industry. However, anonymity causes him trouble, and prompts him to reconsider his anonymous status, and in the interview he admits that the initial decision to be anonymous is not all that justified:

> Initially, I thought it made sense that . . . that I had separated the private and the professional. [. . .] Today, I probably wouldn't do it, because I also think it is inconvenient [. . .]. The problem is that it bites its tail, in a way, because when it is a secret, then, how should I put it, then it is suddenly also important that it doesn't get out [. . .] because then I would appear [to have been] dishonest. (Steven)

Most importantly, what Steven highlights in this quote is that, although anonymity itself is not problematic, a transition from anonymous contributor to the disclosed 'person behind' would be disruptive. A change in behavior might make readers wonder what impelled Steven to write under a pseudonym in the first place. Assuming authenticity as the default norm, in this case, personal disclosure would create uncertainty about the author: the norm of authenticity would be challenged, and judgments of trustworthiness and authenticity would suddenly be actualized in a way they were not before, when readers had no reason to question the authenticity of the author.

Although Twitter users typically generously disclose personal information about themselves in their front-page profiles, they voice a surprisingly strict preference for Twitter users withholding their private lives in their tweets, rather than 'oversharing' either the banalities of everyday life, or the sensitive information and intimate details of their personal lives (cf. Chapter 5). Thus, in comparison with the personal blog, it appears that Twitter involves less pressure for self-disclosure.

Most restrictive is Steven, who claims no interest in the people he follows per se, but only in the information they share. Mirroring his own reflections regarding his self-presentation on Twitter, he clearly orients to professionally and topically interesting knowledge, and strives to filter out knowledge about his interlocutors as irrelevant. Acknowledging that users set individual boundaries for what counts as relevant and what counts as private, Steven talks about a 'common agreement' to not share personal information in an importunate manner (Steven). Rina, for instance, criticizes a couple in her network for 'oversharing' emotions related to their relationship (Rina). Similarly, an otherwise interesting graphic designer oversteps Nick's boundaries by occasionally sharing his depression and strong religiousness in his tweets. Other participants voice a similar distaste for intrusive self-disclosure, although they are generally more inclined to accept personal information as a legitimate part of tweets.

When asked where they themselves draw the line between appropriate content and that which is too private, participants commonly mention details and problems related to their love and sex lives as too private to be tweeted about. Additionally, Nick would never share personal problems, such as 'I have had a very bad day today, or, that I really just want to lie down on the bed and cry' on Twitter (Nick). Betty refrains from directly disclosing on Twitter that she is tired of her job, and John restrains himself from commenting on and interfering with discussions about the company at which he is employed, when it is occasionally discussed on Twitter. By not interfering, he avoids being seen as a spokesperson for the company, and underscores his appearance on Twitter as a *private* individual. Indeed, there are topics that are considered generally unacceptable, and topics that are personally inappropriate, given the work and life situations of the users. When examined, the participants' Twitter feeds from January 2010 include hardly any tweets about the topics that participants characterize as belonging to the private sphere and thus unsuitable for Twitter.

However, when they are written by private individuals, tweets inevitably address the author's personal life and interests. Small snippets of information about spouses and children are occasionally shared, and are largely deemed appropriate. Fun, everyday stories fall into this 'appropriate' category, along with the personal musings and small talk that constitute most of the feeds. For instance, Nick will share 'peculiar, funny little things my kids do' (Nick), because this information is considered superficial and mundane, and generally relatable. A strategy for striking a balance between the personal and the private, when referring to loved ones on Twitter, is refraining from mentioning them by name, and to tweet about them only in the context of everyday household activities and interests. Hence, the participants' significant others and personal lives may give rise to tweets, but careful attention is paid to avoiding exposure of the private. We might say that personal disclosure comes in small doses, is glossed over, and invoked in the portrayal of the mundane and insignificant experiences of everyday life.

The focus on the everyday contributes to the creation of a convincingly authentic impression. Crawford, in her study of microblogging as mundane communication, argues that it is through the revelation of the mundane and the insignificant that readers can connect their own sense of lived experience with that of the writer (Crawford, 2009: 252). Moreover, accounts of the mundane correspond with the notion of sociability. Sociability stipulates balancing information-laden, substantial exchanges, and sharing the subjective and intimate. Only by avoiding these two 'extremes' can sociability become a steering principle for unfolding the interaction (Simmel, 1971 [1910]: 132). As a vehicle for forwarding conversation, the insignificance of daily life fulfills precisely this function. It negotiates and designates Twitter use as personal, not private—ideal for the sort of everyday small talk that is typically exchanged among colleagues at the water cooler in an office space, or among acquaintances who run into one another in the street (Crawford, 2009; Zhao & Rosson, 2009). Perhaps surprisingly, then, it seems that Twitter is actually to some extent used for the sort of mundane and banal small talk of which participants are critical in the interviews.

The participants' experience of closeness to, and intimacy with each other as conveyed in Twitter conversation and reflected in the interviews, is limited. Twitter apparently involves weaker personal relationships between interlocutors. In Chapter 5, I argued that the immediacy of Twitter nurtures a different sense of social presence than the personal blog. Rather than functioning to uphold and develop close personal relationships over time, as on the blog and on Facebook, the conversational atmosphere on Twitter must be attuned to encompass the fluctuating and shifting relationships that are invoked sporadically, in the 'here-and-now' enactments of the genre. This, in turn, involves comparatively fewer perceptibly intimate conversations, and more 'augmented small talk' on Twitter, that is, casual, sociable utterances and exchanges among Twitter peers who happen to enter the Twitter flow simultaneously. Certainly, participants orient to relevant others, seek their company, and may develop more personal relationships with them over time, through repeated conversation. What makes these contact patterns different from those on a blog is that the relationship between relevant peers is not confirmed and maintained on a daily—or even weekly—basis on Twitter. Importantly, along these lines, previous research has found phatic communication to be more prevalent in weaker relationships, for example, among acquaintances and likeminded strangers (for a review, see Meltzer & Musolf, 2000).

Similar to the studied blogs, much of the communication on Twitter is highly phatic in function. It serves to mark an opening of the channel, to signal immediate availability for conversation, and to establish rapport among interlocutors. Hence, phatic communication has a slightly different function in the context of Twitter, than it does on the blog. Rather than being a subtle vehicle for intimacy among close peers, phatic communication on Twitter fulfills its original, contact-making function. It signals approachability, and invites co-present interlocutors to join and continue conversation in the spontaneous here-and-now, subsuming the topic of conversation to the logic of immediacy. A core characteristic of sociability is the primacy of form over content, epitomized on Twitter by the creation of a cheerful and cordial ambience, as driven by stylistic genre conventions. This does not mean that content is not important: it must captivate and unite co-present participants, but its development should not be the goal of the conversation. In the sociable encounter, participants' tact and self-regulation allow topics to change quickly in the flow of conversation, thereby keeping conversation from turning into serious scrutiny or discussion—whether of something personally-disclosing, or information-laden (Simmel, 1971 [1910]: 129–130, 136).

My analyses suggest that, in contrast to Twitter, the personal blog constitutes a much more intimate space. The character of the software strongly influences the enactment and negotiation of genres such as blogs or Twitter as different types of sociable spaces. 'Microblogging encourages the disclosure of simple, easily described moments' (Crawford, 2009: 257), qua the temporal structure and the 140 character limit, whereas the blog—asynchronous and unlimited in space—allows for more substantial writing, including nuanced disclosure and reflection on the self. Furthermore, the blog is first and foremost the blogger's space, whereas as Twitter is little more than a personally customized, collaborative stream of tweets that blend in a public, or semi-public timeline.

Participants stream their everyday doings and engage in small talk with others, while at the same time monitoring other people's conversations, everyday life experiences, and so forth, as they accumulate over time. This option of incessant 'social monitoring' of one another creates a peripheral awareness of others in real-time, that is, the constant possibility of being updated on one another's whereabouts, thoughts, and activities in daily life. In an analysis of live broadcasting on television and its interplay with digital platforms, Ytreberg discusses 'liveness' as a specific experiential quality of television. 'Liveness' is defined as the public and instantaneous transmission of events and happenings, functioning to 'unify disparate sequences in a single flow,' despite spatial fragmentation (Ytreberg, 2009:

477). Twitter encompasses 'liveness' too, as a core feature of the genre. Liveness is created and experienced in the ongoing flow of tweets, weaving together—temporally and spatially—participants' everyday 'life streams' in a communicative flow that not only reflects, but *augments* everyday life, by representing and sharing it in text. The augmentation of everyday life, and the peripheral awareness it facilitates, may function to create a *collective sense of intimacy*, a sense of connectedness in the continued stream, albeit probably a more superficial intimacy than experienced on a personal blog.

FACEBOOK: INTIMACY AT A DISTANCE

As we have seen in the previous chapter, Facebook users are concerned about the exposure of self and others and strive to balance the appropriately personal with the all-too-private exposure, just as do the personal bloggers and Twitter users in this study. At the same time, given the difference from the other genres in terms of networked audience structure and relationships maintained, Facebook could be expected to involve more leeway for personal disclosure.

To be sure, participants share standard personal information on their profiles: their full names, hometown, date of birth, a photo of themselves, and in some cases their relationship status, including information identifying their partner. Some of them even share their phone number and other contact information. The elaborate self-disclosure is supported by the Facebook software. The profile template encourages profile holders to display not only basic personal information, but also political leanings, cultural tastes and so forth. The vivid sharing of personal information must be seen in light of the fact that the profile holder's network is made up of pre-existing relationships. For a large part, the audience thus already has elaborate knowledge of the profile holder—the display of personal information on the Facebook profile does not involve many new revelations.

To counterbalance the disclosure of personal information on their profiles, all participants have limited the access to their Facebook profiles to 'friends only,' by adjusting their privacy settings. Hence, they actively regulate and seek to control to whom they expose themselves on Facebook by making their profiles more of a private space for the invited and knowledgeable few.

The degree of self-disclosure seems to fluctuate with the communicative characteristics inscribed in the software of the genres. If we compare participants from the blog, Twitter and Facebook studies, the three genres represent a gradual move from very restricted amounts of basic personal information being available (as on the blog) to the elaborate sharing of personal information (as on Facebook). This could be because the three genres involve different options for knowing and possibly controlling the potential audience. On the blog, the audience remains undisclosed for the author and figures only at the aggregate level in the blog's statistics. On Twitter the follower-list collects the users that subscribe to the person's tweets and thus provides some indication of the audience, and on Facebook the mutual friending and privacy measures make for even more detailed regulation of the potential audience. Of course, none of these features display the actual audience—those who do in fact see one's contributions.

Concerning the content posted in status updates and so forth on Facebook, several of the study participants state that there are unwritten, tacit rules regarding what it is appropriate and relevant to share, and what is too private, even if each individual user may draw the line between the personal and the private in a slightly different place. This is similar to the other genres. Although difficult to put into words, the boundary between 'personal' and 'private' provides a practical sensibility in the enactment of genre. For instance, Caleb chooses 'not to put up a profile picture of myself in underwear' (Caleb), thereby implying that photos disclosing a lightly dressed body, for instance, overstep his privacy expectations for Facebook. Apart from a greater awareness of privacy as linked to their photo-sharing activities, the Facebook participants do not differ from the Twitter users and bloggers in terms of the content that they consider offensive and outside the boundaries of appropriate self-disclosure. As we saw in Chapter 6, although big life events are announced on Facebook, the participants are generally reluctant to contribute content, and when they do, it often takes on the shape of information sharing or funny musings and small talk about mundane topics, rather than some intimate confession (e.g., about their health or love lives). This is perhaps a bit surprising, given that Facebook is the genre in this study for which public access is most limited, and where the audience is best controlled. Yet, again with Facebook, we see the formation of a communicative space less guided by substantial exchanges and private confessions than by the offering of a casual, sociable encounter.

Similar to the other genres, the norms governing participants' Facebook posting habits suggest that appropriate conduct involves the nuanced sharing of self. Luke explains: 'I would much rather have a photo of me, a little bit chubby and eating donuts than a beautiful fashion photo at the beach' (Luke). As this quote suggests, indeed participants are not careless about how they present themselves through their content contributions. They care and they are very self-aware. However, their careful self-presentation does not involve a polished and perfect communicative expression of self. Instead, participants strive for an informal, nuanced and not too self-conscious self-presentation, similar to that described by Elise and Ben on blogs. This probably reflects the fact that the Facebook audience knows the author quite well from other contexts and will therefore likely be able see through and possibly dismiss a self-presentation that is too strategic and not completely honest. The norms of balanced disclosure of self through the sharing of various content assist in establishing a coherent, authentic and personal portrayal of the individual user without oversharing, just as we have seen with the other genres.

Given the similarity across genres, the 'personal, not private' norm appears to be general for social media use, not just for conveying a coherent and authentic sense of the individual user, but also for creating a sociable ambience and experience among participants. For Twitter and blogs, I argued that phatic communication in different ways represents the key vehicle for achieving sociability. In turn, sociability has its unique conditions and expressions on Facebook. When compared to the sociable spaces produced through personal blogging and Twitter, Facebook seems to land somewhat in-between.

On one hand, the 'friends-only' communication on Facebook stipulates an atmosphere of intimacy and closeness comparable to that seen on the blogs. However, whereas the personal blog is dependent on explicit phatic markers such as the incessant exchange of posts and comments to collaboratively uphold relationships, the direct communicative exchange and display of mutual orientation are in a sense redundant on Facebook. Because the relationship between participants is established before Facebook and already inscribed in the dynamics of friending and grooming of friend networks on the site, participants do not have to reconfirm these relationships by demonstrating mutual awareness in actual conversation. They just have to be there, popping up in each other's newsfeeds from time to time, to remind one another of the existence of their relationship. When participants do engage in communicative exchange, this simply adds an extra layer to relationship maintenance.

One might describe this networked, peripheral awareness of one another as effortless and undirected phatic communication: the markers of presence go out to the entire network at once, simply through checking in and occasionally posting or liking something on Facebook. The direct exchange of messages becomes less important because the participants have already confirmed the existence of a (sometimes-strong) personal affiliation through accepting each other as Facebook friends (cf. the norms of creating friend networks).

On the other hand, Facebook resembles Twitter in the sense that the communication that does play out takes the form of augmented small talk in brief, everyday encounters. As Chapter 6 documented, the conventional, daily rhythm of Facebook use lends itself better to bite-size entertainment, updating and 'hanging out' than for deep and prolonged interpersonal dialogue. Wagman (2010: 64–65) argues that the fast-paced, interstitial nature of Facebook—goofing off, monitoring self and others, and checking things out in-between tasks—locates Facebook as part of the routine that makes op quotidian social life. This makes it more of a space for the convenient seeking out of sociability, and for intimacy at a distance. Along these lines, the intimacy at a distance created on Facebook has closer affinity to Twitter's liveness and the idea that the experience of closeness among participants is first and foremost established in the Facebook stream, which interweaves and augments the mundane activities of everyday life.

THE SOCIABLE SELF: EXTERIORIZED INTIMACY?

The public/private interface finds different expressions on personal blogs, Twitter and Facebook through phatic communication augmentation of the everyday, intimacy, and so on. In this final, analytical section, I want to broaden the perspective to discuss the negotiation of this public/private interface, acknowledging that, while it may be particularly prominent in social media, the negotiation of boundaries between public and private takes a central role in contemporary media culture in general.

> I saw a really good web animation a year ago, when Twitter was all new, where there were a lot of people flying around in a blue room, yelling how they were feeling in this exact second. 'my stomach hurts,' or 'my cat is just so cute,' and it was this worst-case scenario that people would incessantly share which cake they liked, and all those, you know, extremely trivial things about their hamster and so on . . . This self-glorifying . . . [. . .] to say 'isn't it just great, I've been to the loo three times today,' that no one would want to know [. . .] not even if you talked to them in person. You know, people thinking that 'I am the center of the universe and everything I do is super-fantastically important.' (Nick)

This quotation illustrates the common assertion that social media encourage voluntary exposure of what was previously private and screened from the public eye. For instance, David (2009) uses the notion of 'exteriorized intimacy' to examine the public disclosure of intimate personal information, specifically with regard to the personal use of camera phones. Miller and Shepherd (2004) see blogging as epitomizing a cultural 'kairos' of self-exposure and voyeurism. Christensen and Jerslev (2009: 22–27) consider digital media and genres parts of a strong movement in the current media culture towards the intimization and emotionalization of public space, in which the personal 'backstage' is suddenly publicly displayed and scrutinized. Reality and lifestyle television constitute other important media phenomena in this ongoing negotiation of the boundaries between the public and the private.

Originally, intimacy was understood as based on exclusivity and secrecy, that is, the sharing of one's inner life exclusively with one's family, closest friends, and significant others. Hence, the experience of intimacy was tied to the closest interpersonal relationships (Schwarz, 2011). As the three case analyses have suggested, social media may function as vehicles for a more public experience of intimacy, enacted and negotiated with an increasing number of networked connections, beyond the domestic sphere and the special bond between close friends or significant others.

Simmel's writings on sociability describe a different context for togetherness, compared to today's saturated media environment. Has the willingness to share sensitive information in a public space increased? In particular, my analyses of the personal blog and Facebook, but also the Twitter practice of interlinking the self across profiles and genres to allow participants to more extensively monitor one another, suggest that the sharing of personal experiences and public disclosures are coming to be regarded as appropriate. The boundaries of sociability, with respect to the disclosure of the intimate self, may have become porous. Consequently, sociability as an experiential quality is perhaps no longer entirely incompatible with the sharing of something personal, as long as the personal does not overstep the interlocutors' boundaries, and thereby disrupt the ongoing flow of conversation. However, the orientation towards 'the personal, not private' reveals ongoing reflection and effort among participants to sustain a boundary around the private, inner life.

I have argued that intimacy is achieved chiefly through phatic communication and the creation of a sociable ambience. Miller (2008) asserts that, from a critical perspective, blogs, and short forms of communication such as Twitter, in particular, nurture phatic communication, to the extent that substantial conversation is marginalized by superficial blurbs relating to connected presence and peripheral awareness. This argument is suggestive of normative claims that substantive, informational exchanges are more valuable than relational exchanges and sociability. Similarly suggestive is Turkle's argument that online connectivity makes us 'alone together' (2011), that is, constantly tethered to the network of distant others without the certainty of a sustained and real commitment to one another because we may be easily distracted by more interesting conversations elsewhere.

Considering the significance that participants in the highly phatic, ongoing exchanges ascribe to Facebook, Twitter, and blogging in everyday life, such normative evaluations may miss the point. The genres are not void of substance, but foreground the relational function of communication, just as other genres may foreground other functions (Jakobson, 1960; Meltzer & Musolf, 2000). The phatic nature of much of the communication on social media is what enables participants to forge social bonds. As Simmel argues, 'that something is said and accepted is not an end in itself but a mere means to maintain the liveliness, the mutual understanding, the common consciousness of the group' (Simmel, 1971 [1910]: 137; also, Crawford, 2009). Failing to enact these seemingly insignificant exchanges has interactional and individual consequences: it disrupts the experience of sociability that has been achieved, turn by turn in conversation, it challenges the cohesiveness of the dyad or group of closely-knit interlocutors, and it exposes the individual participant as lacking the required skills of being a 'competent user.'

Returning to Nick's description in the quote above, the experiential quality of participation on Twitter, Facebook and blogs does not lie in the individual utterance (a tweet, a blog post, a comment), which may constitute insignificant, even superficial blurbs. The significance of these genres for their users lies in the interweaving and accumulation of individually insignificant utterances and brief exchanges about the everyday, in networks of social affiliation over time. This collaborative augmentation of the everyday fulfills what Simmel (1971 [1910]) describes as the fundamental human need of association.

CHAPTER SUMMARY

Social media evolve at the intersection of personal experience and the publicly displayed nature of communication. Their communicative conventions produce different types of sociable spaces that are collaboratively navigated by participants in adherence to a principle of being 'personal, not private.' In this chapter, I have synthesized the findings from the three case studies to expound on the experiential qualities of social media in quotidian life, and discuss their broader sociocultural implications for the nexus between private and public communication.

As communicative genres, the personal blog, Twitter, and Facebook are negotiated with a view to their ambiguous status as publicly enacted, accessible, and 'on display' for larger audiences, and simultaneously nurturing close-knit groupings and sometimes-intimate relationships among participants in the ongoing, situated genre enactment. Different instances of the genres (individual personal blogs or Twitter and Facebook profiles) may manage this ambiguity in different ways, in and through the participation structures and the collaborative negotiation of relevant topics and interactional conventions of conversation.

8 Social Media, Social Genres

This book builds on a long theoretical and empirical research tradition of studying media usage patterns and media users in everyday life. The goal of the book was to extend and adjust the already viable concepts of genre and sensemaking to the study of social media in everyday life, and this has generally proven analytically useful. Given the sparsely theorized phenomenon of social media in scholarship on digital media, the communicative perspective of genre offers a first attempt at grasping social media as a communicative condition that is inextricably interwoven in the fabric of meaning of contemporary everyday life.

In conclusion, I revisit the theoretical concepts of the 'text' and the 'active media user' with the benefit of a pragmatic, genre-based framework for social media analysis. This framework helps to account for the blurring of production and reception in social media; it also suggests directions for future empirical studies of media use that recognize the multifarious modes of user engagement in the evolving digital media landscape.

FROM TEXT TO COMMUNICATIVE PRACTICE

To ground the study of social media in theories of media and text, I began by establishing a conceptual framework for defining social media as communicative genres, constituted by the interplay between interactive functionalities configured at the software level, and the invocation and appropriation of various software functionalities to achieve certain purposes, in and through users' actual communicative practices. I argued that the software level of social media and other internet-based phenomena complicates the concepts of—and distinctions between—media, genre, and text, because software is malleable, and continuously being revised, and may be adopted differently in different usage situations. Consequently, software is deeply intertwined with the discursive level, and must be taken into consideration as part of a textual analysis of user contributions and their implied understandings and negotiations of the genre. Against this background, I suggested that social media could be seen as particularly dynamic genres, subject to continuous disruption and uncertainty, owing to their deinstitutionalized and participatory character, and the shifting roles of producers and recipients in the communicative practices that make up the text in social media.

I also examined genre as a cognitive device for, or category of sense-making. I elaborated on socio-cognitive reception theory, by introducing a pragmatic approach to cognitive processes, one that emphasizes the social dimension of cognition, and thereby complements the often psychologically based conception and analysis of cognition in audience studies. From this perspective, I suggested that cognition, including relevant genre knowledge, is often tacitly evoked in communicative practice among interlocutors, to demonstrate intersubjective alignment in the situation, and thus ensure a habitual and unproblematic course of interaction. Along these lines, participants in any communicative event draw on genre knowledge appropriate to the situation, in order to master and make sense of it. The concept of genre is intended to bridge gaps between the various constituents in the communicative process; the producer and the recipient orient to one another in situ by means of shared genre knowledge, as expressed in their communicative practices. In social media, where users increasingly become producers, this socio-cognitive understanding of genre knowledge as shared and negotiated by interlocutors in communication is particularly useful.

There are three aspects of crucial importance to the genre perspective that I have advanced in this work, with regard to social media. First, as communicative genres, social media are enacted in communicative practice. The subtle conceptual shift from text to communicative practice entails seeing social media not simply as texts produced and read but something actors *do*, and doing social media accomplishes something for the participants involved. Second, and related to the first point, the meanings of these genres are both *individually anchored and socially negotiated* in communicative practice, that is, they are continuously shaped, adjusted, stabilized, and destabilized through participants' active engagement on Facebook, Twitter, blogs, and so on. Genres constrain communication and regulate behavior because they attune participants in communication to a specific interpretive framework based on 'horizons of expectations' and conventions, but genres are also dynamic, shaped by interaction, and change over time. Finally, as genres, social media involve *belonging to a network of peers* who experience a shared understanding of the purposes, premises, and boundaries of the genre.

To understand social media as everyday phenomena, we need more than a conceptual discussion of them as media, genres, or texts in their own right, and the goal here is not to claim a theoretical primacy of the genre perspective for the study of social media. What is needed is a systematic effort at redeveloping viable concepts and perspectives from the field of audience studies and examining their analytical potential in empirical studies to deepen our understanding of how users communicate on social media and what it means to them. I applied and refined the pragmatic framework of genre in three consecutive case studies of social media in everyday life—case studies that have further served to test emergent hypotheses on the dynamics of genre negotiation at the interplay between software functionalities and usage practices.

One of the main analytic strengths of the genre-based framework is its integration of network, compositional, thematic, and stylistic dimensions into the study of communicative practice in social media. Although the analytic categories are largely derived from textual analysis, they have acquired a slightly different shading and scope, owing to the integration of pragmatic theories of sensemaking as based in communicative practice as well as cognitive processes. The framework paved the way for a very fine-grained, holistic analysis of the phenomena studied. The perspective of genre not only applies to individual cases of social media. Indeed, it is suitable for comparative analysis, for instance, between types of blogs, or, as presented in this book, of different types of social media. The analytic framework presents a systematic for examining similarities and differences between services, including how the variety of uses may tie in with specific software characteristics. The framework may be viewed as an emergent model for the genre analysis of social media, offering a sound, internally consistent, and fine-grained integrative framework for application in future empirical studies of social media uses.

Regarding the role of software and its flexibility, work remains to be done to clarify the ways in which software is socially negotiated. My studies of genre negotiation among ordinary users yielded insights into processes of the adoption and adjustment of (newly) available services in their everyday lives. However, in terms of software and software genres, another system of negotiation—or shaping of technology—enters the equation. Software genres are (also) negotiated in a radically different context than 'the everyday lives of ordinary users,' namely in a socio-structural environment of design innovations, commercial actors, juridical restrictions, IT standards, and so forth, preceding (and following) the launch of new services to a market of ordinary users. In this environment, the creation and negotiation of new software genres and social media services have very little connection with ordinary users' everyday negotiations of meaning in and through active engagement with social media, and they are beyond the scope of the genre framework. Nonetheless, they are important as context and background for the genre analysis, because the dynamics concerning the social shaping of technology underscore the point about software genres being flexible and negotiated at different levels of analysis.

Regarding genre negotiation and dynamics at the intersection of software and actual usage practices, one might argue that the genre perspective tends to foreground user agency at the cost of a more critical assessment of the tensions between agency and exploitation in the relationship between software and usage practices. The lens of genre focuses on how users 'do' and make sense of genres in everyday life, circumscribing the notion of a highly argentic ordinary user. At the same time, the lens partly ignores how software allows service providers to exploit this user agency for commercial gain, through data mining. In fact, service providers may (and often do) use software-based data mining techniques to accumulate a specialized and commercially attractive knowledge of individual users' personal online activities. A critical everyday perspective (Bakardjieva, 2011) might add nuances to the power of ordinary users versus social media software and the companies behind them. Such a perspective recasts the genre negotiations and the implied user agency in light of the structural exploitation that is inevitably part of technology use in everyday life, including the relationship between the users and the companies that harvest personal data, and perhaps use them for personally targeted advertisements online. I have indicated that there are hierarchies and power dynamics at play at the level of communicative practices, by showing how some users, the 'insiders' or core members, are better positioned to validate or sanction other members. However, power as exercised through software, although relevant for understanding the relationship between companies, software, and users of social media, remains to be addressed by the pragmatic framework of genre.

Future research may follow two trajectories. One, to further develop the analysis of network dynamics on social media by examining the relationship between networks and power as enacted in communicative practice. Two, to turn a media system lens on genre development and negotiation, and more broadly, software innovations, to better grasp the context and market mechanisms that drive the rapid development within the field of social media, and thereby inform an understanding of power dynamics at play in social media. Furthermore, a media system perspective may complement the user perspective from which I have argued, to develop a more fine-grained understanding of the tension between users as increasingly empowered participants, and user participation as exploitation and 'big business' for the commercial service providers in the social media market.

TRANSFORMING AUDIENCES INTO INDIVIDUAL AND NETWORKED SENSEMAKING AGENTS

One of the initial goals of this project was the development of the notion of 'the active media user' in audience studies, in light of social media. The conceptualization of text as communicative practice prompts us to integrate theories of interpersonal communication in audience studies. Theories of interpersonal communication underscore the social uses of media as forms of practice to complement the audience-studies idea of active media use in terms of interpretation of texts. Introducing pragmatic theories from microsociology and social psychology to socio-cognitive reception theory of sensemaking, I have theorized that the activity of sensemaking manifests as two interrelated dynamics: a) at an individual level, in which the media user applies personal, cognitive-psychological frameworks for organizing and interpreting experience, and acquires the capacity to master new media and genres (through processes of anchoring); and b) as a social process, in which the individual actively collaborates with fellow media users in ongoing negotiations of meaning through communicative practice (i.e. textual contributions to social media) concerning not only the media in question, but also the sense of self and the everyday social world in which media use is embedded (through processes of objectification).

Pragmatic genre analysis posits an analytical sensibility to individual interpretation as well as social practice. Both aspects are constitutive for user agency vis-à-vis media. Indeed, one of the merits of using a pragmatic framework of genre is that it enables the balancing of the individual-psychological and the social-collaborative components of the sensemaking process, by emphasizing genre as socially negotiated amongst individual users. Arguably, however, the empirical analyses of genre enactments in communicative practice gravitate towards the social level of analysis, rather than towards the uniquely individual contributions to genre, because the notion of 'negotiation' between participants prompts a focus on examining the ongoing social constitution of conventions and expectations of genre, in given social networks. As the analyses have demonstrated, the concrete, individual enactments of genre, manifested in the contribution of blog posts, comments, tweets, and so forth, are framed by a specific network-related logic that creates social pressures for conforming to socially accepted versions of the genre.

To counterbalance the social level of analysis, genre analysis must retain sensitivity to individual variations in expectations and purposes of genre enactment. This is crucial for integrating social practice and individual interpretation in the analysis of media use. Individual level data ground specific purposes and patterns of usage in the concrete—and unique—everyday situations of each of the individual study participants (e.g., accounting for Miriam's very intimate Twitter relationships by connecting them to her disability, or suggesting that Maggie's engagement with a network of Danish bloggers is partly related to her situation as an expatriate). Hence, the analysis connects specific functions of genre to the everyday lives of those who enact it, in line with a long trajectory of mainly qualitative empirical studies of media use in everyday life. Future audience research may continue this trajectory of anchoring media use in social networks as well as individual life circumstances to elicit the multiple ways in which ordinary people do and find meaning in social media in everyday life.

References

Andersen, Michael B. (1994). TV og genre. In P. Dahlgren (Ed.), *Den mångtydiga rutan*. Stockholm: Skriftserien JMK.

Anderson, Richard C. (1978). Schema-directed processes in language comprehension. In A.M. Lesgold, J.W. Pellegrino, S.D. Fokkema & R. Glaser (Eds.), *Cognitive psychology and instruction*. New York: Plenum.

Anderson, Richard C., & Pearson, P. David. (1984). A schema-theoretic view of basic processes in reading comprehension. In P.D. Pearson (Ed.), *Handbook of reading research*. New York: Longman.

Ang, Ien. (1996). Ethnography and radical contextualism in audience studies. In J. Hay, L. Grossberg & E. Wartella (Eds.), *The audience and its landscape* (pp. 247–262). Boulder, CO: Westview Press.

Askehave, Inge, & Nielsen, Anne E. (2005). Digital genres: a challenge to traditional genre theory. *Information Technology & People, 18*(2), 120–141.

Atkinson, J. Maxwell, & Heritage, John (Eds.). (1984). *Structures of social action: Studies in conversation analysis*. Cambridge, UK: Cambridge University Press.

Augoustinos, Martha, & Walker, Iain. (1995). *Social cognition. An integrated introduction*. London: Sage Publications.

Bakardjieva, Maria. (2005). *Internet society. The Internet in everyday life*. Thousand Oaks, CA: Sage Publications.

Bakardjieva, Maria. (2011). The internet in everyday life: Exploring the tenets and contributions of diverse approaches. In M. Consalvo & C.M. Ess (Eds.), *The Blackwell handbook of internet studies* (pp. 59–82). Oxford, UK: Wiley-Blackwell.

Bakhtin, Mikhail. (1986). *Speech genres and other late essays*. Austin: University of Texas Press.

Baron, Naomi S. (2008). *Always on. Language in an online and mobile world*. Oxford, UK: Oxford University Press.

Bartlett, Frederic C. (1932). *Remembering. An experimental and social study*. Cambridge, UK: Cambridge University Press.

Bauman, Marcy L. (1999). The evolution of internet genres. *Computers and Composition, 16*(2), 269–282.

Baumer, Eric, Sueyoshi, Mark, & Tomlinson, Bill. (2008). *Exploring the role of the reader in the activity of blogging*. Paper presented at the Twenty-Sixth Annual SIGCHI Conference on Human Factors in Computing Systems.

Baym, Nancy K. (2000). *Tune in, log on. Soaps, fandom, and online community*. Thousand Oaks, CA: Sage Publications.

Baym, Nancy K. (2010). *Personal connections in the digital age*. Cambridge, UK: Polity Press.

Bazerman, Charles. (1988). *Shaping written knowledge: The genre and activity of the experimental article in science*. Madison: University of Wisconsin Press.

Bazerman, Charles. (2006). The writing of social organization and the literate situating of cognition: Extending Goody's social implications of writing. In D. R. Olson & M. Cole (Eds.), *Technology, literacy and the evolution of society: Implications of the work of Jack Goody*. Mahwah, NJ: Lawrence Erlbaum Associates.

Bechmann, Anja, & Lomborg, Stine. (2013). Mapping actor roles in social media: Different perspectives on value creation in theories of user participation. *New Media & Society, 15*(5), 765–781. doi: 1461444812462853.

Berger, Peter L., & Luckmann, Thomas. (1967). *The social construction of reality. A treatise in the sociology of knowledge*. New York: Anchor Books.

Berkenkotter, Carol, & Huckin, Thomas N. (1993). Rethinking genre from a socio-cognitive perspective. *Written Communication, 10*(4), 475–509.

Bernstein, Michael S., Bakshy, Eytan, Burke, Moira, & Karrer, Brian. (2013). *Quantifying the invisible audience in social networks*. Paper presented at the CHI 2013, Paris, France.

Bhatia, Vijay K. (1993). *Analysing genre—language use in professional settings*. London: Longman.

Bhatia, Vijay K. (1996). Methodological issues in genre analysis. *Hermes, Journal of Linguistics, 16*, 39–59.

Blood, Rebecca. (2005). How blogging software reshapes the online community. *Communications of the ACM, 47*(12), 53–55.

boyd, danah. (2006a). A blogger's blog: Exploring the definition of a medium. *Reconstruction, 6*(4).

boyd, danah. (2006b). Friends, friendsters, and top 8: Writing community into being on social network sites. *First Monday, 11*(12).

boyd, danah. (2007). Why youth (heart) social network sites: The role of networked publics in teenage social life. In D. Buckingham (Ed.), *Identity, and digital media*. Cambridge, MA: MIT Press.

boyd, danah. (2008). *Taken out of context. American teen sociality in networked publics*. PhD thesis, University of California, Berkeley.

boyd, danah, & Ellison, Nicole B. (2007). Social network sites: Definition, history, and scholarship. *Journal of Computer-Mediated Communication, 13*(1), 210–230.

boyd, danah, Golder, Scott, & Lotan, Gilad. (2010). *Tweet, tweet, retweet: Conversational aspects of retweeting on Twitter*. Paper presented at the Hawaii International Conference on System Sciences (HICSS-43), Hawaii.

Brewer, Marilynn B., & Gardner, Wendi. (1996). Who is this 'we'? Levels of collective identity and self representations. *Journal of Personality and Social Psychology, 71*(1), 83–93.

Briggs, Asa, & Burke, Peter. (2002). *A social history of the media. From Gutenberg to the Internet*. Cambridge, UK: Polity Press.

Bruns, Axel. (2008). *Blogs, Wikipedia, Second Life, and beyond: From production to produsage*. New York: Peter Lang.

Bruns, Axel, & Burgess, Jean. (2011). #ausvotes: How Twitter covered the 2010 Australian federal election. *Communication, Politics & Culture, 44*(2), 37–56.

Bruun, Hanne. (2004). *Daytime talkshows i Danmark—om receptionen af en transnational TV-genre*. Aarhus: Forlaget Modtryk.

Bruun, Hanne. (2010). Genre and interpretation in production: a theoretical approach. *Media, Culture & Society, 32*(5), 723–737.

Brügger, Niels. (2013). Facebooks historie. Udviklingen af en tom struktur. In J. L. Jensen & J. Tække (Eds.), *Facebook i den danske hverdag—fra socialt netværk til metamedie*. Frederiksberg: Samfundslitteratur.

Castells, Manuel, Fernández-Ardèvol, Mireia, Qiu, Jack L., & Sey, Araba. (2007). *Mobile communication and society. A global perspective*. Cambridge, MA: MIT Press.

Chayko, Mary. (2002). *Connecting: How we form social bonds and communities in the Internet age*. Albany, NY: State University of New York Press.

Christensen, Christa L., & Jerslev, Anne. (2009). *Hvor går Grænsen? Brudflader i den Moderne Mediekultur*. Copenhagen: Tiderne Skifter.

Cicourel, Aaron V. (1973). *Cognitive sociology. Language and meaning in social interaction*. Baltimore: Penguin Education.

Coulter, Jeff. (1979). *The social construction of mind: Studies in ethnomethodology and linguistic philosophy*. London: Macmillan.

Crawford, Kate. (2009). These foolish things. On intimacy and insignificance in mobile media. In G. Gogging & L. Hjorth (Eds.), *Mobile technologies. From telecommunications to media* (pp. 252–265). London and New York: Routledge.

Crowston, Kevin, & Williams, M. (2000). Reproduced and emergent genres of communication on the world-wide web. *The Information Society, 16*(3), 201–216.

Danmarks Statistik. (2009). Befolkningens brug af Internet 2009. Available at: http://www.dst.dk/pukora/epub/upload/14039/it.pdf

Danmarks Statistik. (2012). It-anvendelse i befolkningen 2012. Available at: http://www.dst.dk/pukora/epub/upload/17443/itanv.pdf

David, Gabriella. (2009). Clarifying the mysteries of an exposed intimacy: Another intimate representation mise-en-scène. In K. Nyìri (Ed.), *Engagement and exposure: Mobile communication and the ethics of social networking* (pp. 77–86). Vienna: Passagen Verlag.

Dijck, Jose van. (2009). Users like you? Theorizing agency in user-generated content. *Media, Culture & Society, 31*(1), 41–58.

Donath, Judith. (2004). Sociable media. In W. S. Bainbridge (Ed.), *Berkshire encyclopedia of human-computer interaction*. Great Barrington, MA: Berkshire Publishing Group.

Donath, Judith, & boyd, danah. (2004). Public displays of connection. *BT Technology Journal, 22*(4), 71–82.

Dyke, Gregory, Lund, Kristine, & Girardot, Jean-Jacques. (2009). *Tatiana: an environment to support the CSCL analysis process*. Paper presented at the CSCL 2009, Rhodes, Greece.

Edwards, Derek. (1997). *Discourse and cognition*. London: Sage Publications.

Ellison, Nicole B., Steinfield, Charles, & Lampe, Cliff. (2007). The benefits of Facebook 'friends': Social capital and college students' use of online social network sites. *Journal of Computer-Mediated Communication, 12*(4), 1143–1168.

Erickson, Thomas. (2000). *Making sense of computer-mediated communication (CMC); Conversations as genres, CMC systems as genre ecologies*. Paper presented at the 33rd Hawaii International Conference on System Sciences (HICSS-33), Hawaii.

Erjavec, Karmen, & Kovačič, Melita P. (2009). A discursive approach to genre: Mobi news. *European Journal of Communication, 24*(2), 147–164.

Finnemann, Niels Ole. (2005). *Internettet i mediehistorisk perspektiv*. Frederiksberg: Samfundslitteratur.

Finnemann, Niels Ole. (2011). Mediatization theory and digital media. *European Journal of Communication Research, 36*(1), 67–89.

Fono, David, & Raynes-Goldie, Kate. (2005). Hyperfriends and beyond: Friendship and social norms on liveJournal. In M. Consalvo & C. Haythornthwaite (Eds.), *Internet Research Annual, vol. 4* (pp. 91–104). New York: Peter Lang.

Frandsen, Kirsten, & Bruun, Hanne. (2005). Mediegenre, identifikation og reception. *MedieKultur, 38*, 51–61.

Furukawa, Tadanobu, Matsuo, Yutaka, Ohmukai, Ikki, Uchiyama, Koki, & Mitsuru, Ishizuka. (2007). *Social networks and reading behavior in the blogosphere*. Paper presented at the ICWSM.

Garcia, Angela C., & Jacobs, Jennifer B. (1999). The eyes of the beholder: Understanding the turn-taking system in quasi-synchronous cmc. *Research on Language & Social Interaction, 32*(4), 337–367.

Garfinkel, Harold. (1967). *Studies in ethnomethodology.* Englewood Cliffs, New York: Prentice-Hall.

Giltrow, Janet, & Stein, Dieter (Eds.). (2009). *Genres in the internet. Issues in the theory of genre.* Amsterdam and Philadelphia: John Benjamins Publishing Company.

Goffman, Erving. (1959). *The presentation of self in everyday life.* New York: Doubleday.

Goffman, Erving. (1967). *Interaction ritual. Essays on face-to-face behavior.* Allen Lane: The Penguin Press.

Gumbrecht, Michelle. (2005). Blogs as 'protected space.' In D. Satish & K.R. Prabhakar (Eds.), *BLOGS: Emerging Communication Media* (pp. 79–91). Hyderabad, India: ICFAI University Press.

Gye, Lisa. (2007). Picture this: The impact of mobile camera phones on personal photographic practices. *Continuum: Journal of Media & Cultural Studies, 21*(2), 279–288.

Hagen, Ingunn. (1998). Creation of socio-cultural meaning. Media reception research and cognitive psychology. In B. Höijer & A. Werner (Eds.), *Cultural cognition. New perspectives in audience theory* (pp. 59–72). Gothenburg: Nordicom.

Hampton, Keith N., Goulet, Lauren S., Marlow, Cameron, & Rainie, Lee. (2012). Why most Facebook users get more than they give. The effect of Facebook's 'power users' on everybody else. *Pew Internet & American Life Project.*

Harrison, Sandra. (2008). Turn taking in email discussions. In S. Kelsey & K. St. Amant (Eds.), *Handbook of research on computer-mediated communication* (pp. 755–772). Hershey, PA: Information Science Reference.

Haythornthwaite, Caroline. (2000). Online personal networks. Size, composition and media use among distance learners. *New Media & Society, 2*(2), 195–226.

Haythornthwaite, Caroline. (2005). Social networks and internet connectivity. *Information, Communication & Society, 8*(2), 125–147.

Helles, Rasmus. (2009). *Personlige medier i hverdagslivet.* PhD thesis, University of Copenhagen.

Helles, Rasmus. (2010). Hverdagslivets nye medier. *Dansk Sociologi, 21*(3), 49–63.

Helles, Rasmus. (2013). Mobile communication and intermediality. *Mobile Media and Communication, 1*(1), 14–19.

Heritage, John. (1984). *Garfinkel and ethnomethodology.* Cambridge, UK: Polity Press.

Hermes, Joke. (1993). Media, meaning and everyday life. *Cultural Studies, 7*(3), 493–506.

Herring, Susan C. (1999a). Interactional coherence in CMC. *Journal of Computer-Mediated Communication, 4*(4).

Herring, Susan C. (1999b). Posting in a different voice: Gender and ethics in computer-mediated communication. In P. A. Mayer (Ed.), *Computer media and communication: A reader.* Oxford: Oxford University Press.

Herring, Susan C., & Paolillo, John C. (2006). Gender and genre variation in blogs. *Journal of Sociolinguistics, 10*(4), 439–459.

Herring, Susan C., Scheidt, Lois A., Wright, Elijah, & Bonus, Sabrina. (2005). Weblogs as a bridging genre. *Information Technology & People, 18*(2), 142–171.

Highfield, Tim, Harrington, Stephen, & Bruns, Axel. (forthcoming). Twitter as a Technology for Audiencing and Fandom: The #Eurovision Phenomenon. *Information, Communication & Society.* doi: 10.1080/1369118X.2012.756053.

Honeycutt, Courtenay, & Herring, Susan C. (2009). *Beyond microblogging: Conversation and collaboration via Twitter.* Paper presented at the Proceedings of the Forty-Second Hawaii International Conference on System Sciences (HICSS-42), Los Alamitos, CA.

Horton, Donald, & Wohl, Richard R. (1956). Mass communication and para-social interaction: Observations on intimacy at a distance. *Psychiatry, 19*, 215–229.

Huberman, Bernardo A., Romero, Daniel, & Wu, Fang. (2009). Social networks that matter: Twitter under the microscope. *First Monday*, 14(1).

Humphreys, Lee. (2013). Mobile social media: Future challenges and opportunities. *Mobile Media and Communication*, 1(1), 20–25.

Höijer, Birgitta. (1991). *Lystfulld glömska, kreativ illusion och realitetsafprövning.* Swedish Radio/PUB nr. 15.

Höijer, Birgitta. (1992). Reception of television narration as a socio-cognitive process: A schema-theoretical outline. *Poetics, 21.*

Höijer, Birgitta. (1998). Cognitive and psycho-dynamic perspectives on reception of television narration. In B. Höijer & A. Werner (Eds.), *Cultural cognition. New perspectives in Audience Theory* (pp. 73–84). Gothenburg: Nordicom.

Höijer, Birgitta. (2007). A socio-cognitive perspective on ideological horizons in meaning-making. In B. Höijer (Ed.), *Ideological horizons in media and citizen discourses. Theoretical and methodological approaches* (pp. 33–50). Gothenburg: Nordicom.

Jakobson, Roman. (1960). Closing statement: Linguistics and poetics. In T. A. Sebeok (Ed.), *Style in language.* Cambridge, MA: MIT Press.

Java, Akshay, Song, Xiaodan, Finin, Tim, & Tseng, Belle. (2007). *Why we twitter: Understanding microblogging usage and communities.* Paper presented at the WebKDD/SNA-KDD '07.

Jenkins, Henry. (2006). *Convergence culture. Where old and new media collide.* New York and London: New York University Press.

Jensen, Klaus Bruhn. (1998). Denmark. In K. B. Jensen (Ed.), *News of the world. World cultures look at television news* (pp. 39–60). London and New York: Routledge.

Jensen, Klaus Bruhn. (2010). *Media convergence. The three degrees of network, mass, and interpersonal communication.* London and New York: Routledge.

Jodelet, Denise. (1991). *Madness and social representations.* London: Harvester/Wheatsheaf.

Jovchelovitch, Sandra. (2007). *Knowledge in context: Representations, community and culture.* London and New York: Routledge.

Kant, Immanuel. (1929). *Critique of pure reason.* New York: St. Martin's Press.

Kendall, Lori. (2005). Diary of a networked individual. System design's effects on online relationships. In M. Consalvo & M. Allen (Eds.), *Internet research annual, vol. 2.* New York: Peter Lang.

Kendall, Lori. (2007). Shout into the wind, and it shouts back: identity and interactional tensions on LiveJournal. *First Monday*, 12(9).

Keyton, Joann. (1999). Relational communication in groups. In L. F. Frey, D. S. Gouran & M. S. Poole (Eds.), *The handbook of group communication theory and research* (pp. 192–222). Thousand Oaks, CA: Sage Publications.

Krishnamurthy, Balachander, Gill, Phillipa, & Arlitt, Martin. (2008). *A few chirps about twitter.* Paper presented at the WOSP '08.

Kuzel, Anton J. (1999). Sampling in qualitative inquiry. In B. F. Crabtree & W. L. Miller (Eds.), *Doing qualitative research* (2nd ed.) (pp. 33–46). Thousand Oaks, CA: Sage Publications.

Lenhart, Amanda. (2009). Twitter and status updating. *Pew Internet & American Life Project.*

Lewis, Jane, & West, Anne. (2009). 'Friending': London-based undergraduates' experience of Facebook. *New Media & Society*, 11(7), 1209–1229.

Licoppe, Christian. (2004). 'Connected' presence: The emergence of a new repertoire for managing social relationships in a changing communication technoscape. *Environment and Planning D: Society and Space*, 22(1), 135–156.

Ling, Richard S. (2008). *New tech, new ties. How mobile communication is reshaping social cohesion.* Cambridge, Mass.: MIT Press.

Ling, Richard S. (2012). *Taken for grantedness. The embedding of mobile communication into society.* Cambridge, MA: MIT Press.

Ling, Richard S., Julsrud, Tom, & Yttri, Birgitte. (2005). Nascent communication genres within SMS and MMS. In R. Harper, L. A. Palen, & A. S. Taylor (Eds.), *The inside text: Social perspectives on SMS in the mobile age* (pp. 75–100). London: Kluwer.

Livingstone, Sonia. (2004). The challenge of changing audiences: Or, what is the audience researcher to do in the age of the internet? *European Journal of Communication, 19,* 75–86.

Livingstone, Sonia. (2008). Taking risky opportunities in youthful content creation: teenagers' use of social networking sites for intimacy, privacy and self-expression. *New Media & Society, 10*(3), 393–411.

Lomborg, Stine. (2009). Navigating the blogosphere: towards a genre-based typology of weblogs. *First Monday, 14*(5).

Lomborg, Stine. (2011). *Social media. A genre perspective.* PhD thesis, Aarhus University.

Lomborg, Stine. (2012a). Negotiating privacy through phatic communication. A case study of the blogging self. *Philosophy & Technology, 25*(3), 415–434.

Lomborg, Stine. (2012b). Researching communicative practice: Web archiving in qualitative social media research. *Journal of Technology in Human Services, 30*(3/4), 219–231.

Lüders, Marika. (2008). Conceptualizing personal media. *New Media & Society, 10*(5), 683–702.

Lüders, Marika, Prøitz, Linn, & Rasmussen, Terje. (2010). Emerging personal media genres. *New Media & Society, 12*(6), 947–963.

Malinowski, Bronislaw. (1923). The problem of meaning in primitive languages. In C. K. Ogden & I. A. Richards (Eds.), *The meaning of meaning* (pp. 146–152). London and New York: Routledge.

Markova, Ivana. (2003). *Dialogicality and social representations.* Cambridge, UK: Cambridge University Press.

Markovsky, Barry, & Lawler, Edward J. (1994). A new theory of group solidarity. *Advances in Group Processes, 11,* 113–137.

Marwick, Alice, & boyd, danah. (2011). I tweet honestly, I tweet passionately: Twitter users, context collapse, and the imagined audience. *New Media & Society, 13*(1), 114–133.

Marwick, Alice E. (2010). *Status update: celebrity, publicity and self-branding in web 2.0.* PhD thesis, New York University.

Matlin, Margaret W. (2005). *Cognition* (6th ed.). Hoboken, NJ: Wiley.

McLaughlin, Caitlin, & Vitak, Jessica. (2012). Norm evolution and violation on Facebook. *New Media & Society, 14*(2), 299–315.

Meltzer, Bernard N., & Musolf, Gil R. (2000). "Have a nice day!": Phatic communication and everyday life. *Studies in Symbolic Interaction, 23,* 95–111.

Mikkelsen, Jan F. (1994). Pragmatisk receptionsteori. In L. Højbjerg (Ed.), *Reception af Levende Billeder.* Copenhagen: Akademisk Forlag.

Miller, Carolyn R. (1984). Genre as social action. *Quarterly Journal of Speech, 70,* 151–167.

Miller, Carolyn R., & Shepherd, Dawn. (2004). Blogging as social action: A genre analysis of the weblog. In L. Gurak, S. Antonijevic, L. Johnson, C. Ratliff, & J. Reyman (Eds.), *Into the blogosphere: Rhetoric, community, and culture of blogs.* Available at: http://blog.lib.umn.edu/blogosphere/blogging_as_social_action.html

Miller, Vincent. (2008). New media networking and phatic culture. *Convergence, 14*(4), 387–400.

Milne, Esther. (2010). *Letters, postcards, email. Technologies of presence.* London and New York: Routledge.

Moscovici, Serge. (1976). *La Psychoanalyse, son image, son public* (2nd ed.). Paris: Presses Universitaires de France.

Moscovici, Serge. (1994). Social representations and pragmatic communication. *Social Science Information, 33*(2), 163–177.

Moscovici, Serge. (2001). *Social representations. Explorations in social psychology.* New York: New York University Press.

Murray, Susan. (2008). Digital images, photo-sharing, and our shifting notions of everyday aesthetics. *Journal of Visual Culture, 7*(2), 147–153.

Murthy, Dhiraj. (2011). Twitter: Microphone for the masses? *Media, Culture and Society, 33*(5), 779–789.

Nardi, Bonnie A., Schiano, Diane J., & Gumbrecht, Michelle. (2004). *Blogging as social activity, or, would you let 900 million people read your diary?* Paper presented at the CSCW-2004.

Neale, Steven. (1980). *Genre.* London: British Film Institute.

Naaman, M., Boase, J., & Lai, C.-H. (2010). *Is it really about me? Message content in social awareness streams.* Paper presented at the CSCW-2010.

Orlikowski, Wanda J., & Yates, JoAnne. (1994). Genre repertoire: The structuring of communicative practices in organizations. *Administrative Science Quarterly, 39*(4), 541–574.

Oulasvirta, Antti, Lehtonen, Esko, Kurvinen, Esko, & Raento, Mika. (2010). Making the ordinary visible in microblogs. *Personal and Ubiquitous Computing, 14*(3), 237–249.

Palmer, Daniel. (2012). iPhone photography, mediating visions of social space. In L. Hjorth, J. Burgess, & I. Richardson (Eds.), *Studying mobile media. Cultural technologies, mobile communication, and the iPhone* (pp. 85–97). London and New York: Routledge.

Palmer, Jerry. (1990). Genrer og medier—et kort overblik. *MedieKultur, 14.*

Paxton, Pamela, & Moody, James. (2003). Structure and sentiment: Explaining emotional attachment to group. *Social Psychology Quarterly, 66*(1), 34–47.

Piaget, Jean. (1952). *The origins of intelligence in children.* New York: International Universities Press.

Polanyi, Michael. (1967). *The tacit dimension.* New York: Anchor Books.

Pomerantz, Anita. (1984). Agreeing and disagreeing with assessments: some features of preferred/dispreferred turn shapes. In J.M. Atkinson & J. Heritage (Eds.), *Structures of social action. Studies in conversation analysis.* Cambridge, UK: Cambridge University Press.

Potter, Jonathan. (2006). Cognition and conversation. *Discourse Studies, 8*(1), 131–140.

Potter, Jonathan, & Edwards, Derek. (1999). Social representations and discursive psychology: From cognition to action. *Culture & Psychology, 5*(4), 447–458.

Potter, Jonathan, & Wetherell, Margaret. (1987). *Discourse and social psychology.* London: Sage Publications.

Rainie, Lee, & Wellman, Barry. (2012). *Networked. The new social operating system.* Cambridge, MA: MIT Press.

Rasmussen, Terje. (2007). *Kampen om Internett.* Oslo: Pax.

Rettberg, Jill W. (2008). *Blogging.* Cambridge, UK: Polity Press.

Rheingold, Howard. (1993). *The virtual community: Homesteading on the electronic frontier.* Reading, MA: Addison-Wesley.

Sacks, Harvey. (1984). On doing 'being ordinary.' In J.M. Atkinson & J. Heritage (Eds.), *Structures of social action: Studies in conversation analysis* (pp. 513–529). Cambridge, UK: Cambridge University Press.

Sacks, Harvey. (1992). *Lectures on conversation.* Oxford, UK and Cambridge, MA: Blackwell Publishing.

Sanderson, James, & Cheong, Pauline H. (2010). Tweeting prayers and communicating grief over Michael Jackson online. *Bulletin of Science, Technology & Society, 30*(5), 328–340.

Schegloff, Emanuel A., Jefferson, Gail, & Sacks, Harvey. (1977). The preference for self-correction in the organization of repair in conversation. *Language in Society,* *53*(2), 361–382.

Schrøder, Kim, Drotner, Kirsten, Kline, Stephen, & Murray, Catherine. (2003). *Researching audiences.* London: Arnold.

Schutz, Alfred. (1971). *Collected papers I. The problem of social reality* (3rd unchanged ed.). The Hague: Martinus Nijhoff.

Schutz, Alfred, & Luckmann, Thomas. (1973). *The structures of the life-world.* Evanston: Northwestern University Press.

Schwarz, Ori. (2011). Who moved my conversation? Instant messaging, intertextuality and new regimes of intimacy and truth. *Media, Culture & Society, 33*(1), 71–87.

Serfaty, Viviane. (2004). Online diaries: Towards a structural approach. *Journal of American Studies, 38*(3), 457–471.

Sessions, Lauren F. (2010). How offline gatherings affect online communities. *Information, Communication & Society, 13*(3), 375–395.

Silverman, David. (1998). *Harvey Sacks. Social science and conversation analysis.* Oxford and New York: Oxford University Press.

Silverstone, Roger. (1994). *Television and everyday life.* London and New York: Routledge.

Simmel, Georg. (1955). *Conflict and the web of group-affiliations.* New York: The Free Press.

Simmel, Georg. (1971 [1910]). Sociability. In D.N. Levine (Ed.), *Georg Simmel. On individuality and social forms. Selected writings* (pp. 127–140). Chicago and London: The University of Chicago Press.

Smith, Aaron, & Rainie, L. (2010). 8% of online Americans use Twitter. *Pew Internet & American Life Project.*

Stake, Robert E. (2003). Case studies. In N.K. Denzin & Y.S. Lincoln (Eds.), *Strategies of qualitative inquiry* (2nd ed.). Thousand Oaks, CA Sage Publications.

Swales, John. (1990). *Genre analysis: English in academic and research settings.* Cambridge, UK: Cambridge University Press.

Sørensen, Anne Scott. (2009). Social media and personal blogging: Textures, routes and patterns. *MedieKultur, 47,* 66–78.

Thorseth, May. (2008). Reflective judgment and enlarged thinking online. *Ethics and Information Technology, 10,* 221–231.

Todorov, Tzvetan. (1990). *Genres in discourse.* Cambridge, UK: Cambridge University Press.

Tolson, Andrew. (1996). *Mediations: Text and discourse in media studies.* London: Arnold.

Turkle, Sherry. (2011). *Alone together. Why we expect more from technology and less from each other.* New York: Basic Books.

Ugander, Johan, Backstrom, Lars, Marlow, Cameron, & Kleinberg, Jon. (2012). *Structural diversity in social contagion.* Paper presented at the Proceedings of the National Academy of Sciences of the United States of America.

Viégas, Fernanda B. (2005). Bloggers' expectations of privacy and accountability: An initial survey. *Journal of Computer-Mediated Communication, 10*(3).

Vitak, Jessica, & Ellison, Nicole B. (2013). 'There's a network out there you might as well tap': Exploring the benefits of and barriers to exchanging informational and support-based resources on Facebook. *New Media & Society, 15*(2), 243–259.

Waldahl, Ragnar. (1998). A cognitive perspective on media effects. In B. Höijer & A. Werner (Eds.), *Cultural cognition. New perspectives in audience theory.* Gothenburg: Nordicom.

Walther, Joseph B., & D'Addario, Kyle P. (2001). The impacts of emoticons on message interpretation in computer-mediated communication. *Social Science Computer Review, 19,* 324–347.

Weick, Karl. (1995). *Sensemaking in organizations.* Thousand Oaks, CA: Sage Publications.

Werry, Christopher C. (1996). Linguistic and interactional features of internet relay chat. In S.C. Herring (Ed.), *Computer-mediated communication: Linguistic, social and cross-cultural perspectives.* Amsterdam: John Benjamins.

Wertsch, James. (1991). *Voices of the mind. A sociocultural approach to mediated action.* Cambridge, MA: Harvard University Press.

Williams, Raymond. (1974). *Television. Technology and Cultural Form.* London: Fontana.

Wittgenstein, Ludvig. (1967). *Philosophical investigations* (2nd ed.). Oxford: Basil Blackwell.

Yates, JoAnne, & Orlikowski, Wanda J. (1992). Genres of organisational communication: A structurational approach to studying communication and media. *Academy of Management Review, 17*(2), 299–326.

Yates, Simeon J., & Sumner, Tamara R. (1997). *Digital genres and the new burden of fixity.* Paper presented at the 30th Hawaii International Conference on System Sciences (HICSS '97).

Yin, Robert K. (1994). *Case study research. Design and methods* (2nd ed.). Thousand Oaks, CA: Sage Publications.

Ytreberg, Espen. (2000). Notes on text production as a field of inquiry in media studies. *Nordicom Review, 2,* 53–62.

Ytreberg, Espen. (2009). Extended liveness and eventfulness in multi-platform reality formats. *New Media & Society, 11*(4), 467–485.

Yuan, Li, & Buckman, Rebecca. (2006, 4 April). Social networking goes mobile: MySpace, Facebook strike deals with cell companies. *The Wall Street Journal.*

Zerubavel, Eviatar. (1997). *Social mindscapes: An invitation to cognitive sociology.* Cambridge, MA: Harvard University Press.

Zhao, Dejin, & Rosson, Mary Beth. (2009). *How and why people Twitter: The role that micro–blogging plays in informal communication at work.* Paper presented at the International Conference on Supporting Group Work, Sanibel Island, FL.

Zhao, Shanyang, & Elesh, David. (2008). Copresence as 'being with.' Social contact in online public domains. *Information, Communication & Society, 11*(4), 565–583.

Index